The Armchair
James Beard

❧ Other books by James Beard ❧

The Armchair
James Beard

Edited by John Ferrone
Foreword by Barbara Kafka

THE LYONS PRESS

All but three of the articles in this volume were previously published in
*American Way, Diversion, Esquire, Gourmet, House & Garden, New York, Town &
Country, Travel & Leisure, Saturday Evening Post,* and *Woman's Day;* and in newspaper columns for Universal Press Syndicate, copyright © 1974, 1977,
1978, 1979, 1981, 1982, 1983, 1985 by James A. Beard and Associates.
They are collected here with the permission of Reed College, residuary
beneficiary under the Will of James A. Beard. "Life at Its Best" is from
Delights and Prejudices by James Beard, copyright © 1964 by James Beard. It
was first published in *Harper's Magazine* and is reprinted with the permission of Scribner, a division of Simon & Schuster.

Book design by A Good Thing Inc.

Printed in the United States of America
10 9 8 7 6 5 4 3 2 1

Library of Congress Cataloging-in-Publication Data

Beard, James, 1903–1985.
　　The armchair James Beard / edited by John Ferrone.
　　　　p.　cm.
　　Articles previously published in various journals.
　　ISBN 1-55821-737-1
　　1. Cookery.　I. Ferrone, John.　II. Title.
TX714. B385　1999
641.5—dc21
　　　　　　　　　　　　　　　　　　　　　98-29728
　　　　　　　　　　　　　　　　　　　　　CIP

❦ Contents ❧

❧ Foreword ❧

Beard Revisited

What a treat John Ferrone has brought us with this book, a feast of articles by James Beard that have never before appeared in book form. As a longtime friend, collaborator, and worker with Beard, Ferrone saved these pieces from oblivion and sifted and annotated them with a knowledgeable eye. Of course, they give great pleasure; but do they matter?

It is natural that I would think so. I miss James Beard, as a friend, an intelligence, a repository of information, a wit, and as a lover of all things to do with food, opera, and gossip. I miss him as a teaching partner, dining partner, and a partner in abstruse gastronomical research that led to rarer and rarer books as well as more of our seemingly endless, crack-of-dawn conversations.

Somewhat less personally, what I miss about Jim, what I feel is the greatest loss to the American food scene, is his distinctively American voice. He fed our nostalgia for an America we may have never known but through which he lived. He recalls in this book, as in many others, the Northwest of his childhood where hams and game hung in the cellar; where Dungeness crabs, oysters, and fish were plentiful and peddlers came to the door selling cooked hominy and fresh vegetables. He was unabashedly enthusiastic, self-taught, forward looking, and eager—until the end of his life—to know the latest innovations of young chefs. He greeted new technologies such as the food processor, the electric stove, and the microwave oven with delight. He researched American food but felt equally connected to the food of his English mother, as well as the food of France, Italy, and South America. And even though he didn't cook it, he grew up with and was very comfortable with Chinese food. He voiced the best of America, the richness of the past, and a vision of the future.

With all the writing assistants and editors that Beard had, the voice in the writing over the years remained remarkably constant.

Many of his culinary passions reflected or predicted the tenor of the country, although he was never a slave to popularity. He loved outdoor cooking and wrote about it many times in his books and articles. Perhaps his large male presence presaged and encouraged the increased presence of men at the barbecue and in the kitchen. There were certainly many men in his classes. He enjoyed picnics and informality. He always served and recommended wine. He researched earlier American and American regional recipes. A substantial breakfast and tea as a meal surfaced repeatedly in his writing, along with the foods that comprised them.

In part, Beard's writings could be read as a serial story of his food-world friendships. He encouraged people who he recognized as talented to enter that world, and carried them along with him from book to book and article to article. He was generous in promoting the work of those he believed in and cared about: Julia Child, M. F. K. Fisher, Helen Evans Brown, Paula Peck, Marcella Hazen, James Villas, and countless others.

The recurring characters of his more personal world included his oldest friend, Mary Hamblet; Leon Leonides of the Coach House, where he frequently lunched; Jeanne Owen (a formidable grande dame who created a vast array of food events) and her fried chicken; his first partners, Bill and Irma Rhode; Helen McCully, the first non–home economics food editor of a major woman's magazine; Clementine Paddleford, the idiosyncratic food editor of the *Herald Tribune;* and many others, including James Nassikas of the Stanford Court in San Francisco, where James Beard and I taught and where Beard virtually lived for part of the year. The list of names, even those in this wonderful book, could go on.

He took us into dozens of restaurants and introduced us to their chefs, from Lucas Carton in Paris to Quo Vadis in New York and the London Chop House in Detroit. He sponsored younger chefs and remembered those who contributed in the past, such as Louis Diat of the Ritz-Carlton.

Wherever his inquiring mind took him—to books, people, or places, James Beard found recipes to share that enriched our lives. I will always miss him, but he lives again in this book. Thank you, Jim; thank you, John.

—Barbara Kafka
Spring 1999

❧ Introduction ❧

James Beard was one of the country's most influential and most publicized food authorities, and by now his history must be known to just about everybody who qualifies as a reasonably serious cook. But for those who are still in the dark about the origins of this extraordinary man, it wouldn't hurt to repeat a few facts of his life, leading up to his defection to the food world.

He was born in Portland, Oregon, in 1903. His father, who had come to Oregon from Iowa by covered wagon, was an appraiser at Portland's customs house. His mother, of English and Welsh ancestry, had owned and managed a small residential hotel. It was from her that Beard acquired a love of food and the theater, along with a precocious sophistication. He aspired to be a singer or actor or both. Not yet twenty, he went off to London to study voice with an assistant of Enrico Caruso, and lived for a time in Paris. When his goal of becoming a heldentenor seemed unpromising, he returned home to seek a career on the stage and in radio, sometimes keeping afloat with teaching and cooking jobs. His rotund six-foot-four frame limited his prospects, but he even had a go at Hollywood.

In 1937 he moved to New York to look for theater work, lived hand to mouth, and once again taught school to help pay the rent. The event that would steer him toward his true calling came late in 1938, when he met a German-born brother and sister as passionately interested in food as he was. They decided to form a catering service, Hors d'Oeuvre Inc., to exploit New York's cocktail habit. World War II brought it to an end, but out of it came Beard's first cookbook, *Hors d'Oeuvre and Canapés.* In 1946 he appeared on the first cooking program ever televised, NBC's *I Love to Eat.* Theater and food had fused, and Beard was on his way up as gastronomic guru and champion of America's culinary wealth. He died in New York in January 1985 after years of poor health, but preached good food right to the end.

James Beard's twenty-some cookbooks (the count is debatable) are his most visible legacy, but he had just as much to say and said it louder and longer in hundreds of articles that lasted a month, a week, or a day and then disappeared into the void. For forty years or so in over thirty-five magazines and newspapers, he dispensed recipes and advice that collectively were nothing short of encyclopedic. Portions of this material were harvested for Beard's cookbooks—it could be said that the short-lived writing did legwork for the more enduring—but a good deal has stayed buried. This volume brings sixty-five articles to light.

Magazine assignments kept Beard's pot boiling. They gave him needed income in the early years and were the chief stimulus for food research. Before he acquired a full-time staff in the seventies, he lived at the stove, playing with every conceivable facet of cookery. Even—reluctantly—packaged mixes. The assignments were usually dreamed up by food editors. Sometimes they were inspired by Beard's latest travels. A 1963 stay in St.-Rémy-de-Provence produced a "Provençal Cook Book" for *House & Garden* (included here as "The Food of Provence"). Tours of Ireland and the starry restaurants of France in 1966 spawned articles for *Town & Country*.

On home ground, "Dishes to Fight Over" was clearly an echo of Beard's research on regional food for his magnum opus, *American Cookery*. A further, seemingly inexhaustible source of materials was his Pacific Northwest boyhood. Time after time he looks back to the seasonal pleasures of his mother's kitchen, wagons of fresh produce sold door to door, and clamming and cooking at the Oregon seaside.

When Beard began a syndicated column in 1970, in collaboration with former *House & Garden* editor José Wilson, he was free of assignments on at least one front and acquired his biggest audience. He could speak on any culinary topic that came into his head. He could teach, pontificate, or reminisce. Maybe best of all, he could be up to the minute, scolding a young Chez Panisse for failing to mash its green peppercorns or singing the praises of Europe's hottest new chef. "Beard on Food," as the column was called, became his weekly pulpit right up to the time of his death.

Beard made his magazine debut in 1942, just three years after taking up food as a profession, with a piece in *The House Beautiful* (as it was then called), "It Tastes Better Outdoors," built around "A Man's Dinner" of broiled sirloin steaks. The next month, his "Charcoal Cheer" appeared in the new food magazine *Gourmet*, an association that had its ups and downs during the next thirty years. He contributed to *Woman's Day*, too, and to *McCall's*, *Apartment Life*, and *Harper's Bazaar*. His longest, most productive run was at *House & Garden*, beginning in December 1942, for which he later assembled compilations of recipes known as cookbooks and wrote a monthly column, "Corkscrew," on wines and spirits.

At first he spoke primarily to the women's market—the readers then labeled as "homemakers"—but turned up in unexpected places like *Popular Mechanics* and *Ski Life*, and in 1950 he had become the food and drink expert for he-man readers of *Argosy*, with articles on outdoor cookery and "Good Grub from the Galley." In the sixties and seventies he would greatly broaden his readership with his syndicated column and appearances in *Travel & Leisure*, *Esquire*, *New York*, *Town & Country*, *American Way* (American Airlines' in-flight magazine), and the newer, gender-neutral food magazines. One of his last pieces was written for *Diversion*, a magazine "for physicians at leisure."

Three of the selections included here—on lobster, sauer-kraut, and berrying—have never been published and, unlike the rest of the collection, were not written as magazine or newspaper assignments, although they qualify as armchair Beard. The unedited manuscripts I worked from are almost certainly transcripts of tapes Beard made in the last years of his life for a book in progress to be called *Menus and Memories.* A number of people—Barbara Kafka, Judith and Evan Jones, Irene Sax, and myself, among others—tried to coax the memories out of him, but Beard managed to produce only a few fragments, the most significant of which were published by Kakfa in *The James Beard Celebration Cookbook.*

There have been two previous collections of Beard's articles—the first, *Beard on Food,* composed of his syndicated columns, and the second, *James Beard's Simple Foods,* of articles written for *American Way.* This is the only collection to draw on the full scope of his food journalism.

Although it contains more than one hundred thirty recipes, *The Armchair James Beard* is meant for browsing rather than cooking. It could just as easily have been called *The Bedside James Beard,* if that's where you like to meditate on food, or *The Patio Beard,* or *The Poolside Beard.* Wherever it is read, Beard's infectious love of good food and drink is sure to send the reader back into the kitchen.

❧ *E*ditor's Note ❧

From the start of his culinary journalism, Beard needed a helping hand. He had greater patience at the stove than he did at his
portable typewriter, where he pounded out pieces with convic-
tion but without a second glance. His writing had all the
authority one could want, as well as gusto and charm. It needed
organizing and heavy polishing, and in later years, when Beard
was likely to talk the substance of an article into a tape recorder,
it required a fleshing out of ideas. For these services he relied on
several cowriters during his forty-year career—initially, his
Portland friend Isabel Callvert. I followed, working on more
than a hundred articles, including a number in this collection.
José Wilson, an alumna of *House & Garden*, came next, collabo-
rating on a syndicated column until her death in 1980. From
that time until Beard's death in January 1985, the column was
coauthored by Jacqueline Mallorca.

We tidied up Beard to varying degrees—sometimes, appar-
ently, too much. His friend and colleague Helen Evans Brown
once complained to him that a newly published cookbook
lacked his usual pithy remarks. "I feel it's more Isabel than you."
More often than not, Beard's distinctive voice came through.

Most of the pieces collected here are reprinted from the
publications in which they first appeared. In some cases, I was
unable to locate tearsheets and was obliged to work from final
manuscripts—the two may differ—and a few times, from rough
drafts. Although I did a fair amount of cutting throughout, an
occasional overlapping of material could not be helped. I also
provided titles where necessary and engaged in minor editorial
tampering along the way. James Beard, I feel reasonably certain,
would not have minded.

I thank Morris J. Galen and Reed College for making this book possible; Caroline Stuart and Jacqueline Mallorca, for their help in tracking down aging manuscripts; Naomi Barry, for a special errand in Paris; Deirdre Bair, for elusive information; Olivia Blumer and Barney Karpfinger, for putting the project in the right hands; and Lilly Golden at the Lyons Press, for her unfailing support and sound judgment.

*W*hen I first met James Beard, in 1954, he occupied a second-floor studio apartment in a handsome brownstone on Twelfth Street in Greenwich Village, where he had lived for thirteen years. His improbable kitchen ran neck and neck with bathroom facilities along a corridor, and he had a choice of doing dishes in a tiny sink or in the bathtub with the shower turned on. It was this maddening arrangement, together with cooking by gas, which he hated, that drove Beard down the street in 1957 to an ugly new brick apartment house, where he triumphantly installed an all-electric kitchen. He remained only two years before moving to a charming little house on Tenth Street across from the Women's House of Detention.

Here he was able to have his first teaching kitchen, organized around a U-shaped bank of electric burners and work surfaces, which he called his grand piano. Watermelon-colored Formica panels could slipcover the entire U, making a spacious serving table for Beard's lavish cocktail buffets. Here, too, is where the now-famous black and white wallpaper of colossal pineapples originated. When he outgrew the Tenth Street house and moved to one two blocks north, the kitchen retained the same pattern, with the U of cooking units growing wider and shallower. Beard presided over classes from a high canvas director's chair. It was this kitchen, his "fifth," that Beard was outfitting in the second of these articles, "Tools of My Trade." It is now the centerpiece of Beard House, run by the James Beard Foundation.

The Stomach, Heart, and Spirit of the House

In a house without a genuine kitchen, one of the delights of growing up is lost. No other room can gather the family together with such a feeling of warmth and security. And now, after a long decline, the American kitchen is finally regaining its status as the family room.

What a change has come over its design since the thirties and forties, when that room was all but forgotten. Architects turned it into a corridor—it still exists in all too many houses and apartments—where the sink was too small, the opening of the refrigerator required clever maneuvering, and much of the storage space was up out of reach. There was no thought of a place for sitting and eating unless one balanced on a step stool, and there was surely little incentive to produce good food. No child growing up with such a kitchen could ever know the fun of watching his mother turn out cookies, licking the spoon from a bowl of cake batter, cranking the ice cream freezer. Nor the joys of taffy pulls, making fudge, and many of the rites of Christmas.

I grew up in a kitchen that was the hub of the house and the crossroads of the entire neighborhood. It was enormous in size, and like many kitchens of the previous century, its supplies filled the adjoining pantry—as large as most New York apartment kitchens—and the basement as well. It was a pleasant room with wallpaper of red polka dots on a cream-colored background and with cream enameled woodwork. Unbleached muslin curtains trimmed with red braid piping were hung at the windows. When we ate, we sat at a large round table that accommodated six to eight people. It was a friendly spot in which to enjoy our food, which was prepared nearby on a great range. When I was very young, this was an immense black wood-burning stove that heated the room in addition to cooking our food. A second stove, a gas stove, was tucked away in the pantry. These were later replaced by a giant white stove that burned both wood and gas—a wood oven below and gas ovens and broilers above. It was a joy to work with and as dependable as any stove could be.

One of the kitchen's many doors led to the basement, where the stove wood was stored, together with fruits and vegetables and other items to be kept cool, as well as wine and liquor. During the game season, ducks, teal, and pheasants hung from a rope strung across the basement, and occasionally a ham or two was hung for aging. The mingled smells were wonderful to me—pitchy wood, apples and pears, the strange, gamy scent of hanging birds.

A second door led to the screened back porch, where we sometimes sat to have breakfast or lunch, looking out on the Gravenstein apple trees, whose fruit could be colossal, the towering Bing cherry trees, and the smaller Royal Anne cherry tree. And there was a small herb plot where parsley, shallots, chives, thyme, and sage grew, and frequently basil or tarragon. In spring, a lilac bush at the foot of the porch stairs sent its perfume through the kitchen door.

The pantry was the stockroom for the kitchen. It held rows of plates and hanging cups—a set of blue willow dishes and a set of peach-blossom dishes from China that we were all fond of and generally used for lunch and dinner. At the far end of the pantry was a large, heavy working board for pastry making, cutting and chopping, and general preparation of food. A bin under the worktable held fifty pounds of flour at a time, and sugar and other staples were stored in proportionate quantities. It was a wonderful pantry to wander into. Mouthwatering mysteries were stored away in the meat safe and in jars and drawers, china and glass sparkled everywhere, and there was an intriguing array of gadgetry ready for action.

For years, a sewing machine was kept in the kitchen at the window opening onto the porch. Here a seamstress, who came every three or four months, did bits and pieces of sewing for the family and brought gossip from the neighborhood. The machine was one of the beautiful Victorian models, with a wrought-iron base and a wooden lid, and it was not at all obtrusive in a room dedicated to food.

We were a family of individuals, my mother, my father, and I. Though we were compatible, each had his own life apart from the others, and for each the kitchen played a different role. My father found his greatest privacy in the early morning hours. He made it known that he would prefer fixing breakfast and sending it upstairs on trays rather than have any company. In winter, one could hear him getting the fire going with papers and kindling, and the reassuring rush of air through the damper as the fire caught. In summer, he first opened all the doors to let in the fresh morning air. Then he proceeded with his menu, which might be a traditional combination of fruit, bacon or country ham, eggs, and toast or rolls. On Sunday mornings in winter, his specialty was homemade sausage, deliciously blended with thyme, a bit of bay leaf, and pepper. In the spring and fall—we were always at the beach in summer— he invariably sautéed young chicken, which would be served with country bacon, cream gravy, and hot biscuits.

As soon as my father went upstairs to groom himself for the day, my mother took possession of the kitchen, which was truly her realm. No other part of the house provided so appropriate a background for this warm, independent, sometimes fearsome woman. Here she entertained for lunch—her intimate friends preferred to eat in the kitchen—here she blended teas, did preserving and pickling, and chatted with neighbors, exchanging pungent confidences over tea, scones, and mock macaroons.

The kitchen was mine late at night. I enjoyed having one or several friends in for a drink, a supper of scrambled eggs, or a sandwich. We used to sit up late and talk, comparing ideas that were current during the early years of the Depression. At times like these, the kitchen became a smoke-filled supper club.

When the family gathered at the kitchen table, frequently with an old family friend, the room took on the air of a coffeehouse or a tavern. We were not of one mind politically, and there were heated discussions over the League of Nations, new taxes, Prohibition. Often the talk was simply about food. We disagreed about how certain dishes should be prepared or raved about our favorite foods as they came into season—the first shad roe and shad, tiny new potatoes, white and green asparagus, alligator pears. . . . We ate well, and there seemed to be a constant flow of good things into our larder. Once, years after my mother had died and I had long been away, I visited the house where I grew up. When I stepped into the kitchen, I knew at once it had become just another room.

The kitchen where I now cook and teach, forty years later, is a world apart, but it perpetuates some of the ideas of our family kitchen.[1] Naturally, I was opposed to a purely functional laboratory. Thus, I planned with Agnes Crowther, an interior designer and friend of long standing, to make this a functional kitchen with beauty—again, a kitchen to live in. In every respect, it has triumphed. It is without question the center of the house. Whenever there are guests, whether few or many, the kitchen

---

[1] This was Beard's kitchen on West Tenth Street in New York.

draws them. Even sixty or seventy people manage to stuff themselves into the kitchen, leaving the overflow rooms empty. It is a huge kitchen by normal standards, but its elements are so harmonious that one is unaware of its size. Its walls are covered with paper (treated to make it spotproof) in three different designs. The major equipment was planned for teaching as well as for household use. The central piece is a U-shaped unit mounted on legs, outfitted with ten electric burners and with shelves below. Four chopping boards are set in at convenient places between the burners. Formica covers trimmed with rosewood fit over this unit, converting it into a buffet table, a demonstration table, or a combination of buffet and stove.

Elsewhere in the room is a high worktable on wheels that is useful for cutting, display, and demonstration. Two sinks, one with a swan's-neck faucet for washing vegetables and the other for washing dishes and pots, are near the double ovens and broilers and the refrigerator-freezer. On one side of the room are racks that hold jars of staple items, and beneath are hooks for skillets and pans of varying sizes. A wine rack for spirits and liqueurs is attached to the wall. (Storage for wine is in the basement.) Shallow cupboards hold quantities of bowls and dishes. Two rosewood chests of drawers contain small equipment. A fine old Swiss painted wooden rack, faded in color, holds glassware, and a pine cabinet stores herbs, spices, and additional glassware.

Between the windows is a small marble table, whose wrought-iron base is from an old sewing machine—an echo of my childhood kitchen. And above the table is a handsome French copper lavabo of the type used in kitchens and dining rooms during the eighteenth and nineteenth centuries.

To dine in this kitchen is ever a satisfying experience. My preference for kitchen dining never seems to wane. It is not nostalgia but a natural expression of my love for food and its preparation. It seems to me that the pleasure of eating is heightened if one is there amidst the delightful smells to witness the moment when the finished dish comes out of the pot or the oven. And usually the less time lost between stove and table, the better.

Wherever old kitchens are being renovated and new ones designed, the trend is toward spaciousness and familial warmth. Kitchens are getting bigger, better equipped, more efficient, less laboratorial, more fun, more lived in. Antique utensils sit side by side with sleek modern appliances. Tiffany lamps spotlight cozy corners. It is fashionable to own an old butcher's block and yards of maple work surfaces. The uncomfortable overhanging oven, the poorly insulated oven, and the stove top crowded with burners are on the way out. On the way in are Pyroceram stove tops, smooth and glowing; auxiliary broilers; and electronic ovens for instant cookery. Everywhere there is evidence of sturdier equipment, more intelligent design, and greater beauty.

The cause of it all is the pursuit of good food. Since the midforties, Americans have become more adventurous and more sophisticated in their food habits. Cookbooks by the dozens are published and bought each season, cooking schools are burgeoning throughout the country, the service magazines feature kitchen design in nearly every issue, and the *New York Times* devotes columns to culinary matters. On television, Julia Child has brought French cooking within reach of adoring amateur cooks of both sexes, young and old. And from coast to coast, shops devoted exclusively to the kitchen offer wares from France, England, Spain, Italy, and Mexico.

As a result of the proliferation of what I like to call "pot shops," the new kitchen has a *batterie de cuisine* that would have baffled a housewife thirty years ago—omelet and crêpe pans, unlined copper bowls for beating egg whites and batter, fish broilers large enough to hold ten- and twelve-pounders, electric mixers capable of kneading dough and puréeing, electrically run ice cream makers, chef's knives, boning knives, slicing knives.

In many families, both husband and wife enjoy the pleasures of cooking, and in this event the kitchen is sometimes planned to provide two separate working areas—occasionally, different stoves, too—for the pair of cooks. I know of a remarkable kitchen in a house in Syracuse, New York, that boasts three stoves, each producing a different type of heat: a professional electric stove and an electric wall oven, a gas stove with a Pyroceram top, and an indoor charcoal grill with a blower and exhaust system of its own. All are in use. The kitchen embraces a large dining area furnished with an enormous table and handsome eighteenth-century-style chairs, and it has a work surface as large as the whole kitchen in some city apartments. A relatively large family flows in and out of this room, and everyone from the adults to the tiniest child loves it above any other part of the house. Recently I attended a dinner party there. We were thirty-eight guests at table—all in the kitchen.

Other kitchens like this one are being built these days on a scale that lets them serve as a dining room, and in many vacation houses the kitchen is so open to the rest of the house that the cook at work can stay in constant touch with family and guests. Frequently, too, the kitchen portals open on a terrace, where the family takes its meals according to the season. A kitchen in Southern California that uses the indoor-outdoor principle was created by Philip Brown, a fine cook and food writer, and his late wife, Helen Evans Brown. While the kitchen itself is cozily small and functional, its cheer extends to the adjacent garden in an almost magical way. The garden was incorporated as part of the kitchen through the Browns' experimenting with charcoal cookery over the years. They have done as much as anyone in this country to change backyard cooking into an art as carefully executed as indoor cooking. The other rooms in the Browns' household serve as a library, containing one of the largest cookbook collections in the country. It could be said that this entire house and garden are one great kitchen.

In many families, of course, kitchen dining has always been taken for granted. The breadwinner, home from a hard day's work, and the children, in from play, feel more comfortable at the kitchen table. The dining room is reserved for Sunday dinner and state occasions. Here, fashion plays no part, but the kitchen is, in a completely honest and basic way, a gathering place for the family.

It should come as no surprise that Julia Child shares my euphoria about kitchens. She says, "It's the most important room in the house; not only is it the stomach, but the heart and the spirit as well. In addition to the kitchen, a house needs only bathrooms and bedrooms. Besides being a workroom and a studio, the kitchen should also be a family room. So it should be utterly efficient, beautiful, and comfortable." She and Paul Child have been true to this ideal in their two kitchens—one in Cambridge, Massachusetts, and the other near Grasse in the South of France. Both of these kitchens have great space and work surfaces, fine equipment, comfort, beauty, and an abundance of personality. Anyone who walked into either of Julia's kitchens would immediately recognize it to be the stomach, heart, and spirit of the house.

Today's kitchen, which evolved from the fight to emancipate women from drudgery, has now reached a standard of push-button efficiency that Catharine Beecher and her successors—Marion Harland, Mrs. Rorer, and Fannie Farmer—never dreamed of. We have self-cleaning ovens, waste disposals, exhaust fans, dishwash-ers, automatic timers, ice-making units, rotisseries, and small appliances for every culinary operation. Combined with this is the introduction of an old-world touch—cabinetry in the French or Spanish modes, eye-catching tiles, and handsome light fixtures, making a setting that calls for shining copper, utensils of inter-esting shapes, exotic oddments and whimsical bits of Americana. And it was high time we softened our sterile space-age look with the mellowness of Europe, whence came our most important cooking traditions.

For many housewives, it is true, the glorious modern kitchen only provides a backdrop for the reconstitution of quick convenience food and a congenial spot where the family can eat it. Fortunately, in increasing numbers of families, the kitchen is where the heart lies, and everybody, including Dad and the teenage children, is finding food a creative pursuit, a favorite indoor sport, a passion. It stands to reason that a beautiful, well-equipped kitchen is an incentive to good cook-ing, and a family will always rally around a good cook.

[1968]

Tools of My Trade

I have been cooking for nearly sixty-five years out of my three score and ten, and during that time I have used every piece of kitchen equipment invented. In my early years at the beach in Oregon, I cooked on a small woodstove that could hardly hold one big pan and required an intricate regulation of heat. Elsewhere around the world, I have cooked with gas, coal, oil, butane, and electricity. My first dishwasher, and in some ways the best, was my bathtub. I simply piled in the dishes, drew the curtain, and turned on the shower. As for pots and pans and other utensils, I have run the gamut from the ghastly granite-ware of fifty or sixty years ago to enameled iron and Teflon. The point is, I can put up with anything if I have to. But I know what I like, too, and as I begin to equip my fifth kitchen for personal and professional use, I am taking another ruthless inventory of the utensils and appliances in my life. Here are my views on the matter this time around.

First of all, I am an electric cook. If I had a second choice of heat for my stove, it would probably be wood. I loathe gas. I know that one is supposed to have a professional gas stove in order to qualify as a gourmet cook, but maybe I am just never going to be one. I think that people who do not like electric cooking have not bothered to master the technique of antici-pating its flow and ebb of heat. Once you know how to operate the keyboard, it is a joy. An electric oven gives even, gentle heat for baking, and I like the cleanliness and accuracy of electric stove-top cooking, the way it treats my pots and pans, and the results I get from it. I can't say that I have per-suaded any of my students to switch from gas to electricity, which they are obliged to use in my classes, but so far no one has been outraged enough to drop out.

I also like Corning's new smooth-top ceramic ranges—the feel of the surface and the idea of it. Another piece of avant-garde equipment I approve of is my microwave oven. It is a handy booster for performing a number of kitchen chores like melting chocolate and melting or clarifying butter. It does some fish dishes very well, too, such as shad roe or fillets stuffed with a fish mousse, and it's good for cooking bacon and certain veg-etables. I find it most useful when I am pan-broiling chops, steaks, or hamburgers for guests who like their meat in varying degrees of pink. The portions needing more cooking can be tossed into the microwave for a minute or a half-minute to create the difference. It is not as yet the one oven to have in a kitchen, but if you have space and can afford it, it is a luxurious gadget.

I do not know who designs the interiors for dishwashers— in most cases, badly. I once had a perfectly wonderful General Electric mobile dishwasher that provided space for tall-stemmed wineglasses and had racks that allowed plates to be inserted and removed with ease.[1] When it grew old, it was replaced with a new machine with spikes on its racks, no stacking plan, and a top shelf so shallow that glasses of decent size were crushed. I have graduated to a small heavy-duty Hobart professional dishwasher with trays in it that are so much more sensible than anything else on the market. Some manufacturer ought to take the initiative in designing a practical household dishwasher that will hold glasses without breaking them and good plates without chipping them.

My two most valuable and lovable kitchen appliances are the Robot Coupe and the Hobart KitchenAid mixer. Both come with accessories that permit a large range of functions. The Robot Coupe chops, pulverizes, shreds, slices, mixes, and makes pastry. It is quick, clean, functional. It is like having another person in the kitchen and can be talked into doing practically anything. I am sure that Montagné, Carême, or any of the great chefs of the past two centuries would have been enchanted with the prospect of chopping mushrooms for a duxelles or of making beautiful mayonnaise in the Robot

---

[1] I inherited the old dishwasher until Beard demanded to have it back in exchange for the brand-new one.—J. F.

Coupe (not that anything will really replace the flavor and texture of mayonnaise made by hand with fork and plate, good olive oil, and egg yolks). With the Robot Coupe, I now grind my own beef in seconds to the degree of fineness I want for steak tartare and hamburgers. Apart from the advantage of having it absolutely fresh, I can control the amount of fat and grind the seasonings right in with the meat. As for more classical food, the Robot Coupe will produce, in exactly twenty-six seconds, a wonderful *pâte brisée* for making pastry. The method is practically foolproof; the *pâte* is not touched by human hands until it comes out in a little ball ready to be chilled and rolled.

The KitchenAid mixer does things that the Robot Coupe cannot. The larger models like mine come equipped with a hook for kneading bread dough, which saves a lot of energy, although I happen to enjoy kneading by hand. There is also an ice cream freezer attachment that I like to use for making a sherbet or ice cream for dinner at the last minute. The purée attachment is another asset, although it is not strong enough to do certain foods. (The Robot Coupe also purées.) I have prepared a *brandade de morue* in both machines with equal success. If I were banished to a remote spot, I would take the Robot Coupe and the KitchenAid with me. They would see me through almost any kitchen maneuver.

There are times when I am feeling antimachine and prefer the hard work but more aesthetic process of making a *brandade* or aïoli in my treasured marble mortar, slowly grinding the ingredients into a lovely finished texture. A marble mortar has the advantage of keeping the ingredients cool during grinding and can be chilled beforehand to the point where it will hold its cool for a long, long time. Besides which, it is beautiful to look at, and it feels good to the touch. For the same reasons, I like marble for other uses in the kitchen—slabs for kneading bread and rolling pastry. Eventually I hope to own a refrigerated marble top for this purpose, a magnificent bit of equipment I have seen in France and covet greatly.

Along with the marble mortar, a utensil that is more satisfying to use than its mechanical counterpart is the copper bowl for beating egg whites. Again, it's a handsome object and nice to handle, and again, it means work. You must exert a good deal of energy with a large whisk to build the egg whites to the perfect point. Also, you must keep the copper in fine condition, wiping the bowl after each use with vinegar or lemon juice and salt and then rinsing with water. A mixer will, of course, produce comparable volume quite effortlessly.

While I admit to the beauty and capabilities of copper, I don't use much of it because it requires such upkeep. I cannot stand to use it unless it is kept highly polished, and this is too time-consuming for the pace of life today. I realize that it is unmatched as a conductor of heat by any other cooking medium, but I am not going to spend half of my life polishing on that account. If I do occasionally use a copper pan, I prefer one of the older kinds with tinned lining rather than copper-clad stainless steel, which doesn't distribute heat as evenly and is quite heavy to handle besides. I am an admirer of cast aluminum, which I think does an extraordinarily good job, especially the large hotel-ware sauté pans and cookers cast in the classic design.[2] And I still enjoy pan-broiling and sautéing (chicken, for example) in good old iron skillets—"spiders," if you want to call them by their provincial name. I am devoted to Teflon skillets, too, for certain functions, particularly those made with heavy-duty aluminum. Aesthetically, though, Teflon and similar products have their drawbacks,

---

[2] Of course, unlined aluminum has long been discredited as an ideal cooking medium because of its chemical interaction with foods.

because it is not pleasing to stare into a lifeless black, brown, or gray interior. Furthermore, Teflon tends to wear relatively fast, but here is a case where I would uphold efficiency over other considerations.

I choose glass, porcelain, or enameled iron saucepans for making delicate sauces—pans that are heavy enough to provide even heat without using a *bain marie* when you are trying to produce a custard sauce, a hollandaise, or a béarnaise. As for omelet pans, I do not belong to the school that says you must never wash them out but merely wipe them, lest they cause your omelet to stick. (I once watched Fanny Craddock on British television instructing a group of guests on the art of omelets, and they had been told to bring their most disreputable pans.) I have found that heavy pans of cast aluminum or cast iron, properly cleaned and heated, make fine omelets; Teflon-lined pans with rounded sides also give good results.

The advances in ovenproof glass technology by Corning and other manufacturers have put some highly attractive new clear-glass baking dishes on the market. They are simple in design, delicate in weight and appearance, easy to clean, and very effective—in all, a delight to use. I find the soufflé dishes elegant, and the *kugelhopf* mold is almost as nice. There is strong appeal in being able to watch through clear glass as the contents brown to perfection in either of these dishes.

My views on salad bowls are similar to those on omelet pans. I am president of the anti-wooden-salad-bowl association. The oil residue in wooden bowls becomes rancid, the garlic flavors grow stale, and the surface acquires a dank, rather slimy patina that is unpleasant to the touch and is certainly disastrous to delicate salad greens. I believe in making salad in spotlessly clean glass, porcelain, or earthenware, and one of my standbys is a handsome crystal bowl.

Another item I have always been a crank about is knives. I collect good knives the way other people collect fine porcelain. I am particular about the feel of a knife, its heft and balance, but beyond that, the range of my taste is wide. I own French, German, Chinese, and Japanese knives, with a few English and American ones thrown in. I can't say which I like best; it depends on the job to be done. For routine chopping, I enjoy a mammoth French knife. I am also fond of working with a Chinese cleaver or cutter, a versatile instrument that I use for everything. Serrated knives are highly useful, too. I favor one that is called a pâté knife or a serrated slicer, which is long and coarsely edged. The American Gerber knives, made of special steel, deserve attention. I find the slicers and smaller knives good—the company makes a slim, supple boning knife and a little French knife that is excellent—but most of its other knives are not as well balanced as they might be. One of my prizes is a tiny poultry knife from France with a triangular blade less than two inches long. It is superb for its intended purpose, but it has also replaced the common paring knife in my kitchen, and I now keep six on hand.

I suppose a word is in order here about the electric knife. I would no more think of using one on a fine roast or a steak than I would a pruning saw. But it is incredible in principle and has its uses, which in my kitchen is to slice large, crusty loaves of bread, a job it performs wonderfully.

Good knives must be properly cared for by being stored in a rack. I have an impressive one designed for me by my friend Agnes Crowther. It is adapted from an old churn and holds about twenty-five knives in slots or in racks along the sides. Being made of wood, it doesn't ruin the blade edges the way magnetic racks do. Furthermore, it is on wheels and can be rolled around into position anywhere in the kitchen I happen to need it. It is one of my most guarded possessions. Not only is it important to protect knife edges, but the blades must be kept thoroughly clean. Unless made of stainless steel, they should be wiped off after use and dried immediately after washing.

What do I cut, chop, slice, and carve on? Wood, of course. I often serve a meal of cheese, sausage, a bottle of wine, and a good loaf of bread, in which case I carry a breadboard to the table and cut the loaf to order. Now we are told that bread-boards of wood are unsanitary, and I have been sent a board made out of glass, and another of plastic, that are supposed to be the ideal modern surfaces on which to slice bread. Well, I can't stand to use them. Cutting on glass gives me the constant fear that I am going to crack it, and the plastic board is so revolting to the eye that it almost destroys the joy of cutting into a delicious loaf. Are aesthetic considerations of no importance? The same is true of plastic cutting and chopping boards, which are turning up in professional kitchens with greater frequency. A horrid gray in color and dead in sound, they resemble nothing so much as a paving block and are hardly apt to make gastronomy an inviting pursuit. Chopping on a good responsive piece of hardwood gives you the warm feeling that only work with honest materials can bring.

As for the countless smaller utensils, there are a few I would like to single out. I could not live without a Mouli julienne. Although there are many electrical appliances that shred, this hand-operated machine has its unique qualities. Small and rather fragile, it is equipped with three interchangeable cutters that make shreds of different sizes. I use it for zucchini, radishes, carrots, potatoes, and orange peel, among other items. For the money, it is one of the most useful utensils I have. I can put in a good word for the Mouli food mill, too, which has a variety of uses, such as puréeing and ricing.

I have an assortment of wire and aluminum strainers and colanders, but I take special pleasure in using my porcelain strainer. I might as well note here that I am violent on the subject of using cheesecloth to strain and clarify broth, which is universally prescribed. I hold to the old tradition of lining a sieve or colander with linen, and I keep several enormous dinner napkins on hand for this purpose.

Some people stir with spoons, and some don't. Well, I like wooden spatulas. I like the feel of them, the flatness of them, and the quality of the wood. For my hands, they seem to be a natural. Where many people would use a whisk, I might use a spatula. I guess I have developed a technique for it. I have wooden spatulas in sizes ranging from those about the size of a large teaspoon to enormous paddles.

The only type of meat thermometer allowed in my kitchen is a Taylor professional thermometer, which has a slender shaft and a dial the size of a quarter, registering 0° to 220°. Unlike conventional meat thermometers, which are jabbed into a roast and left there like a fatal arrow, this one is inserted into the meat for a reading and then removed, somewhat like a fever thermometer and just as dependable. I also disapprove of conventional meat thermometers because they tell us to cook our beef to 140° for rare. The surface heat of a roast continues to penetrate the meat after it is removed from the oven, and if you wait until the center registers 140° you will not have rare beef, I assure you. I like to take out a roast at 125° and let it stand for ten or fifteen minutes before carving.

My last advice is to be utterly cold-blooded in taking a stock check of your own kitchen. Forget what you paid for certain items or who gave them to you. Whatever is inefficient, ugly, or ersatz should go. It is an easy matter to dispose of unloved objects in New York. Simply put them out on the street, and they will disappear before your back is turned. I did this the last time I cleaned out my kitchen, and people fought over pots and pans in front of my door.

[1973]

To Grind or Not to Grind

There is much to be said for modern appliances in the kitchen, but there are times when we revert to primitive tools simply because they do the job so much better. One of the oldest of these tools (actually two, but we speak of them together) is the mortar and pestle. The mortar may be big enough to hold ten pounds of food or so tiny it can take only one clove of garlic, but the size is secondary to the fact that it fills a very special need. I may be at odds with technology, but if I want to make a small amount of herb butter or perform some similar task, I find that the mortar and pestle cannot be equaled by any machine such as a blender or food processor.

Originally, this was the one and only way to make a really fine purée or a smooth mixture for mousses, mousselines, and galantines. Professional kitchens were equipped with huge mortars and pestles so heavy they had to be operated by ropes and pulleys. In countries like Mexico and India, where chilies and grains are ground by hand, mortars may be made of lava rock or rough stone. The Japanese have a very unusual pottery mortar and pestle with a rough, ridged, glazed interior that almost grinds as it crushes. Then there are other nifty little stone and marble varieties that are very handy in the kitchen. I have a marble mortar about five inches high and two and one-half inches wide, just big enough for a couple of garlic cloves and some fresh herbs, that I use all the time.

In former times, many dishes depended on the mortar and pestle for success. One was the Provençal aïoli, a version of mayonnaise made with garlic, eggs, olive oil, and sometimes bread crumbs. Nowadays you can make an aïoli in a mortar, with great patience, or in a food processor, with great speed. It is up to you, although some people feel that the emulsion of oil, egg, and garlic made in a huge marble mortar, as is done in Provence, results in a more flavorful aïoli. I have tried to be impartial about this, and I find that while it's fun to make the mixture in a big marble mortar, should you happen to own one, you get an equally luscious, thick, wondrous sauce by using the food processor.

However, for small jobs, the mortar and pestle does have distinct advantages. This is true, for example, if you are making a dish with green peppercorns—the newest taste sensation in a century—which few people know how to use properly. Recently, while dining in a fascinating small restaurant called Chez Panisse in Berkeley, California, I had a perfectly cooked duck with green peppercorns, a lovely blend of flavors, but the peppercorns were floating around in the sauce. Had they been crushed to a paste before being added, you would have savored their special flavor without having to bite into the peppercorns themselves, which is not as pleasant to the palate. I feel that a rich, unctuous sauce shouldn't be interrupted by whole peppercorns, green or black.

It's so simple to keep a little mortar around for just such a purpose. When you introduce garlic to a sauce (unless it happens to be one where you want chunks), you can mash the cloves in the mortar, with a little salt to make the grinding easier. Then stir the paste into the sauce, which results in a smooth texture without the bite that pieces of garlic impart.

When I work with certain spices, such as caraway, cardamom, or anise seeds, I often pulverize them in a mortar, which gives more flavor and delicacy when they are added to the finished sauce. I have a great goulash recipe that a friend perfected, in which caraway seeds finely pounded with lemon peel and garlic are added near the end of the cooking time. This brings a finish and distinction to an otherwise bourgeois dish. Here it is.

❧ Viennese Goulash ❧

Peel and thinly slice 6 medium onions. Simmer until golden in 4 tablespoons of butter and 2 tablespoons of oil. Add ¼ cup of Hungarian paprika and ¼ cup of vinegar. Cook 4 minutes, then add 3 pounds of beef rump or chuck cut into 2-inch cubes. Brown the beef all over, and season to taste with salt and pepper. Add 1 teaspoon of dried thyme and ½ cup of tomato purée, and simmer until the liquid is almost reduced to a glaze. Sprinkle with 3 to 4 tablespoons of flour, mixing until the flour is well colored. Add 2 cups of beef broth or enough to immerse the meat, and simmer, covered, until tender—about 2 hours. In a mortar, grind to a paste 1 tablespoon of caraway seeds, the finely chopped zest of 1 lemon, and 2 garlic cloves. Stir into the goulash, and cook another 10 minutes. Serve with spaetzle or noodles. Serves 6.

[1974]

2

*B*eard mourns the passing of breakfast as a full-scale meal in this next group of articles, recalling feasts of sautéed chicken, country ham, and clam muscles cooked in bacon fat and observing breakfast rites around the world. But by the time he was exhorting readers to rise and eat, he himself was reduced to a large cup of tea and a sliver of toast—although he was known to breakfast on leftover asparagus.

"Hearty Luncheon Dishes" prescribes a sensible time to enjoy such classics as *choucroute garnie* and *bollito misto,* too rugged for an evening meal but too good to be missed. "In Search of Cassoulet" reports on "the great bean happening of all time" at a three-star Paris restaurant and searches out New York's own best versions of the dish. I was on the trail with Beard and remember sharing a tasty cassoulet with him at Les Pyrénées, where it is still served daily.

Other articles discuss the joys of teatime and summer food, regional dishes, holiday meals in Provence, and the art of outdoor cookery. Beard was a master at the grill, thanks to an early start in his boyhood days, and wrote four books on the subject. After a collaborative effort with Helen Evans Brown, he told her, "I feel we are the king and queen of charcoal cookery." So they were, and their book is alive and well.

Whatever Happened to Breakfast?

My first breakfast memories are of calling to my mother for tea, toast, fruit, and an egg. This was standard fare for many, many years, except on Sunday morning when my father prepared a certain menu that I suppose went back to pioneer times and his school days. This consisted of fruit—fresh if possible, never orange juice—and sautéed chicken, topped with strips of bacon and a cream sauce and served with hot biscuits and pear or peach preserves—not strawberry, raspberry, or apricot, although sometimes my mother and I would sneak in pineapple or apricot in defiance of the household rule. On winter Sundays, instead of chicken we often had big cakes of sausage cooked to a delicious brown and served with fried apple rings and biscuits.

Come spring and summer, when we went to our house on the Oregon coast, hardly a fortnight passed that we didn't have a remarkable breakfast on the beach, usually for twelve to eighteen people. A driftwood fire was started and allowed to burn down to coals, and then the cooking began. There might be country-cured ham or bacon and sausage cakes; or if some of us had been clamming, we'd have the digging muscle of the clam, cooked in bacon fat and served with rashers of bacon. Nearly always there would be golden brown hotcakes, made with sour cream and served with melted butter and honey. Fruit, eggs, and coffee cake were also part of our feast. We would sit drinking coffee from mugs and eating this hearty food while members of the party took turns manning the griddles. Under an almost cloudless sky, with the exciting roar of the surf, these picnic breakfasts gave pleasures that I still cherish.

I also have memories of visiting an aunt who owned an enormous sheep ranch in eastern Oregon. There, the front door was always unlocked so close friends could come and go as they pleased, and two or three rooms were kept ready to welcome the weary traveler. You never knew whom you'd see at breakfast, which was a hearty and often protracted meal. There would be cornmeal or oatmeal porridge; thickly cut country ham and bacon or sometimes pork chops if an animal had been slaughtered; eggs in many styles; pancakes with honey, syrup, and sweet butter; hot biscuits and muffins or a quick coffee cake; and marvelous home-fried or hash-brown potatoes. (I think that must be where my passion for potatoes for breakfast began.) This was country eating in America sixty years ago.

Breakfasts nowadays are seldom on such an impressive scale. Though I think many people secretly yearn for a big breakfast, they have become so calorie and cholesterol conscious that they routinely limit themselves to coffee, orange juice (which I have never learned to like, except with champagne), toast, and occasionally an egg. Just watch those same people on the road and you'll see them tuck away fruit, bacon and eggs, wheat cakes, and sausage—whatever is on the menu. The delicious self-indulgence of a big breakfast is made even more enjoyable by the sense that one is misbehaving.

Breakfasts, I have discovered, differ greatly throughout the world. The most entertaining ones I recall took place during three mornings in Norway. There, where lunch is a sparse meal, breakfast is traditionally a form of smorgasbord, with cured, smoked, and fresh fish; cold meats; eggs; fruit; cheeses; cereals; and different breads—a great spread. On the first morning, I watched with amusement and some horror as tourists wandered around a huge table piling cold meat, a little cheese, smoked fish, and a few salad greens on one plate. Suddenly they would spot prunes, applesauce, cornflakes, and other familiar foods, which they heaped on the meat, cheese, and fish. They never learned to take more than one plate. This performance was repeated for two more mornings.

Breakfast in other countries is a much slimmer affair. Coffee, chocolate, or tea with rolls, croissants, brioche, and other baked things are what you get in France, Italy, and Spain. In Holland, one has cheese, cold meat, and rolls, while in Japan you might be served fried or smoked fish and salted plums. The British, however, have always been stalwart breakfast eaters. They have loved their porridge, eggs, sausages, ham, bacon, grilled kidneys, mushrooms, tomatoes, finnan haddie, and kippers, always accompanied by pots of tea, cold crisp toast, and marmalade. Although you still see substantial breakfasts being set down in front of old-timers in England, the new generation seems to have adopted the fast-food-style breakfast of juice, toast, and coffee, which I find a shame.

There has been a similar decline in our own great national breakfasts, but a few hearty dishes survive in various parts of the country. At some point—and I'm not sure where or when—an unknown cook got the idea that hash would make a divine breakfast dish, which it certainly does. Unfortunately, good hash is extremely hard to find these days. Mostly what one gets is something out of a can, ground beyond all recognition, and artificially flavored. Even when cooked fairly crisp, it bears little resemblance to good old-fashioned corned-beef hash, made with well-cooked corned beef, rather coarsely chopped by hand, and blended with chopped potato, chopped onion, and a touch of nutmeg. There should be enough fat left on the corned beef to give it a moist texture. Cooked until crisp and brown on the outside and topped with fried or poached eggs, this can make a truly memorable morning meal.

There are many other good egg dishes to be had, too. For one, take a baked potato, split and butter it, break an egg over each half, and return it to the oven to bake until the eggs are set. Serve with a few rashers of bacon. Or you might opt for quick French omelets, filled with all manner of things, according to one's taste and pocketbook—with caviar, if money is no object, or with chili if you long for palate-searing pungency.

Growing numbers of people, I find, like nothing better than eating leftovers for breakfast. I have friends, for example, who always overbuy steak so they will have enough left for breakfast with toast or maybe leftover potatoes fried in a skillet. I've known others who munch salads and vegetables or cold chicken.

Then at the opposite pole there are those from the catch-it-and-eat-it school, who get up early to catch a mess of trout, roll them in cornmeal, cook them in bacon fat, and serve them with crisp bacon and hot biscuits and cornbread.

If I could choose any place in America for a breakfast to revel in, I would choose Kentucky. Here the tradition of aged hams still lingers, and one can find specimens that taste the way they did when I was young, with that salty, tangy, smoky flavor. A bountiful breakfast in Kentucky would start with melon, not too mushy and not too sweet, that had been cooled in springwater. After this I would have strong, well-brewed coffee, minus cream and sugar, followed by a ham steak, blanched to remove some of the salt, and sautéed very gently until cooked through and delicately colored. With this should come redeye gravy, made from the ham drippings and strong coffee, cooked down and poured over the ham; then two fresh eggs, cooked sunny-side up in butter, and home-fried potatoes.

On the other hand, if I should be with friends in New York, we might start breakfast with a collection of smoked fish—whitefish, chub, sturgeon, paper-thin slices of smoked salmon—with fresh cream cheese; thinly sliced onion; perhaps split, toasted, and buttered bagels; and a bowl of watercress. Then we'd move on to coffee with fresh toast and honey or tea with heated brioche, sweet butter, and raspberry jam.

The one time we are apt to go all out for a festive breakfast is during the holidays. For many years now, I have invited fifteen or twenty friends to come on Christmas Day for champagne and breakfast. The two seem to go together, and if I could live as I choose, a bottle of champagne at 11 A.M. or just before a late breakfast would be my idea of heaven. To nibble with the champagne, since I usually serve a Portuguese codfish-potato dish, I take the skins of the potatoes I baked for the dish, butter them well, sprinkle them with salt and pepper, and pop them into a hot oven or under the broiler until the butter melts and they get crisp and delicately brown. Sometimes I make them free-form; other times, I cut them into neat strips.

After this, we have a sit-down buffet. The featured item is the Codfish Portuguese. I put a huge mound of the puréed codfish, potato, cream, and garlic mixture in a baking dish, sprinkle it with buttered bread crumbs, put it in the oven, and out comes a gorgeous crustily golden pile. I also serve a cold ham, for which I have an abiding weakness, and perhaps Italian sausages, sweet and hot, or cakes of sausage meat that I make myself. If asparagus is available in the markets at holiday time, I might serve a huge platter of it. If not, a big bowl of watercress or baked tomatoes, if there are any decent ones to be had. For breads, I traditionally have a Sally Lunn and sometimes a brioche loaf, stollen, or favorite fruitcake, or a carrot cake brought by a friend. And of course, jams, marmalades, and tea or coffee.

One Christmas, I was living in the Stanford Court Hotel in San Francisco. Being an early riser, I had a very early breakfast all by myself. It was a beautiful sunny day with blue sky and crisp air. In my room I had a tiny Christmas tree. What could be better, I thought, than raspberries—they were late that year—with sugar and thick cream? I had a huge bowl of them, and they were all raspberries should be—ripe, flavorful, and a festive red. I also ordered buttermilk pancakes, made from a family recipe I'd given the pastry chef. The pancakes were tender, and I lavished plenty of butter and maple syrup on them.

With a few rashers of bacon, not too soft and not too crisp, and a pot of good tea, my Christmas breakfast was complete.

ᾱ Codfish Portuguese ᾰ

2 pounds dried salt codfish,
  soaked 12 hours or overnight
  in cold water
6 to 8 potatoes

1/3 cup olive oil
3 cloves garlic, minced
About 1/3 cup cream
1/2 cup buttered crumbs

Drain the codfish and pull apart into small pieces. Put in a saucepan, cover with cold water, and bring to a boil. Simmer for 5 minutes or until flaky and tender. Drain well and cool. When cool enough to handle, shred or chop very fine and pound in a mortar.

Meanwhile, bake the potatoes. Remove carefully from their skins. Add the codfish, oil, garlic, and cream. Beat by hand or in an electric mixer, or whirl in a food processor to make a light, fluffy mixture. Taste for seasoning. Codfish is salty, so you might not need any more salt.

Turn into a well-buttered baking dish or casserole, and sprinkle with the crumbs. Bake in a 350° oven until very hot, about 35 minutes.

ᾱ Herb Sausage ᾰ

2 pounds coarsely ground pork
  from the butt
1/2 pound fresh pork fat cut in
  1/2-inch cubes
4 finely chopped cloves
  of garlic

1 teaspoon salt
2 teaspoons dried basil
1 1/2 teaspoons anise seed
*1 teaspoon freshly ground
  black pepper*

Combine all ingredients and mix well by hand. Make a small patty, and sauté it to taste for seasoning. Fill sausage casings with the mixture or form into patties. (If using casings, follow instructions that come with the hand or electric sausage stuffer.)

To cook: Prick the sausage links all over with a needle. Place in a skillet with $1/4$ inch of water. Cook over medium heat, turning sausage frequently, until the water has evaporated and the sausage is nicely browned all over.

If cooking sausage patties, place them in a heavy skillet over moderately low heat. Cook until well browned on both sides, pouring off some of the fat as it accumulates.

❧ Buttermilk Pancakes ❧

2 cups all-purpose flour　　*$1^1/_2$ cups buttermilk*
1 teaspoon baking soda　　*3 eggs, separated*
1 teaspoon salt　　　　　　*$1/4$ cup butter, melted*

Sift the dry ingredients into a mixing bowl. Stir in the buttermilk and well-beaten egg yolks. Add the butter and beat until smooth. Beat the egg whites until firm but not dry. Fold into the batter very gently. Drop the batter by spoonfuls on a lightly greased hot griddle and cook until brown. Turn and brown the other side.

[1978]

ℋearty Luncheon Dishes

Time was when one ate the principal meal of the day in the afternoon, which I think was a civilized and congenial practice, and in Europe you still find the habit of large luncheon parties. Not only is it a charming way to entertain, but it also provides an opportunity for offering certain dishes in the French, Italian, and English cuisines that, when served at dinner, are difficult to digest and become persecutors of sleep. I am often appalled to be a guest at a supper or dinner party where such things as *pot-au-feu, cassoulet,* or *choucroute garnie* are served at eight-thirty or even at midnight, after the theater.

Rather than banish these delicious dishes from our menus, why not choose a sensible time when they may, in good conscience, be prepared—say, for a Saturday or Sunday luncheon. Every Saturday during the winter, Manhattan's Quo Vadis restaurant makes a midday specialty of *bollito misto,* and the number of devotees seems to grow each year. It is a colossal and extraordinarily good meal. After you have passed a couple of hours devouring it, with some good wine and perhaps a bit of cheese to finish, you can go forth content for an afternoon's shopping or gallery hopping.

✐ Bollito Misto ✐

A true *bollito misto* encompasses several meats, so it should always be planned for a large number of guests, twelve being ideal. The usual display might include chicken or capon, pork, veal, beef, tongue, and sausage, with vegetables and sauces. If a calf's head is added, that rules out veal, and sometimes both beef and veal tongues are used. The choice is flexible, but there must be variety.

In a very large kettle, combine 4 pounds of brisket of beef; 2 or 3 onions, one of them stuck with 2 cloves; several leeks; 2 or 3 carrots; 2 garlic cloves; 2 tablespoons of salt; 1 bay leaf; a pinch of rosemary; and water to cover. Bring the mixture to a boil and simmer for 1^1/$_2$ hours. Add a calf's head, boned and rolled (cook the brains separately in salted water for about 25 minutes), or 2 veal tongues, and cook for $1^1/_2$ hours more. Add one 3- to 4-pound roasting chicken or capon and 1 or 2 *cotechino* sausages, and cook until the meats are tender. If the calf's head and chicken are done first, remove them and keep them warm. Taste the broth for seasoning, and add salt if necessary.

While the meats are cooking, prepare additional vegetables, timing them so they will be done at the same time as the meats: boil 12 or more medium peeled potatoes in salted water until tender; separately, cook carrots, leeks, and onions.

Arrange the meats and vegetables on a large heated platter, and have a carving board at your side. Carve the meats to each person's taste, and offer a potato and vegetables. Serve the rich broth in cups.

Typical accompaniments for a *bollito misto* are coarse salt, mustard fruits (available in jars or cans from Italian or specialty food shops), and horseradish sauce or freshly grated horseradish. I think a good herbed vinaigrette sauce is one of the nicest complements. Serves 12 or more.

❧ Herbed Vinaigrette Sauce ❧

Combine $^3/_4$ cup of olive oil and $^1/_4$ cup of wine vinegar with 1 teaspoon each of salt and freshly ground black pepper, 3 tablespoons of chopped Italian parsley, 2 tablespoons each of chopped chives and one other fresh herb—such as basil, mint, thyme, or rosemary—and finely chopped garlic to taste. Blend thoroughly. The sauce should be really thick with the fresh green herbs.

With such a meal, a little cheese and fresh fruit are about as much as one would wish to serve. For wine, an Italian Barolo or an Hermitage from the Rhône Valley would be ideal.

❧ Bourride ❧

One of the more delectable dishes in southern French cuisine is a bourride, a soup that is highly aromatized with garlic and has a creamy, velvety texture that is supremely satisfying to the palate and tongue.

Buy 4 fillets of flounder, snapper, bass, or similar fish. Also ask for a fish carcass and a couple of heads for the stock. If you are deft with a knife, buy whole fish and fillet them yourself.

Put the fish bones and heads in a kettle with 1 onion stuck with 2 cloves, 3 or 4 garlic cloves, 4 sprigs of parsley, 2 teaspoons of salt, 3 to 4 cups of water, and 1/2 cup of white wine or dry vermouth. Bring the mixture to a boil, skim off any scum that forms, and simmer for 25 or 30 minutes. Strain and keep hot.

Prepare an aïoli: To make it by hand, crush 3 or 4 garlic cloves in a mortar and mix in 3 egg yolks. Work in a fruity olive oil, a few drops at a time, until the aïoli begins to thicken like mayonnaise. Increase the flow of oil, while continuing to stir, until the aïoli is literally thick enough to cut. You will need about 2 cups of oil in all. Add salt to taste and a squeeze of lemon juice.

To make the aïoli in a blender, put the garlic and egg yolks in the container with 1 tablespoon of lemon juice and 1 teaspoon of salt. Turn the blender on and off. Then turn it to high and slowly pour the oil into the center of the container and blend the sauce until it is thick. Transfer to a bowl or saucepan. [To make in a food processor, first blend the egg yolks and garlic together for 2 or 3 seconds, then slowly pour in the olive oil, with the machine running, until the mixture begins to thicken. The rest of the oil can be added more rapidly. When the sauce is quite thick, season with salt and lemon juice.]

Measure the fish fillets at their thickest point with a ruler. Heat a skillet or sauté pan large enough to hold the fish in one layer, butter it lightly, and add 1 or 2 crushed garlic cloves. Lightly salt the fillets, sprinkle with freshly ground pepper, and arrange them in the pan. Pour the hot fish stock over them, and poach them for 10 minutes per inch of thickness, no more. Remove the fillets to a hot platter, cover them with foil, and keep them warm.

Rapidly reduce the stock over high heat by slightly less than half, add 1/4 cup of heavy cream, and cook for a few seconds without letting the mixture boil. Strain into the aïoli, stirring vigorously, until the liquid has the consistency of heavy cream. Put each fillet in a soup plate, ladle the rich, garlicky broth over them, and sprinkle with chopped parsley. Serve with boiled tiny new potatoes and toasted garlic-scented French bread. You may also pass a bowl of extra aïoli, so it can be added to the broth, to taste. For hearty eaters, you may need to double the recipe. Serves 4.

Follow the bourride with cheese and fruit or a delicate mousse or sorbet. Drink a brisk white wine, such as an Hermitage blanc or a Muscadet.

❧ Choucroute Garnie ❧

This dish happens to be one of my all-time favorites, and I've found that it is a great stimulus to the appetite. The sight of the glistening mound of sauerkraut surrounded by delicate pink pieces of smoked pork loin and sausage is calculated to nudge the most jaded palate. If you are serving *choucroute,* make it for a large group of people so you can have an interesting selection of meats.

Wash 4 pounds of sauerkraut well and drain thoroughly. Wash a 2-pound piece of rather lean salt pork. Cut several fairly thick slices (about 1/2 pound) of the pork, and parboil them for

10 minutes in water. Drain, and arrange in the bottom of a heavy 8-quart kettle. Cover with the sauerkraut, and bury the remaining salt pork in the center. Add 3 to 4 cups of chicken or beef broth, or enough to cover the sauerkraut, bring to a boil over brisk heat, and boil for 5 minutes. Add 2 finely chopped garlic cloves and $1/2$ teaspoon of freshly ground black pepper, and simmer, covered, for $1^{1}/_{2}$ hours. Add 1 or 2 good-sized *cotechino* sausages (more readily available than the traditional French *saucisson à l'ail*), and simmer for another 40 minutes. Add 10 to 12 juicy knackwurst and 1 or 2 rings of Polish sausage or ring bologna, and simmer for 20 minutes more.

Meanwhile, brown a 3- to 4-pound smoked loin of pork in a 350° oven. Most smoked pork loin is already cooked and merely needs heating through. It can be kept separate after browning or added to the sauerkraut mixture for the last few moments of cooking.

Boil 16 potatoes, peeled and trimmed to fairly equal size, in salted water to cover until they are tender. Drain, return to the pan, and set over low heat to dry for 1 or 2 minutes.

Gently heat 8 fairly thin slices of cooked ham in white wine barely to cover, but do not let them simmer.

To serve the *choucroute garnie:* Mound the sauerkraut on a large platter. Slice the smoked pork loin, the *cotechino,* and the Polish sausage or ring bologna, and place them around the sauerkraut, along with the whole knackwurst. Put some slices of the salt pork at one end of the sauerkraut. Roll the ham slices, and place them at the other end.

Serve with the boiled potatoes, lightly dusted with chopped parsley, mustards of all types, and rye or French bread. Drink an Alsatian Riesling or a California Johannisberg Riesling. This makes a truly gargantuan feast. The meats can be varied still further to include boiled beef, fresh pork, spareribs, pig's feet, duck, or goose. Serves 8 or more.

❧ Bouillabaisse ❧

Bouillabaisse, a specialty of the South of France and another hearty and flavorful dish that really shines at the midday meal, is not a soup. The best description of it would be a fairly liquid fish stew. Although it is basically simple, its excellence lies in the fact that the taste and texture of each type of fish come through. Timing is all, or you will end up with a mess of overcooked fish in a broth.

Although in this country, we cannot find the same fish used in the South of France, it is perfectly possible to make substitutions, which will depend on where you live. On the Atlantic coast, you have a choice of halibut, rockfish, cod, or even swordfish for the firmer fish; flounder, snapper, or lemon sole for the less firm; and lobster and mussels for the shellfish. On the West Coast, you can use halibut, black cod, or sablefish for the firm-textured fish; sand dabs, snapper, or rex sole for the softer; and crabs and small clams for the shellfish. You will need 5 pounds of fish, 2 lobsters or 4 crabs, and 1 quart of mussels or 24 small clams.

Clean all the fish and cut them into slices about 1 inch thick. If heads are available, cut them in half. Separate the firm fish from the less firm.

In a wide braising pan or kettle large enough to hold all the seafood, heat $1/2$ cup of olive oil. Add 5 or 6 garlic cloves and 2 large onions, both finely chopped; 4 or 5 ripe tomatoes, peeled, seeded, and chopped; a stick of dried fennel or about 2 teaspoons fennel seed; a good pinch of saffron; 2 tablespoons of salt; and $1^{1}/_{2}$ teaspoons of freshly ground pepper. Add the firm fish, the lobsters or crabs, the fish heads, and boiling water to more than cover the seafood. Boil briskly for 7 to 8 minutes, which makes the oil and water combine and gives a richer broth. Add the softer fish and cook for 5 to 6 minutes more, but at a less brisk heat. Be careful not to overcook.

While the fish are cooking, put the mussels, well scrubbed and bearded, or the clams in another kettle with 1½ cups of water, and cook them, covered, over high heat until the shells open. Discard any that do not open. Strain the broth into the bouillabaisse, and reserve the mussels or clams, keeping them warm.

Transfer the fish and shellfish to a hot serving dish, and cover them with a linen napkin. Reduce the broth over high heat for several minutes. Correct the seasoning.

Line a tureen or large bowl with slices of French bread, lightly toasted. Add the fish and mussels or clams. Cut the lobsters or crabs into serving pieces, discarding the inedible parts but leaving the shells on. Arrange them on the bread. Pour the broth over all.

Serve immediately in bowls or soup plates with more toasted French bread. You may also want to serve a peppery rouille, which is part sauce, part condiment. A dry Provence white wine is traditional with bouillabaisse, but a Muscadet or California pinot blanc would be just as good. Serves 8 to 10.

✾ Rouille ✾

Soak 4 or 5 dried hot red peppers in water to cover for several hours. Drain and pound in a mortar. Work in 3 garlic cloves, a touch of salt, and 4 or 5 tablespoons of olive oil until the mixture is smooth and well blended. If you like, stir in about 1 cup of bouillabaisse broth and 1 tablespoon of hot paprika.

✾ Couscous ✾

Every year, it seems to me, more and more people are making couscous, which takes its name from a particular grind of wheat.

Traditionally, couscous is steamed over broth in a two-part wasp-waisted steamer called a *couscoussière*, but you can improvise a suitable steamer by putting a colander over the pot containing the broth and covering it well with a sheet or two of foil. As the grains of wheat are rather fine, I usually place a layer of cheesecloth on the bottom of the steamer or colander to prevent them from falling through the holes. This is the kind of meal that turns a Sunday lunch into a great ceremony.

For the broth, brown 2 pounds of cubed fat-free shoulder of lamb in 4 or 5 tablespoons of olive oil. Add 2 very large or 3 medium onions and 3 garlic cloves, both finely chopped. Stir the ingredients together, and cook gently for 5 to 8 minutes. Transfer to the bottom part of a *couscoussière* or a deep kettle over which you can place a colander or steamer. Add $1^1/_2$ cups of Italian plum tomatoes with their juice and 4 fairly small zucchini cut into $1^1/_2$-inch lengths. Add 1 can of drained chickpeas and water or stock to cover. Bring the mixture to a boil, and skim off any scum that forms. Add $1^1/_2$ tablespoons of salt, 1 or 2 dried hot red peppers, and 1 teaspoon of freshly ground pepper. Cover and simmer for 1 hour. Add 4 carrots, cut into thin slices; 4 small white turnips, cut into $1^1/_2$-inch dice; and 2 or 3 green peppers, cut into thin strips. Simmer for 15 minutes.

Wash $1^1/_2$ pounds of couscous thoroughly, rub it through the hands, and squeeze it dry. Put in a cheesecloth-lined steamer or colander and place over the simmering broth. Cover tightly and seal with foil. Steam for about 45 minutes.

In a mortar, place 8 peppercorns, 12 coriander pods, 3 or 4 small dried hot red peppers or 1 chili jalapeño, 1 garlic clove, and 2 to 3 tablespoons of olive oil and pound until the mixture is well blended. Add a little of the broth from the pot and a goodly amount of Tabasco.

Transfer the steamed couscous to a bowl. Put the broth, meat, and vegetables in another dish. Serve along with the sauce. With this, drink a chilled rosé or a very young Beaujolais.

Some people like to serve chicken kebabs with the couscous; others use chicken stock for the broth and serve it with broiled chicken. In any form, it qualifies as a remarkable dish, although not the lightest fare in the world. Serves 8.

≈ Cassoulet ≈

There are many versions of cassoulet, all of them good and all monumentally substantial. One of the versions of which I am fondest was originated by an older Frenchwoman who lived in this country for many years and adapted the recipes of her native land to the best raw materials available in New York, San Francisco, or wherever she happened to be. I have made her adaptation of cassoulet many times and still think it is one of the best I've ever eaten.

Soak 2 pounds of Great Northern beans overnight in water to more than cover. Add 1 tablespoon of salt; 1 onion stuck with 2 cloves; 3 or 4 garlic cloves; 1 bay leaf; and 1 pig's foot, split. Bring to a boil, skim off any scum that rises, and simmer until the beans are just tender. Be careful not to overcook them.

While the beans are cooking, salt and pepper well 1 small leg or half leg of lamb (about 3¹/₂ pounds) and 3 pounds of loin or shoulder of pork. Put the meats in a roasting pan and roast at 325° for 1¹/₂ hours, basting from time to time with 1¹/₂ cups of red wine. Let the meats cool, then chill so that the fat in the pan juices congeals. Skim off the fat and reserve the juices. Cut the meats into 2-inch cubes.

Poach 8 to 10 French *saucissons* or Italian sausages in water to cover for 5 minutes. Or use a larger sausage, such as *saucisson à l'ail, cotechino,* or Polish kielbasa, cutting it into slices about $1/2$ inch thick.

Finely chop 4 to 6 garlic cloves, and blend them with $1^1/2$ teaspoons of crumbled thyme and 1 teaspoon of freshly ground pepper. Remove the pig's foot from the cooked beans, and cut away the skin and meat from the bones. Drain the beans, reserving the liquid, and discard the bay leaf, onion, and garlic cloves.

Put a layer of beans in a deep earthenware or enameled iron pot, sprinkle with some of the garlic-herb mixture, and add some of the diced meats, including the meat and skin from the pig's foot and the sausages. Continue making layers until all the ingredients are used, finishing with a layer of beans.

Combine the reserved pan juices with the bean liquid, $1/2$ cup of red wine, and 2 tablespoons of tomato paste. Pour enough into the pot to reach almost to the final layer of beans. Top with a few strips of salt pork, cut rather thin, and cover lightly with foil. Bake at 350° for 1 hour. Remove the foil, sprinkle the top with dry bread crumbs, and bake for 1 hour more or until the liquid is absorbed, the top is glazed, and the crumbs are brown. If the liquid is absorbed too quickly during the first hour or so, add more.

Serve with crisp bread and a hearty wine, such as a Châteauneuf-du-Pape. Serves 10 to 12.

You can vary this cassoulet by adding roast or preserved goose or crisp roast duck, or you can make it just with lamb and sausages, omitting the pork. Also leave out the tomatoes, if you like, or add more garlic. The recipe is very flexible, and any way you prepare it, the result is likely to be superb.

❧ Poule-au-Pot ❧

I believe it was Henri IV who first advocated a chicken in every pot, and *poule-au-pot* has passed down through the years as his memorial. It is a perfect dish for Sunday lunch, and you might wish to double the recipe, for the cold edition is almost better than the hot.

Blanch a good-sized head of cabbage in boiling salted water for 15 to 18 minutes or until the leaves can be separated easily.

Prepare a forcemeat for the leaves: In a heavy skillet, sauté 2 medium onions and 1 garlic clove, both finely chopped, in 4 tablespoons of butter until the vegetables are barely wilted. With a fork, blend in well 1$\frac{1}{2}$ pounds of ground pork and $\frac{1}{2}$ pound of finely chopped mushrooms. Add 3 or 4 chopped chicken livers, 2 teaspoons of salt, and 1 teaspoon of thyme. Cook for about 10 minutes, tossing from time to time. Add $\frac{1}{2}$ cup of fresh bread crumbs, $\frac{1}{4}$ cup of cognac, and 2 lightly beaten eggs. Cook until the mixture is thickened. If it is too liquid, drain it carefully.

Remove the leaves from the cabbage and spread them out flat. Put some of the forcemeat on each leaf and carefully roll it up, tucking in the ends. Arrange the stuffed leaves snugly side by side in a skillet or saucepan so they won't unroll, cover with some of the cabbage liquid or with stock, and simmer gently for 15 minutes.

Truss a 4- to 5-pound roasting chicken and put it in a large kettle with a beef marrow bone, 4 to 6 well-cleaned leeks, 4 medium onions, 4 carrots, 2 medium turnips, a rib of celery, 1$\frac{1}{2}$ tablespoons of salt, 1 teaspoon of thyme, 2 or 3 sprigs of parsley, and water to cover. Bring to a boil, skim off any scum that rises, and reduce the heat. Simmer, covered, for 50 minutes to 1$\frac{1}{4}$ hours or until the chicken is just tender. Be careful not to overcook. If the chicken is done before some of the vegetables, remove it and keep it warm.

Just before serving, add a little of the chicken broth to the stuffed cabbage and simmer it for about 15 minutes more. Transfer the chicken to a platter and surround it with the stuffed cabbage and the vegetables from the pot. Serve the broth separately. Boiled potatoes are a must with this dish. It is also usually accompanied by coarse salt, *cornichons,* and grated Gruyère cheese. A Moulin-à-Vent or a Fleurie is the best wine to have with this. Serves 4.

⁊ Beefsteak and Kidney Pudding ⁊

Not all the dishes I consider appropriate for midday fare are French or Italian. One of them is English. Steak and kidney pudding is completely different from the better-known steak and kidney pie. When I was first in England as a young man, I well remember eating at a small bistro near the office of some friends. If you were a regular, you got a fresh napkin on Mondays and kept it in a napkin ring in your own pigeonhole for the rest of the week. Although the proprietor was a Belgian, there was always a magnificent beefsteak and kidney pudding on Wednesdays, to which he gave a Continental touch by using wine instead of the usual water for the liquid. Savory and heartwarming, this was a meal I looked forward to each week.

The pastry for this recipe is different from the usual one in that it is lubricated by suet. Combine $1/2$ pound of cold suet, very finely chopped, with 4 cups of flour and $1^1/2$ teaspoons of salt. Rub together until the mixture resembles coarse meal. Add 6 to 8 tablespoons of ice water. Pull the pastry together by rolling it into a ball and kneading it well until it is thoroughly blended and very smooth. Sprinkle with a little flour and chill for 30 to 40 minutes.

Divide the pastry into 2 pieces, one about double the volume of the other. Roll the larger piece into a circle $1/4$ inch thick, drape it over the rolling pin, and unroll it over a 6-cup pudding basin or bowl. Let it ease into the bottom of the basin and around the sides, leaving it untrimmed for the time being.

Cut 2 pounds of top round of beef or beef chuck into $2\frac{1}{2}$-inch cubes, toss them lightly in flour, and put them in the pastry. Add 1 or 2 veal kidneys, trimmed of fat and cut into 1-inch cubes, sprinkle lightly with flour, and mix with the beef. (If you can't find veal kidneys, use 6 to 8 lamb kidneys, soaked in milk for $1\frac{1}{2}$ hours, dried, and cut into 1-inch dice.) Add 2 large onions, finely chopped; 1 cup of thinly sliced mushrooms; 3 tablespoons of chopped parsley; 1 tablespoon of salt; and 1 teaspoon each of thyme and freshly ground pepper. Mix well with the hands, and add $1\frac{1}{2}$ cups of boiling water or stock.

Roll out the remaining piece of pastry into a circle large enough to fit the top of the basin. Trim the excess from the overhanging bottom pastry, dampen the edge with water, and put on the top crust. Pinch and crimp the two edges together to seal them well. Cover the pudding with a piece of foil, and then set it on a tea towel that has been wrung out in hot water, sprinkled well with flour, and shaken. Tie the towel securely under the rim of the basin with string or twine, then bring up the diagonally opposite corners of the towel, two at a time, and knot them over the top of the basin to provide a handle for lifting.

Lower the basin with this handle into an 8- to 10-quart kettle and pour boiling water into the kettle until it reaches the point below the rim of the basin at which the towel is tied. Bring the water to a boil, reduce the heat to a simmer, and steam the pudding for $4\frac{1}{2}$ to 5 hours. As the water boils away, renew it from time to time.

Lift out the pudding and remove the cloth and foil. Dry the basin and wrap it in a linen napkin. Serve the pudding directly from the basin, accompanied by boiled potatoes and red wine. Salad and fruit are all you need to complete this substantial meal. Serves 4.

[1971]

𝒥n Search of Cassoulet

Cassoulet has come into fashion in this country only in the last ten or twenty years, but in France it has been one of the most cherished dishes of bourgeois cookery for centuries. Montaigne deified it as "the God of Cookery" in three persons, the trinity being the cassoulets of Castelnaudary, Carcassonne, and Toulouse, and if this tribute seems irreverent for a dish of beans and meat, we must remember how seriously the French have always taken their food. Yet the appeal of cassoulet *is* sometimes sublime, which is hard to explain of a dish so hearty it can only be eaten safely at midday with plenty of time for a digestive stupor. Certainly it is unthinkable to eat cassoulet at night and go to bed, a lesson I learned the hard way a number of years ago in Paris.

On that occasion, the Great Bean Happening of all time, several gastronomes, mostly French, were invited to an evening of cassoulet tasting by Raymond Oliver, proprietor and chef of the three-star Paris restaurant Grand Vefour. I was the only American in the group, which included the late Simone Arbellot, Jean Arnobauldi, and Robert Courtine, who considers himself Mr. Food in France. M. Oliver had asked us to come between eight-thirty and nine that night. For a first course, he plied us with a generous helping of his famous shrimp toast. After that came not three but four cassoulets. We began with the celebrated progenitor, the cassoulet of Castelnaudary, which classically contains fresh pork, ham, pork skin, sausage, bits of *confit d'oie*, and beans. After an intermission, we went on to the equally famed cassoulet of Toulouse, which resembles the first, save for the inclusion of salt pork, Toulouse sausages, and lamb—usually either boned breast or shoulder—and sometimes substitutes duck for the preserved goose. Thirdly, we tasted the cassoulet of Carcassonne. Here, in addition to pork, ham, sausage, pork skin, and lamb, the distinctive ingredient (in season, and it was in season for this event) is partridge. For the finale, we had M. Oliver's own version of a cassoulet, which was based on all the others but was cooked longer and was greatly different in seasoning.

This marathon meal, set awash by gallons of new Beaujolais, lasted until one o'clock in the morning, at which point we heaved ourselves out into the night. I remember walking from the Palais Royale around the Place de la Concorde, across the bridge, up the Boulevard St.-Germain, over to the Place St.-Sulpice, and then to my apartment. Enough action to shake down Castelnaudary, Toulouse, Carcassonne, and M. Oliver, I thought—but no. I was up again at two-thirty and walked for another two hours along the Seine.

Although I wouldn't have missed that evening for anything in the world, it was many months before I could look at a bean. I have long since recovered, and I find myself on the cassoulet trail again. Good ones are hard to come by. They are not made by cutting a pork chop and a lamb chop, mixing them with canned kidney beans, throwing in some nondescript sausage, and topping it off with a few crumbs; yet I have had many like this in my time. I have also eaten cassoulet when it seemed to be made with chili powder and an abundance of tomato, which smothered the beautiful blending of the essential flavors. I have had tinned cassoulet from France that was inexcusable and frozen cassoulet that was even worse. Simple though the dish is, it takes careful preparation to make it a great experience.

In New York, there are several French restaurants where cassoulet is more or less a regular on the menu, and the quality ranges from good to mediocre. Also, some of the city's outstanding French chefs, in a burst of nostalgia, will produce a cassoulet from time to time—not in the classic styles but according to personal taste. The beans differ, the meats differ, the preparations differ. In fact, you will find as many versions of this dish as there are cooks. One could make a case for calling Boston baked beans a cassoulet Américaine, for that matter, and several years ago I saw Texas chili on a Paris menu under the name "Espèce de Cassoulet du Far-Ouest," and so it is.

Among New York's rarer cassoulets, one of the noblest can be found at Lutèce as an occasional winter plat du jour on the lunch menu. It bears the distinctive touch of chef André Soltner and is pleasing for its gelatinous, lip-sticking character, derived from the slow cooking of pig's feet, pork skin, and salt pork along with the beans—pea beans in this case, luscious to the bite. The other principal ingredients are roast goose; breast of lamb, defatted by high heat and cut into small pieces; and *saucisson à l'ail*, made by one of the best charcutiers in the city—not as pungent as the real Toulouse sausage, but nonetheless exceedingly good. Soltner adds a little tomato to his cassoulet, coloring it delicately without upsetting the balance of flavors. A brisk '73 Beaujolais accompanied this tasting and cut the richness, where a heavier wine might not have done so. If you try Lutèce's cassoulet, order nothing to start with, I beg you, and have only a bit of salad and fruit sherbet after, and of course plenty of wine.

I have been eating cassoulet at Quo Vadis for over twenty years. The present chef, Eugène Bernard, is from Pau, in the southwest of France on the fringe of the cassoulet country. Therefore, he is very much at home with its traditions. At the recent tasting, Bernard created an ingenious substitute for *confit d'oie* by immersing a duck in a *saumure*—a brine bath—for two or three days before roasting it. The flesh of the duck becomes sweeter with this treatment and absorbs almost enough salt to season the entire dish. The beans, Great Northern, were cooked with *les couennes*—pieces of pork skin—tied together and flavored with onion, garlic, and pepper. In addition to the duck, the meats consisted of lamb, pork, salt pork, and a wonderful sausage closely resembling *cotechino*. Bernard believes in baking his cassoulet until it forms a crust, folding the crust in, and baking it till another forms, sometimes repeating the process once more. This introduces nice crisp bits among the other textures. The wine this time was a great fruity Châteauneuf-du-Pape, which had a friendly kinship with the earthiness of the cassoulet. And I succumbed to *anguilles au vert* as a first course.

At the Coach House, Leon Lianides occasionally offers a cassoulet with Greek overtones, which is not surprising, since he is Greek, and he tells me it reminds him of a native bean soup called *fasoulada*. His chef is a black American. So this French-Greek cassoulet has an American accent as well and proved to be the most peasantlike and strikingly different of all the cassoulets I sampled. White cannellini beans were used, the meat was chunky, the combination of flavors was robust, and a good natural crust was achieved without the use of many crumbs. With our cassoulet, we drank an extraordinary '61 Château la Grâce-Dieu from St.-Emilion, which might seem too refined a wine for such a dish, though the dish and the wine held up nicely with each other.

A few of New York's more modest French restaurants feature cassoulet, too. It has been a staple on La Toque Blanche's menu for years, where it is listed as "Toulousain" and is described as containing lamb, duck, goose, and sausage. Though the somewhat tomatoey flavor is acceptable, the meats are cut into such minia-ture pieces that they look and nearly taste alike, and the sausage is rather undistinguished. In general, the dish lacks the necessary body to make it interesting.

Les Pyrénées is one of several West Side bistros supervised by the Pujol family. They all specialize in regional bourgeois dishes such as *tripes à la mode de Caen*, coq au vin, *boeuf à la Bourguignonne*, and cassoulet. The last is on the menu at Les Pyrénées practically every day, and since the Pujols hail from the region around Toulouse, this Toulousain version has authenticity. It contains *les couennes,* lamb, duck that is roasted separately, and well-seasoned sausages. The beans are small—navy or pea beans—and the sauce is rich and flavorful, with a good bouquet and perhaps less garlic than I found elsewhere. This is a truly hearty bourgeois interpretation of the dish, which is cooked in quantity for two or three days' supply, reheated on order, and served in its casserole.

I ordered a pleasant Beaujolais to go with my cassoulet, and instead of salad I had a first course of *céleri rémoulade.* Strawberries in red wine finished off the meal. The day I lunched at Les Pyrénées, six people in my neighborhood also ordered cassoulet. Some were coming back to it after previous visits, and the others had obviously been told to ask for it. So this restaurant has a reputation among cassoulet hunters.

I wonder how many of us there are. Several of the restaurateurs I spoke with reported that Americans shun beans, which is the reason proprietors produce cassoulet only on demand. Is it a question of calories? Flatulence? Snobbery? In the land of the baked bean, it would seem that cassoulet is not yet even a demigod.[1]

[1974]

$\mathcal{T}$ea and Crumpets

The days when people gathered in the afternoon at four or five o'clock for a relaxing interlude of tea, sandwiches, toast, and cakes have vanished, along with other pleasant social practices.

---

[1]Quo Vadis, the Coach House, and La Toque Blanche all closed their doors some years ago.

Tea bridged the gap between lunch and dinner, restoring the body on cold days and giving a brisk lift on hot ones, but now that we are cooled by air-conditioning and warmed by central heating, the custom has lost much of its raison d'être.

Happily, tea itself, the most stimulating drink in the world, has not disappeared. For me a fine, fresh, clear cup of tea is a way of life, something I look forward to the first thing in the morning and in late afternoon.

Tea bags may have their place, but the best cup of tea is made with loose tea in the pot, and in my opinion, that pot should be made not of porcelain but of nonporous earthenware with a fine, heavy glaze. The choice of tea is a personal matter, whether it be a full, round India tea such as a Darjeeling; a tea from Ceylon; an orange pekoe; a delicate, pale oolong; a Keemun; or one of the aromatic teas—Earl Grey, for instance, with its orange overtones, or smoky Lapsang souchong, so earthy, brisk, and refreshing. Then there are the fragrant flower teas, such as jasmine, with the blossoms in it, or a lesser-known tea containing white chrysanthemum flowers, which give it a rather bitter aftertaste that tea lovers find immensely pleasing.

The making of any of these teas requires care. To brew tea, put fresh cold water on to boil in a kettle or saucepan. Meanwhile, warm the teapot with hot water from the tap or pour in some of the almost boiling water from the kettle. Let the water stand a few minutes, pour it out, and measure tea into the warmed pot. For a four- to six-cup pot, I put in a heaping tablespoon of most teas; or gauge a teaspoon to a cup unless you like a very pale, delicately flavored tea, in which case a half teaspoon would suffice. When the water comes to a brisk, noisy, rolling boil, pour it over the tea and put the lid on at once. If you own a knitted tea cozy, which fits over the pot like a sweater, leaving the handle and spout free, put it on to keep the tea warm. Let it steep for six to eight minutes, then pour it into thin teacups. Milk may be added, never cream, and sugar; or thin, thin slices of lemon, perhaps with a clove stuck in each slice. Those who really love the flavor of tea will eschew such fripperies and drink the clear, amber liquid for what it is.

If the tea is too strong or if you want to replenish the supply, always add freshly boiling water. Warm water will not do. Finally, tea should not stand too long, so if you enjoy several cups, it is best to wash out the pot and make it anew.

That's the Beard method of making tea. Other people have their own. I know that in one household where tea is in demand three or four times a day, it is made in a stainless-steel saucepan. About two or three tablespoons of tea are put in and about eight to nine cups of boiling water. The pan is put on a burner just warm enough to keep the tea hot without letting it come to a boil. It is covered and allowed to steep for six to seven minutes, after which it is strained into a warm pot. If you follow this excellent method, be sure to use the saucepan solely for making tea.

When I was young, many people drank what was called Russian tea. It was often served in glasses, with a thin slice of lemon stuck with a clove, one or two lumps of sugar, and a jigger of rum, which made a most invigorating and delicious drink. You might try it as a change from ordinary tea, especially on an icy afternoon.

What does one serve with tea? I can think of all kinds of things: toast and jam; paper-thin slices of bread lavishly buttered; hot crumpets and muffins; cookies; melting little tartlets; slices of spongy, spicy, or fruity cakes; and tea sandwiches.

Tea sandwiches differ from other sandwiches in that they must be extremely thin, almost transparent. Good homemade white bread or an unsliced loaf from a fine bake shop is an absolute necessity. The bread should be sliced as thin as possible and generously spread with softened butter to hold the sandwiches firmly together. Two normal slices of bread with a filling will make about four tiny sandwiches, an adequate serving for one. Trim off the crusts and cut into any desired shape—rounds, fingers, triangles, or diamonds. If the sandwiches are prepared well ahead of time, they should be packed in plastic wrap, put in plastic bags, and stored in the refrigerator until just before serving.

Good tea sandwiches should be attractive to the eye and rewarding to the bite. Any of the following fillings make delicious sandwiches.

Cucumber: Split cucumbers lengthwise, remove the seeds, and slice thinly. Sprinkle the slices with salt and let stand for about 30 minutes. Wash off the salt, dry the slices well, and toss with a tiny bit of mayonnaise or simply with salt and pepper to taste. If the cucumbers are very young and tender, the seeds may be left in, but even these cucumbers are best seeded.

Tomato: Peel, seed, and coarsely chop tomatoes, and season with a touch of salt and pepper. Very firm tomatoes may be sliced instead of chopped, but for some reason, chopped tomatoes seem less apt to soak into the bread.

Deviled ham: Thinly slice and grind smoked ham, preferably Virginia or Smithfield, and blend with finely chopped sweet or sour pickles; tiny pinches of ground ginger, cloves, and nutmeg; and enough mayonnaise to make a spreadable mixture.

Smoked salmon: Use very thin slices of high-quality smoked salmon, with perhaps a grind of pepper.

Chicken or turkey: Thinly slice the breast meat of chicken or turkey and season with a little salt and pepper.

For sandwiches that are a bit fancier, roll very thin slices of buttered bread around watercress sprigs, asparagus tips, or any of the fillings given above. Tie them lightly with string, pack loosely in a box, and cover with plastic wrap. Let stand for one or two hours before removing the strings and serving. These rolled sandwiches are extremely popular at tea parties and look most engaging on a plate with a green sprig or asparagus tip peeking out of the end.

℘ Crumpets ℘

Crumpets, which once could be found all over England and in many places in New York City, have becomes less and less available. They are flat, about $1/2$ inch thick, and very porous. When toasted, they will absorb vast quantities of butter. Served with raspberry or strawberry jam and Devonshire cream, they are about as habit-forming as any teatime specialty can be.

In a bowl, combine $1/2$ cup of milk with $1/2$ cup plus 2 tablespoons of boiling water. Let cool to lukewarm. Sprinkle 1 envelope of active dry yeast over the mixture, add 1 teaspoon of sugar, and let the yeast proof for 10 minutes. Combine with $1^3/4$ cups of flour sifted with 1 teaspoon of salt. Stir the batter well, and let it rise in a warm place until it is very bubbly and almost double in bulk. Mix $3/4$ teaspoon of baking soda with 3 tablespoons of hot water, beat it into the batter, and let it rise again until double in bulk.

Arrange twelve 3-inch muffin rings or flan rings on a moderately hot griddle. (Or use 7-ounce cans, such as tuna fish cans, with the tops and bottoms removed.) Spoon the batter into the rings to a depth of $1/2$ inch, and cook until brown on the bottom and dry and bubbly on top. Turn quickly and let brown slightly on the other side. Allow to cool. Toast, butter lavishly, and serve with preserves.

❧ Treacle Tartlets ❧

At how many teas have I eaten treacle tart? Sometimes I was served from a large tart cut into wedges; sometimes, tiny tartlets, with a light, flaky crust and a beautiful sugary filling, which were barely a bite. Either way, treacle tart is irresistible to me.

Into a mixing bowl, sift $1^{1}/_{2}$ cups of flour, 4 teaspoons of sugar, and $^{1}/_{8}$ teaspoon of salt. Work in 3 tablespoons each of butter and lard or vegetable shortening until the mixture resembles coarse meal. Blend in 1 egg yolk and enough cold water to make a stiff but malleable dough. Roll out $^{1}/_{8}$ inch thick on a lightly floured board, and with a fluted $2^{1}/_{2}$-inch cutter, cut out 24 rounds. Fit the rounds into buttered $1^{1}/_{2}$-inch tartlet tins. Prick the bottoms with a fork, and bake in a 400° oven for 7 minutes. Remove from the oven and allow to cool.

In a bowl, combine $1^{1}/_{4}$ cups each of golden corn syrup and loosely packed flaked coconut, and $^{1}/_{2}$ cup of bread crumbs. Put 1 tablespoon of the mixture into each shell. Bake at 350° for 15 minutes or until the pastry is golden brown. Remove from the tins and let cool on a rack.

❧ Maids of Honour ❧

Maids of Honour, those delectable, short, almond-flavored little cakes that hail from Richmond in Surrey, England, are said to have been invented for Henry VIII, which goes to show that the boisterous monarch was a connoisseur of other things than wives. They have been a part of the traditional English tea for centuries.

Into a mixing bowl, sift $1^{1}/_{2}$ cups of flour, 4 teaspoons of sugar, and $^{1}/_{8}$ teaspoon of salt. Work in 3 tablespoons each of butter and lard or vegetable shortening until the mixture resembles coarse meal. Blend in 1 egg yolk and enough cold water to make a stiff but malleable dough. Roll it out $1/8$ inch thick on a lightly floured board, and with a fluted $2^{1}/2$-inch cutter, cut out 16 rounds, reserving the leftover dough for another use. Fit the rounds into buttered $1^{1}/2$-inch tartlet tins.

In a saucepan, combine 1 cup of milk with $1/4$ cup of soft white bread crumbs, and bring the mixture to a boil over moderate heat. Remove the pan from the heat and let the mixture cool for 4 minutes. Stir in 1 stick of butter, cut into small pieces; 6 tablespoons of sugar; and the grated rind of 2 lemons. Beat in 2 large eggs, and blend in $1^{1}/3$ cups of ground almonds. Fill the pastry shells with the mixture and bake in a 425° oven for 20 minutes or until the pastry is browned and the filling set. Transfer to a rack and let cool.

☞ Gingerbread ☜

The special gingerbread one has for tea in England and occasionally in this country is very different from the gingerbread we are used to, which really is a bread. English tea gingerbread is a cake, and it has a rather different texture and flavor.

Into a mixing bowl, sift 3 cups of flour, 2 teaspoons of ground ginger, and 1 teaspoon of baking soda. Mix in $2/3$ cup each of currants and coarsely chopped blanched almonds. In a saucepan, gently heat $1/2$ cup each of vegetable shortening, golden corn syrup, and molasses, and $1/3$ cup of sugar until the shortening is melted and the sugar dissolved. Let the mixture cool, and with a wooden spoon work it into the flour mixture with $1/3$ cup of milk. Then beat in 1 large egg.

Grease an 8-inch square baking pan, cover the bottom with wax paper, and grease the paper. Spread the batter in the pan. Bake in a 375° oven for 35 minutes or until a cake tester inserted in the center comes out clean. Let cool in the pan for 10 minutes, then turn out on a rack. Serve warm with butter.

❧ Eccles Cakes ❧

Eccles Cakes are yet another English specialty—crisp on the outside, fruity on the inside, and quite delectable. I know they are considered tea food, but we used to make extra-large cakes and take them on picnics as well.

Thoroughly combine 6 tablespoons of butter with 6 tablespoons of lard or vegetable shortening. Chill until firm and cut into small cubes. Into a mixing bowl sift 2 cups of flour and $1/4$ teaspoon of salt. Stir in the cubes, coating them well. Blend in $1/2$ teaspoon of strained lemon juice and enough cold water to make a soft but not sticky dough. Roll out on a lightly floured board into a rectangle about $3/16$ inch thick and fold it into thirds, overlapping the ends completely. With an open side of the dough facing you, roll out and fold the dough as before, turning it again so an open side faces you. Repeat the procedure three more times. Chill the dough for 15 minutes, then roll it out to slightly less than $1/4$ inch thick. Cut out 10 rounds $4^1/2$ inches in diameter.

In a bowl, cream 1 tablespoon of butter with 2 tablespoons of sugar. Mix in $1/2$ cup of currants and 2 tablespoons each of finely chopped glacéed orange and lemon peel. Put 2 teaspoons of the filling on one-half of each round of dough. Brush the edges with milk, and press them together so the filling is thoroughly sealed. Turn the cakes over, and with a rolling pin, lightly flatten them until the dough is thin enough for the currants to show through. Brush the tops with milk and sprinkle with 3 tablespoons of sugar. Cut 2 small slits in each. Arrange on a baking sheet and bake in a 400° oven for 25 minutes or until they are golden brown.

❧ Queen Cakes ☙

Queen Cakes and their variation, Fruity Cakes, are childhood memories for me. These simple, tiny cupcakes are just right with a pot of tea.

In a bowl, cream together 1 stick of butter and $2/3$ cup of sugar until the mixture is light and fluffy. Beat in 2 eggs, one at a time, and stir in $1/2$ teaspoon of vanilla. Lightly dredge $1/2$ cup of seedless raisins with flour and add them to the egg mixture with 2 tablespoons of finely chopped mixed glacéed fruit and 1 tablespoon of milk. Sift together $1^1/3$ cups of flour, 1 teaspoon of baking powder, and $1/8$ teaspoon of salt, and gently fold them into the batter. Pour into 24 small well-buttered muffin tins, lined with $1^1/2$-inch paper baking cups. Bake in a 350° oven for 20 minutes or until a cake tester inserted in the center of a cake comes out clean. Turn the cakes out on a rack and let them cool.

To make Fruity Cakes, substitute $1/3$ cup of combined chopped glacéed cherries, angelica, and almonds for the raisins and mixed glacéed fruit.

❧ Rock Cakes ☙

Rock Cakes, which are much more appetizing than their name would indicate, have been a favorite of mine for many years. Although I have always eaten them cold, I recently found that they can also be eaten warm, with a little butter, which makes them quite different.

Into a mixing bowl, sift 2 cups of flour; $1/2$ cup of sugar; $1^1/2$ teaspoons of baking powder; $1/2$ teaspoon of salt; and $1/8$ teaspoon each of cinnamon, cloves, and nutmeg. Thoroughly work in 6 tablespoons of butter. Stir in $3/4$ cup of dried currants and

2 tablespoons of finely chopped mixed glacéed fruit. Mix in 1 lightly beaten egg, and add $1/2$ cup plus 2 tablespoons of milk or just enough to make a stiff batter. Drop by tablespoons onto a buttered baking sheet, and bake in the top third of a 400° oven for 20 minutes or until the cakes are golden brown and firm to the touch. Let them cool on a rack. Serve them whole or split while warm and spread with butter.

❧ Shortbread ❧

Shortbread, a crisp, sweet cookie, is popular throughout the world under different names. It is found in Scandinavian, French, Italian, and British cuisines. The buttery, crumbly texture of shortbread is wonderful with tea.

In a mixing bowl, cream 1 stick of butter with $1/3$ cup of sugar. Blend in 2 cups of flour sifted with $1/4$ teaspoon of salt to make a very firm dough. Roll out $1/4$ inch thick on a lightly floured board, and with a fluted $2^{1}/_{2}$-inch cutter cut into 18 rounds. Lightly butter a large baking sheet and arrange the rounds on it. Bake in a 350° oven for 5 minutes or until well browned on the bottom. Turn over with a metal spatula and bake for 5 minutes more or until the other side is lightly browned. Sprinkle the tops with sugar and let cool on the baking sheet for 5 minutes. Transfer to a rack and let cool completely.

❧ Swiss Roll ❧

To me, no tea would be complete without two light cakes—the Jam Sandwich, which consists of two thin layers of sponge cake sandwiched with jam and dusted with confectioners' sugar, and the Swiss Roll or Jelly Roll.

In a bowl, beat 4 egg yolks with $1/4$ cup of sugar until they ribbon when the beater is lifted. In another bowl, beat 4 egg whites until they are stiff but not dry. Fold them into the yolk mixture. Sift together $1/4$ cup each of flour and cornstarch. Fold into the egg mixture with $1/2$ teaspoon each of vanilla and grated lemon rind.

Butter an 11 x 16-inch jelly roll pan, line it with wax paper, and butter the paper. Spread the batter evenly in the pan. Bake in a 400° oven for about 12 to 15 minutes or until lightly browned. Turn the cake out on a damp towel, remove the paper, and spread the cake with a thin layer of strawberry or raspberry jam. Roll up in the towel from the short side, and let cool. Unwrap and sprinkle with sugar. Serve in slices.

⚶ Currant Cake ⚶

Currant Cake, not as rich as fruitcake, is very pleasant in the morning or evening with a cup of tea. We used to quadruple the recipe and give the cakes to our friends at Christmas.

Into a bowl, sift together 2 cups of cake flour, 1 teaspoon of baking powder, and $1/8$ teaspoon of salt. Work in 6 tablespoons of butter until the mixture resembles coarse meal. Stir in $2/3$ cup each of sugar and currants and 2 lightly beaten eggs. Then add $1/3$ to $1/2$ cup of milk or enough to make a firm batter.

Butter a 6-cup loaf pan, cover the bottom with wax paper, and butter the paper. Pour in the batter and spread evenly. Bake in a 350° oven for 1 hour or until a cake tester inserted in the center comes out clean. Let the cake cool in the pan for 5 minutes, turn it out on a rack, and let it cool completely. It will stay moist for several days if well wrapped in foil or plastic wrap.

❧ Seedcake ❧

Another childhood taste I will always treasure is that of Seedcake. If you like the flavor of caraway, Seedcake is quite addictive. The amount of caraway seed in this recipe can be varied, or poppy seed may be substituted, but I think it is the caraway—and a good deal of it—that gives such a wonderful flavor.

In a bowl, thoroughly cream 2 sticks of butter with $1^1/_2$ cups of sugar. Beat in 4 eggs, one at a time. Stir in 3 tablespoons of caraway seed. Gently fold in 2 cups of flour sifted with 2 teaspoons of baking powder and $^1/_4$ teaspoon of salt. Butter an 8-inch round cake pan, cover the bottom with wax paper, and butter the paper. Spread the batter in the pan, and bake in a 375° oven for 1 hour or until it begins to shrink from the sides of the pan and is firm to the touch. Let cool in the pan for 2 to 3 minutes, then turn out on a rack, peel off the paper, and let cool completely.

❧ Citrus Bread ❧

Citrus Bread is something the English borrowed from the American quick breads, and very nice it is when thinly sliced, heavily buttered, and offered with a good lemon or ginger marmalade. It is equally welcome at the breakfast table or with afternoon tea.

In a bowl, cream 1 stick of butter with 1 cup of sugar. Beat in 2 well-beaten eggs. Sift $1^1/_2$ cups of flour with 1 teaspoon of baking powder and $^1/_4$ teaspoon of salt. Stir $^1/_2$ cup of milk into the egg-sugar mixture, 2 tablespoons at a time, alternately with the flour, $^1/_2$ cup at a time. Then stir in the grated rind of 1 lemon and 1 teaspoon of finely grated orange rind.

Butter a loaf pan, line the bottom with wax paper, and butter the paper. Pour the batter in the pan, and bake in a 325° oven for 45 minutes or until a cake tester inserted in the center comes out clean. Just before the bread is done, combine in a saucepan the strained juice of $^1/_2$ lemon, an equal quantity of strained orange juice, and $^1/_3$ cup of sugar. Stir over moderate heat until the sugar is dissolved. When the bread comes out of the oven, brush the top with this mixture and let it cool in the pan.

[1972]

Dishes to Fight Over

One evening many years ago, I attended an unforgettable performance of Stravinsky's *Firebird* on the West Coast. Two women sitting in front of me were keeping up a rather noisy conversation during the louder section of the score when suddenly it arrived at the lullaby sequence. At that point, one of the women was saying to the other in a ringing voice, heard by the entire audience and the conductor, "Well, I always fry mine in lard." The episode demonstrated to me once and for all the importance people attach to their own ways of cooking. They will do battle to prove they have a superior recipe for this or that dish, and I frequently have been upbraided in letters because my published version of a recipe did not agree with Grandmother's. Sometimes two families compete over a cherished dish and, on a larger scale, whole populations can take sides—which is how some of our most delightful regional cooking was created. What follows, therefore, is my sampling of some common dishes that have been fought over throughout our culinary history.

Perhaps the most disputed of our regional foods is clam chowder, which has appeared in many different guises since its invention in the early history of this country. First and foremost in the field was the New England chowder, which was originally made with readily available local clams and probably salt pork and pilot biscuits. Just when milk was added to the dish, no one seems to know. Onions came along later, too. Certainly it started out potatoless, because chowder was eaten in New England long before potatoes were in general use. This recipe for clam chowder from Mrs. Crowen's *American System of Cookery* was published in New York in 1847. It is as close to the original dish as we are likely to come—and no potatoes. The result is a rather thick, buttery stew-soup, very clammy in flavor and quite delicious.

❧ Mrs. Crowen's Clam Chowder ❧

4 to 6 dozen shucked clams
(about 1 quart with liquid)
1 cup cracker crumbs
1 cup finely chopped parsley

1/4 cup butter or margarine,
cut in small pieces
2 cups milk, scalded
Freshly ground pepper

Strain the clams, reserving the liquid. With a sharp knife, chop the clams into 1/2-inch pieces. In a 2 1/2-quart casserole, make a layer of the clams, cracker crumbs, 1/2 cup of parsley, and the butter. Add the clam liquid, milk, and pepper to taste. Cover and bake in a preheated 350° oven 30 minutes, stirring twice.

Ladle into bowls. If you like, add a pat of butter to each bowl. Sprinkle generously with the remaining parsley. Makes about 2 quarts.

There have been numerous variations of New England clam chowder, including those developed by settlers in the Northwest, many of whom came from New England. Since dairying was one of the great industries of the Northwest, it was an easy step to a chowder that called for cream as well as potatoes and bacon, and the clams in this case were the delicate Pacific razor clams, ground or minced and added to the chowder at the last minute. This, essentially, is the clam chowder I maintain to be the best of all.

⫍ My Favorite Clam Chowder ⫎

2 dozen shucked razor,
  cherrystone, quahog, or
  littleneck clams; or about
  1½ cups with liquid
1 medium onion, finely
  chopped
3 thick slices bacon, fried
  crisp and finely crumbled
  (reserve 2 tablespoons of fat)

2 medium potatoes,
  thinly sliced
2 cups boiling salted water
Salt and freshly ground pepper
3 cups half-and-half or milk
Butter
Thyme
Chopped parsley

Strain the clams, reserving the liquid. With a sharp knife, finely chop the clams and set them aside. Sauté the onion in 2 tablespoons of bacon fat until lightly browned. Simmer the potatoes in the salted water until tender. Add the reserved clam liquid, bacon, onion, and salt and pepper to taste. Simmer 5 minutes. Add the half-and-half, bring to a boil, and add the clams. Cook until they are barely heated through. Taste and correct the seasoning.

To each serving, add a dollop of butter, a pinch of thyme, and chopped parsley. Makes 7 cups.

Note: Salt pork can be substituted for the bacon. Also, the size of the clams will determine the number. We used medium cherrystones.

The biggest rift among chowder fans is the one between the New England school and the school that prefers the radically different version known as Manhattan clam chowder. It may have come to fame in New York, but it is definitely a soup of Italian or Greek heritage. It can be quite good or really horrible, depending on how well it is made. Although many diners and restaurants serve Manhattan clam chowder full of potatoes, this recipe ignores them and is much more delicate and interesting as a consequence.

⌘ Manhattan Clam Chowder ⌘

3 dozen shucked medium
   cherrystone clams or about 2
   to 3 cups with liquid
1/2 cup each chopped onion
   and green pepper
2 cloves garlic, minced
4 thick slices bacon, fried crisp
   and coarsely crumbled
   (reserve the fat)

1 1-pound can stewed tomatoes
1/2 cup cooked rice
1/2 teaspoon thyme
1/4 teaspoon oregano
Salt and freshly
   ground pepper

Strain the clams and reserve the liquid. With a sharp knife, finely chop the clams and set them aside. Sauté the onion, green pepper, and garlic in 3 tablespoons bacon fat over low heat until tender but not browned. Add the reserved clam liquid, tomatoes, rice, thyme, oregano, and salt and pepper to taste. Simmer 5 minutes. Just before serving, add the chopped clams and bring to a boil. Remove from the heat and sprinkle with the crumbled bacon and chopped parsley. Makes 1 quart.

In the early days of the century, when people had basket socials, there were always arguments about whose potato salad was best, and the arguments continue. In fact, I am going to give you a recipe that has been kept secret for over fifty years by the family of one of my friends. Finally my friend said, "Well, hell. Why not let people share it?"

It's a rich one, using a dressing that appears to draw on all three of the dressings most commonly used for potato salad—

boiled dressing, French dressing, and mayonnaise—which always play a large part in the dissension. "My," I have heard people say, "it doesn't begin to taste the way it does made with boiled dressing." I myself happen to think that mayonnaise doesn't make a particularly brilliant potato salad unless it's mixed with another ingredient, such as sour cream. At any rate, here is the secret family recipe that my friend claims makes the greatest potato salad anyone has ever known. It is best made with potatoes that have been in storage a while.

❧ Mrs. Rockey's Potato Salad ❧

6 old potatoes, about
  2¹/2 pounds
1/3 cup vinegar
4 eggs, beaten
1 tablespoon butter
1 cup heavy cream
4 tablespoons finely
  chopped parsley

2 tablespoons finely chopped
  onion
1 teaspoon dry mustard
1 teaspoon salt
1/2 teaspoon white pepper
Dash of cayenne

Cook the potatoes in their jackets. Peel and slice while steaming hot. Bring the vinegar to a boil, and with a small whisk, gradually beat it into the eggs. Transfer to the top of a double boiler and stir over simmering water until thickened. Stir in the butter and cook a minute more. Add the cream, 2 tablespoons of parsley, the onion, and the seasonings. Mix with the hot potatoes. Allow to cool, then sprinkle with the remaining parsley and refrigerate until serving time. Makes 4 to 6 servings.

Another extraordinarily good potato salad I have used through the years was created by a woman who worked for me in the early thirties and into the forties. Dora swore by this recipe:

☙ Dora's Potato Salad ☞

3 pounds potatoes
  (about 8 medium)
$1/4$ cup finely chopped onion
$1/4$ cup finely chopped
  green onions
$1/4$ cup wine vinegar

1 clove garlic, finely chopped
1 teaspoon salt
Freshly ground pepper
$1/2$ cup finely chopped celery
Boiled dressing

Cook the potatoes in their jackets. Peel and slice while warm. Combine with the onions, vinegar, garlic, and salt and pepper to taste. Cover and refrigerate 12 to 24 hours. Just before serving, add the celery and toss with boiled dressing. Makes 4 to 6 servings.

Boiled dressing: With a small whisk, blend $1/2$ cup of olive oil, $1/4$ cup of wine vinegar, 1 tablespoon of flour, 1 teaspoon of sugar, $1/4$ teaspoon of salt, $1/8$ teaspoon of dry mustard, and freshly ground pepper to taste. Transfer to the top of a double boiler, beat in 2 egg yolks, and stir over hot, not boiling, water until thickened. Remove from the heat and stir in $1/4$ cup of sour cream. Cool. Makes 1 cup.

Now here is what I like to think of as *my* potato salad, one that I have done for over forty years. I have toted it to picnics, served it at home, and used it for many occasions.

☙ My Own Potato Salad ☞

$2^1/2$ to 3 pounds small new
  potatoes (22 to 27)
$1/2$ cup olive oil
$1/4$ cup wine or tarragon
  vinegar
2 teaspoons salt

Freshly ground pepper
$2/3$ cup finely chopped
  green onions
$1/2$ cup finely chopped parsley
3 chopped hard-cooked eggs
Capers

Boil the potatoes in their jackets until tender. Do not over-cook. Rinse in cold water and peel while they are as hot as you can handle. Slice and combine with the oil, vinegar, salt, and pepper to taste. Allow to cool, then cover and refrigerate 12 to 24 hours. Bring to room temperature and add the green onions and parsley. Garnish with the eggs and capers. Makes 4 to 6 servings.

Variation: Add $3/4$ cup of finely chopped celery and approximately $1/3$ cup of mayonnaise. Sprinkle with chopped egg and serve with salad greens.

The question of how to make fried chicken has been one of the most intense of all the food controversies. Now, fried chicken is not, as many people think, an American invention. It was probably adapted from a Viennese dish. There is even an Italian dish that could have been its inspiration. But we Americans have taken it over, and it has been closely identified with the South, where chicken has been batter-fried, parboiled and fried, fried with cracker crumbs, deep-fat fried, fried in lard, fried in butter, and fried in olive oil. In our household, when I was growing up, my mother and father and Let, our Chinese cook, all had different ideas on fried chicken. My father liked it for breakfast with hot biscuits.

◈ Father's Fried Chicken ◈

6 *thick slices bacon*
1 *broiler-fryer (about 3*
  pounds), cut up

Flour
Salt and freshly ground pepper
$1^1/_2$ cups milk

Fry the bacon in a heavy skillet. Drain on paper towels and keep warm. Reserve the fat. Coat the chicken with flour and sprinkle with salt and pepper. Brown quickly in hot bacon fat in a large, heavy skillet. Cover and cook over low heat 20 minutes or until the chicken is tender. Transfer to a hot platter. Pour all but 2 tablespoons of fat from the skillet. Stir in 2 tablespoons of flour and cook over low heat, scraping up the residue in the skillet. Add the milk and stir over low heat until slightly thickened. Strain and season generously with salt and pepper. Serve with the chicken and bacon. Serves 4.

Many people would contend that chicken must be fried in much deeper fat and at the same temperature throughout. Here is a recipe that nods in the direction of the deep-fat technique but finishes the chicken in the oven. It comes from Virginia friends and has been handed down for several generations.

⌇ Virginia Fried Chicken ⌇

2 broiler-fryers (about 3 pounds each), cut up
Flour
3 eggs, beaten
1/2 cup milk
3 cups coarse cracker crumbs
Lard or oil
Salt and freshly ground pepper
Chopped parsley
Gravy

Coat the chicken with flour. Combine the eggs and milk. Dip the chicken in the egg mixture, then coat with cracker crumbs. Using two heavy skillets, brown the chicken in 1 inch of hot lard or oil, being careful not to crowd the pieces. Turn carefully with tongs to keep the crumbs intact. When golden brown, transfer to a shallow roasting pan and season well with salt and pepper. Bake in a preheated 350° oven 20 to 25 minutes or until the chicken is tender.

Transfer to a hot platter and sprinkle generously with chopped parsley. Serve with gravy and mashed potatoes or boiled new potatoes. This chicken is also good served cold. Makes 6 servings.

Gravy: Pour all but 3 tablespoons of fat from one skillet. Blend in 3 tablespoons of flour, and cook over low heat, scraping up the residue from the skillet. Gradually stir in 1 cup each of milk and heavy cream, and continue to stir over low heat until thickened. Season to taste with salt and freshly ground pepper. If you like, add 2 to 3 tablespoons of sherry or Madeira. Makes 2 cups.

A friend of mine preferred to fry her chicken in olive oil because she liked the flavor of it and felt it was far superior to any other method. I must say, it made delicious chicken and is worth including in our controversy. If you are not fond of the taste of olive oil, peanut or corn oil works equally well.

❦ Jeanne's Fried Chicken ❦

*1 broiler-fryer (about 3
    pounds), cut up*
Flour

Olive oil
Chopped parsley

Coat the chicken with flour. Heat 1 inch of oil in a large, heavy skillet to 350° on a deep-fat frying thermometer. Carefully lower the chicken pieces into the oil to prevent spattering and cook quickly until golden brown, turning once. Drain on paper towels. Arrange in a baking dish and bake in a preheated 325° oven 15 minutes or until tender. Serve sprinkled generously with chopped parsley. Makes 4 servings.

Although many of us consider lamb the most delicate and delicious of all meats, it is greatly disliked in some parts of the country. People say it smells and tastes like tallow. Because of this prejudice, lamb is difficult to find except in and around large cities. I support the theory that overcooking has been the chief reason for the case against lamb. As a matter of fact, the Lamb Council itself has been at fault in telling people to cook lamb until it reaches an internal temperature of 180°, which will give you a pale, gray meat that is indeed unattractive. The lamb controversy, therefore, comes down to two points: whether it is edible at all and how well done it should be. Assuming that it *is* edible, I am going to present three different ways of cooking a leg of lamb, beginning with what I consider to be the best treatment.

First of all, remove the fell, if present. (Or have your butcher do it.) This is the thin membrane covering the leg. Sometimes it can be loosened and torn off with a quick tug. Otherwise, it must be cut bit by bit, using knife or scissors. I emphasize this step because the fell has an odd flavor that can affect the taste of the meat.

❧ Leg of Lamb Provençal ❧

1 leg of lamb (5 to 6 pounds)
2 to 3 cloves garlic, cut
*   in slivers*
2 teaspoons salt

$^1/_2$ teaspoon freshly
*   ground pepper*
$^3/_4$ teaspoon rosemary,
*   finely crushed*

With the point of a knife, make slits in the lamb at even intervals and insert a garlic sliver in each. Rub the meat well with salt, pepper, and rosemary. Place on a rack in a roasting pan. Sear in a preheated 450° oven 10 minutes. Reduce the temperature to 325° and continue roasting 10 minutes per pound or until a meat thermometer registers an internal temperature of 130° for very rare or 140° for medium rare.

Remove from the oven and let stand 15 minutes before carving. To carve, hold the leg at an angle and cut down along the meat in thin slices, with the grain. It slices much better this way, looks better on the plate, and is just as tender as it would be if cut against the grain. If you like, remove all fat from the roasting pan and swirl a small amount of broth in the pan to deglaze. Serve this juice with the meat, along with sautéed or fried potatoes, sautéed mushrooms, and chopped spinach. Makes 6 to 8 servings.

Variation: Wrap half an anchovy around each sliver of garlic before inserting in the lamb. Reduce the salt by half. This gives a delicious, mysterious flavor to the roast.

For those who want their lamb well done, here is an interesting recipe for a braised leg of lamb from Fannie Merritt Farmer, one of our greatest molders of culinary taste. (The original recipe called for leg of mutton.)

☞ Miss Farmer's Braised Leg of Lamb ☜

1 leg of lamb (about
    7 pounds), boned
    but not tied
Stuffing (see below)
7 tablespoons butter or
    margarine
1 slice each onion, carrot, and
    turnip, diced

$1/2$ bay leaf
1 sprig thyme or $1/4$ teaspoon
    dried thyme, crushed
1 sprig parsley
3 cups boiling water
$1^1/2$ teaspoons salt
12 peppercorns
4 tablespoons flour

Spread the leg meat out. Spoon the stuffing onto it, spreading slightly. Roll up the meat and secure with a few skewers. Then tie, using approximately 6 pieces of heavy string 12 inches long. Remove the skewers. Heat 4 tablespoons of butter to sizzling in a large Dutch oven. Add the lamb, diced vegetables and herbs, and cook about 5 minutes, turning the lamb frequently to brown. Add the water, salt, and peppercorns. Cover and cook slowly over low heat or in a 300° oven 3 hours, uncovering the last 30 minutes.

Remove the lamb to a hot platter. Boil the broth until reduced to half or about 1³/₄ cups, and strain. Melt the remaining butter in a saucepan, and blend in the flour. Stir over low heat until the mixture begins to brown. Slowly add the reduced broth, and continue to stir until thickened and smooth. Serve with the sliced lamb. Makes about 8 servings.

Stuffing: Combine 1 cup of cracker crumbs, ¹/₄ cup each of melted butter or margarine and boiling water, 1¹/₂ teaspoons of poultry seasoning, ¹/₄ teaspoon of salt, and ¹/₈ teaspoon of pepper.

For those who like lamb falling apart, here is an unusual French recipe that turns the meat almost into a pâté. It is quite delicious.

☙ Seven-Hour Lamb ❧

¹/₂ pound salt pork or
    fatback
1 leg of lamb (about
    6 pounds), boned
    but not tied
3 cloves garlic, slivered
2 cups beef stock
6 medium onions, sliced

6 carrots, sliced
1 celery top
1 sprig parsley
2 teaspoons salt
1 teaspoon thyme
³/₄ teaspoon pepper
Pinch each of cinnamon,
    nutmeg, and fennel

Rinse the salt pork, if salted. Cut off 2 slices about ¹/₄ inch thick and dice. Set aside the remainder. Spread out the lamb meat. Make small slits in it, and insert the garlic slivers and pork pieces at even intervals. Roll and fasten with skewers, then tie securely. Remove the skewers. In a large Dutch oven or roasting pan, add the remaining ingredients and the reserved salt pork and bring to a boil. Place the lamb in the pot, cover, and simmer over *very low* heat or in a 200° oven 7 hours. The meat will reduce to an almost pâté-like consistency and can be served with a spoon and fork, accompanied by the broth (fat removed) and vegetables. Serve with red kidney beans cooked with a little olive oil and red wine or with a dish of lentils or white beans. A salad or coleslaw is another good accompaniment. Serve with red wine. Makes 8 servings.

How do you like your apple pie? Some early recipes used whole cloves, but many people chose to use cinnamon, nutmeg, or mace. Others used no seasoning at all except butter. Do you like a two-crust or a deep-dish pie? And how do you eat it—with cheese, à la mode, or plain? These are a few of the controversies centering on our national dessert. I'm not too fond of cinnamon myself, although I have grown up with people who thought no apple pie was right without it, and I prefer greening, pippin, Gravenstein, or transparent apples to other varieties. So here is my idea of a perfect all-American apple pie.

❧ Two-Crust Apple Pie ❧

Crust:

2 cups flour
1 teaspoon salt

$^2/_3$ cup shortening or $^1/_3$ cup
    butter or margarine and
    $^1/_2$ cup shortening
$^1/_4$ cup (about) ice water

Filling:

5 cups peeled, cored, and
    thinly sliced apples
    (about 2 pounds)
$^1/_2$ to $^3/_4$ cup sugar, depending
    on sweetness of apples

$^1/_2$ to 1 teaspoon mace or nutmeg
$^1/_4$ teaspoon salt
Dash of lemon juice
3 tablespoons (about)
    butter or margarine

Stir the flour with the salt. Cut in the shortening with a pastry blender, fork, or two table knives until you have pieces the size of small peas. Sprinkle with water, a few drops at a time, and toss the mixture with a fork to distribute the water evenly. The dough should be moistened just enough to form a ball. (The type of flour used and the temperature of the mixture will make a difference in the amount of water required.) Don't handle too much. Wrap the dough in wax paper and refrigerate about 30 minutes.

Meanwhile, prepare the filling. Combine the apple slices, sugar, mace, and salt, and toss to mix thoroughly. Add a few drops of lemon juice. Roll out half the dough on a lightly floured pastry cloth or board an inch larger than a 9-inch pie pan. Fit into the pan and fill with the apple mixture. Dot with butter. Roll out the upper crust. Moisten the edge of the bottom crust and set the top crust in place. Crimp the edges to seal, trim off excess dough, and cut a vent in the middle for steam to escape.

Bake in a preheated 450° oven 15 minutes. Reduce the heat to 350° and continue baking 20 to 35 minutes or until the crust is golden. Remove from the oven and let cool slightly. Serve warm or cold (warm being much better), without embellishment, with aged cheddar cheese, in the fashion of the early 1900s and 1920s, or à la mode. I've even had it with hot cheese sauce on it, and very good it was.

Deep-dish or English apple pies are prepared in a slightly different way. To hold up the center of the crust during baking, it is best to use an inverted eggcup, coffee cup, or one of the gadgets designed especially for the purpose. Some deep-dish recipes call for what is known as a rough paste, although you are free to use the pastry given for the two-crust pie.

This is a genuine deep-dish apple pie, and it needs no spice. Of course, it would do no harm to pour another spoonful or two of applejack or brandy through the vent in the crust after you take the pie out of the oven.

❧ Deep-Dish Apple Pie ❧

Rough Puff Pastry:

2 cups flour
1 teaspoon salt

12 tablespoons hard butter
   or margarine, cut in
   3/4-inch cubes
1/4 cup or more ice water

Filling:

6 cups peeled and cored apples,
   cut in sixths (about 3
   pounds)
7/8 cup sugar (1 cup less 2
   tablespoons)
2 to 3 (or more) tablespoons
   butter or margarine, cut up

Pinch of salt
1 teaspoon lemon juice
2 tablespoons (or more)
   applejack or brandy
1 egg yolk mixed with
   1 tablespoon water
   or cream

Stir the flour and salt together in a large bowl. Add the butter cubes and water, and mix all ingredients lightly with a wooden spatula until the mixture begins to ball. (The butter should not break up too much.) Turn out onto a floured surface, gather into a ball, and knead just a little. Shape into a rough rectangle, then roll out to a strip about 12 x 4 inches and about 3/4 inch thick, keeping the edges straight. Butter will appear as yellow streaks in the pastry. Fold into thirds, the upper third covering the bottom third like an envelope. Seal the edges lightly with your fingers. Turn the pastry so a narrow end faces you. Roll out again to a rectangle about 18 x 6 inches and about 1/2 inch thick. Fold and roll out four more times, giving the pastry a quarter turn each time. After two rollings, place the pastry in a plastic bag and refrigerate for 20 minutes. Let rest 10 to 15 minutes before the final rolling.

Meanwhile, place an inverted cup or other support in the center of a large oval baking dish, about 12 x 9 x 3 inches. Surround it with apples tossed with the sugar, building up toward the center to help support the crust. Dot with butter and sprinkle with salt. Add the lemon juice and applejack.

Using the baking dish as a guide, roll out the pastry so it is $1/2$ inch larger in circumference than the dish and about $1/4$ inch thick. (I like a rather thick crust for this particular pie.) Trim off excess dough, roll it out, and cut it into several $1/2$-inch-wide strips. Brush the edges of the dish and the pastry strips with water. Fit the strips around the edge of the dish to make a base for the crust. Press down firmly and moisten again with cold water. Brush the edge of the pastry with water and invert it on the dish. Press the edges down to seal, using the tines of a fork, if you like. Make a steam vent in the center, preferably one about $1/2$ inch to $3/4$ inch in diameter. Brush the surface of the pastry well with the egg mixture.

Bake in a preheated 450° oven 15 minutes, then reduce the heat to 350° and bake another 25 to 35 minutes, depending on the type of apples used. When done, remove from the oven and cool slightly. To serve, cut the crust in wedges, place a wedge on each plate, golden brown side up, and spoon apples over or beside it. This is best eaten warm with heavy cream or ice cream.

[1974]

Summer Food

I have always been a lover of cold food. Often I deliberately buy more meat than I need for dinner for just this reason. In some ways I enjoy roast beef more the second day, thinly sliced and served with a salad. One of the most satisfying of all summer dishes is cold roast loin of pork served with a fragrant, spicy mustard mayonnaise and crushed green peppercorns. Another is cold roast or braised veal with mustard mayonnaise, or a veal salad.

When you plan a meal of cold food, try for an interesting contrast of flavors. You might start with a crisp salad of seafood, celery, and greens, then have cold roast beef with mustard mayonnaise and a big bowl of watercress, without dressing, or sweet, crunchy snow peas.

Another thing I like to do is take fresh Rock Cornish game hens that weigh about a pound, poach them in chicken broth, and cool them until just tepid; then arrange them on a platter with a border of sliced or shredded raw vegetables, such as carrot, celery, and cucumber, that have been marinated in a vinaigrette sauce. With one dish, you have your entrée and vegetable or salad course complete. Beforehand you might have something cool and creamy, such as cold tomato bisque or an avocado and yogurt soup, and for dessert, a fruit tart or perhaps strawberries masked with a purée of raspberries.

Cold fish is perfect summer food. Probably as elegant a dish as one can find is cold poached salmon served with mayonnaise tinted green with the finely chopped leaves of parsley, tarragon, chives, and wilted spinach. With the salmon, I like to serve tomatoes, hollowed out and stuffed with strips of peeled and seeded cucumber, first salted to draw out the juices, then rinsed, drained, and mixed with a combination of mayonnaise, yogurt, and finely chopped dill. I also serve tiny boiled new potatoes, tossed with butter, chopped parsley, and chopped mint. Another winner is a platter of cold boiled lobster surrounded by a glorious frieze of poached vegetables à la grecque, such as young green beans, tiny white onions, baby pattypan squash, and carrots.

Leftover seafood can be a source of many delicious cold meals. If I have poached or sautéed fish fillets left from dinner, I arrange them in a single layer in a baking dish, put thin slices of onion, green pepper, and orange over them, and add olive oil just to cover, with a sprinkling of chopped dill or tarragon and salt and pepper to taste. The dish is covered with plastic wrap and refrigerated overnight. The next day, with a rice salad, this marinated fish makes a lovely light lunch.

Summer meals can also benefit from a contrast of temperatures. When I have a dinner in the garden, I wait until everyone has finished their cocktails and then hand around demitasses of steaming, rich chicken consommé. It gives the palate a welcome jolt before we sit down to the cold food. After this, I might have poached trout or perhaps tiny roast squab chickens or Rock Cornish game hens (the fresh, not the frozen), served tepid with a choice of salads.

For roast squab chickens, allow 1 bird per serving. Rub the cavities with a cut lemon, and if you have fresh tarragon, put a few sprigs inside. Arrange the birds on their sides on a rack in a shallow roasting pan, and rub the topmost side with soft butter. Roast in a 400° oven for 20 minutes, turn, rub with butter, and roast 20 minutes more. Finally, turn the birds breast up, baste well with the pan juices or melted butter, and sprinkle with salt and pepper. Roast 10 or 12 minutes longer. Do not overcook. To test for doneness, wiggle the legs to see if they move easily, and puncture the skin at the thigh joint with a small, sharp knife. The juices should be faintly tinged with pink for a moist and juicy bird. (If you are roasting fresh Rock Cornish hens, follow the same procedure, but roast for only 45 minutes.)

Remove the birds to a platter, and let them cool at room temperature until just tepid. Garnish the platter with watercress, and serve with a well-chilled light white wine, such as an Alsatian Sylvaner or Riesling, or a light chilled young Beaujolais or California gamay Beaujolais. For salads, you might have a rice salad; a salad of sliced raw mushrooms marinated in vinaigrette sauce and sprinkled with chopped tarragon; or the marvelously refreshing Middle Eastern salad, tabbouleh, which is made with cracked wheat, green onions, tomatoes, chopped parsley, and fresh mint, with a very lemony dressing.

[1977]

Outdoor Chefmanship

I'm a veteran in outdoor cooking. As a matter of fact, the first book I wrote on the subject (and I have done four) was also the first on the market. I wrote it back in the days when people spent small fortunes building, in their backyards or gardens, enormous and imposing brick or stone fireplaces that housed a fairly small grill and a firebox. Unfortunately, these were not too efficient. It was a major operation to get a fire going and not something one did casually, for wood or charcoal had to be burned down to a good bed of coals, and that took time and trouble. The owners of these vast fireplaces, which looked like something out of the *Ring of the Nibelung*, loved to show off in front of them, but more often than not the hamburgers they produced were little black pellets and the steaks so well done they resembled pot roast. What happened with chicken is better left unsaid.

Yet for years hunters, fishermen, and campers had done their cooking on the simplest sort of grills set over fires like those my mother used at the beach when I was a child, and they worked magnificently. Finally, the manufacturers and backyard chefs learned that this kind of equipment made the most sense, and all sorts of small and large portable grills appeared on the scene, some badly designed and unusable and others pretty good. Gradually we evolved well-designed, well-made portable outdoor cooking equipment that even an idiot could handle with some degree of success—round, square, and oblong grills with various types of fireboxes that burned the latest in fuels, such as charcoal briquets. As a result, there was less cremation, and grilling became rather more scientific.

Many of the good grills had fireboxes that could be lowered or adjusted to several positions to give varying degrees of heat and better ventilation to distribute the heat more evenly. At this point, we can buy efficient grills at reasonable prices that do a very satisfactory job. I won't guarantee that a little hibachi will do as much as a far more expensive grill with a larger firebox and perhaps an electrically driven spit, but it is possible to cook things like chops, steaks, and chicken on small grills with some degree of artistry. Grilling or broiling—or barbecuing, as some people call it, although that is not really a correct term to use for our kind of outdoor cooking—is one of the major culinary arts and certainly one that has become a way of life in this country. In summer, many Americans count on outdoor cooking for a great deal of their meal planning, because it is so pleasant to sit on a terrace, in a garden, or by a pool, grill your main course, and bring the rest of the meal from the kitchen. We really have portable kitchens. Even if you are cooking at the beach, you can take along your grill, a cold pack of food, utensils, and everything you need to turn out a decent meal.

I am more and more encouraged to find that people have learned you don't have to build a funeral pyre to grill properly. A few briquets or a small amount of charcoal burned down to lovely, ashy, glowing coals will do the trick. The secret is to have an adjustable grill that can bring the food as close to the heat as necessary. Start at a medium temperature and then, if you want to char the meat, raise the firebox toward the end of the cooking time to give that crusty brown finish and what most people consider to be delectable flavor. Thirty to forty briquets are enough for an average grill. Let them burn down to glowing, ash-covered coals, and then spread them around evenly so they give a temperature at grill level of about 350° to 375° when you are ready to put the meat on. (For charring, adjust the firebox to increase the temperature to 450° to 500°.) To check the temperature, use a flat grill thermometer or an oven thermometer. It's very important to get the right heat.

The choice of foods that can be grilled outdoors is so great that it is senseless to stick to the standard hamburgers, frankfurters, steaks, chops, and chicken. If you are fond of variety meats, you can grill kidneys, liver steaks, chicken hearts, or a split veal heart. The number of kebab combinations that can be grilled on skewers is practically endless. You might go Persian with cubes of lamb marinated in yogurt and spices or cubes of chicken with the same marinade. Or you can marinate chunks of lamb or beef in lemon juice, oil, and herbs, changing the herb flavoring to taste. Grilled duck, squab, and tiny quail are delicious and delicate—and don't be afraid of undercooking them. I don't mean you want a bloody bird, but a trace of pink in the meat is not going to kill you, and the meat will be moister and more succulent.

If your grill has a spit attachment, there is no end of things you can roast over coals—boned roasts, for example, such as eye of the rib, eye of the round, filet of beef, top sirloin, or boned leg of lamb; and any kind of bird. Here again, the secret is to keep an even temperature as your roast revolves on the spit, with a catch basin for the drippings to prevent flare-ups. Many of the better outdoor grills have these catch basins, but if yours doesn't, you should sink an ice cube tray or metal pan in the center of the coals to do the job. In the old days, you had to be equipped with one of those little spray bottles of water to douse the flames, and sometimes you were spraying more than grilling.

One of the most common mistakes on the outdoor grill is cooking certain foods too long that should be whisked through in a hurry to keep them juicy—most notably hamburgers. I have been served hamburgers that were grilled so slowly they were as dry as sawdust and just about as palatable. I'm sure over-cooked hamburgers have driven more people away from the outdoor grill than anything else, except possibly overdone frankfurters. To my mind, a hamburger is better pan-broiled or cooked on a flat surface, such as a griddle. If you do like charcoal-broiled hamburgers, they must be prevented from drying out. There are various ways to combat this. One is to add a bit of grated onion and heavy cream to the meat mixture before making the patties, although I warn you, the cream and onion will make the meat come out sort of pinky gray inside rather than a luscious rare red. Or you can follow Philip Brown's method of putting a chip of ice in the center of each hamburger before grilling. Or lastly, give a hamburger more heat than you would a steak so that it browns very quickly on the outside, then lower the firebox to reduce the heat and allow it to cook to the desired state of doneness. Steaks are no problem unless you have one that is very thin, in which case you must keep turning it quickly and giving it a good deal of heat or it will become well done and bloodless. And when you turn it, for heaven's sake don't use a fork or all the juices will run out. Turn it with tongs. This goes for anything you are grilling.

I happen to be a lamb freak, and one of the foods I most enjoy is a broiled boned leg of lamb that is opened out and cooked flat like a giant steak. This technique is called butter-flying a leg, except that I prefer to leave the shank bone in, which is not normally done. I also like to remove all of the fat from the lamb and marinate the meat for a day or two. First I rub the meat with a touch of olive oil, coarse pepper, fresh rosemary, and well-pounded garlic, then I put it in a dish with a little red wine, cover it, and turn it several times a day.

I broil it for about eighteen minutes a side, so it is crusty on the outside and pink inside. Or you can leave the fat on, stud the meat with garlic slivers, and rub it with salt, freshly ground black pepper, crumbled bay leaf, and a light coating of oil. Grill it fat-side down first, so the drippings from the fat fall into the catch pan rather than being absorbed into the meat. Turn it flesh-side down for the second part of the cooking time and brush with a bit of oil. Finally, just before removing it from the grill (the meat should have reached an internal temperature of 120° to 125° for rare, tested in the thickest part with a meat thermometer), turn it onto the fat side again, bring up the heat, and let the fat almost char, which gives a wonderful flavor. Either method is good. The meat has a glorious taste, and the carving of the boned leg is incredibly easy. As it will be uneven in thickness, serve the thickest, pinkest slices to those who like it that way and the thinner, better-done slices to those who prefer it medium rare. This is one of the most delicious outdoor foods I know. Serve it with crisp fried potatoes, a good salad, and plenty of red wine—a California zinfandel, for instance. It can also be served with a rather interesting variation on béarnaise sauce that uses chopped fresh mint in place of the usual tarragon. Follow your favorite recipe. A fresh mint béarnaise has nothing at all to do with that sugary, vinegary mint sauce so dear to the English, which I happen to abominate.

If you don't want a whole boned leg of lamb, there are other lamb cuts you can grill. One is a loin or rib chop cut three inches thick—and if a loin chop, with the kidney fat removed as well as a good deal of fat from the edges—and then tied, either boned or with the bone in, or secured with a small metal skewer so it holds its shape during the grilling. It should be grilled on all sides, not just two, and turned with tongs so it cooks evenly. Test it by inserting a thermometer very carefully into the thickest part of the meat without touching the bone. For rare, it should register 125°, and for medium rare, 130° to 135°. You can brush the chop with olive oil and tuck a garlic clove in the middle before putting it on the grill to give a nice distribution of flavor, or rub chopped rosemary into the meat—fresh, if you have some in your garden; otherwise, use crumbled dried rosemary. This is almost a one-person-sized roast. Serve it with a good coleslaw or with a bowl of fresh garden peas, very lightly cooked and smothered with butter. Again, a good sturdy red wine like a zinfandel, a Côtes du Rhône, or an Italian Barolo would be nice with the lamb.

There was a time when we used to get wonderful thick mutton chops, now almost a thing of the past, but if you have a butcher who can occasionally get good mutton—not the awful, scrawny kind—order a chop prepared as for the lamb loin or rib chop. It will have a stronger flavor than lamb but is excellent cooked the same way. For accompaniments, no delicate sauce, just good sturdy fried potatoes and a selection of mustards—a Dijon mustard, a tarragon mustard, or any of the herb-flavored mustards—along with a platter of peeled and sliced garden tomatoes, dressed with a dribble of olive oil, a touch of vinegar, and lots of finely chopped fresh basil, plus some crisp French bread. For dessert, luscious fresh raspberries, strawberries, or peaches.

When I grill chickens, I don't like skinny little broilers. Instead I buy 2- to 2$^{1}/_{2}$- or 3-pound chickens and have them split and the backbone removed—it is easy to do this yourself if you are deft with a Chinese cleaver or poultry shears. Slice right down the back, cutting out the whole spinal column, so that the chicken lies flat on the grill and cooks evenly.

Many things go well with grilled meats and poultry and can be cooked on the grill along with them—vegetables, in foil, or fruits. A mixture of vegetables, such as a ratatouille or a sauté of vegetables, can be kept warm on the grill after having been cooked in the kitchen.

If you are at the shore, freshly caught fish is great grilled, but you should use one of those square-hinged grills that hold the fish while it is turned. As with other cooking methods for fish, measure the fish at the thickest part and grill it for 10 minutes per measured inch. Overcooked fish is as good to eat as grilled cardboard, so don't be afraid if it seems slightly undercooked; it is better for you. With grilled fish, a sauce of yogurt flavored with Dijon mustard, chopped onion, and a little crushed garlic is a more pleasing and less caloric accompaniment than tartar sauce, hollandaise, or any of those rich, emulsified sauces we all love but that do put on the pounds. Good for the palate, bad for the belly, is what I say about such things.

Time was when outdoor grilling was considered to be a man's job, and the woman was supposed to supply him with accompaniments from the kitchen. I know a number of women who are much better at the outdoor grill than their husbands. So, along with all the other stale male traditions, like men's bars, I think this should be forgotten, too.

[1977]

The Art of Picnicking

Eating out of doors has always been one of my great joys. Just to munch a sandwich, drink something from a thermos, and talk with friends is a liberating experience never achieved in any dining room. Even the simplest of picnics can be a delight. All it takes is the right state of mind and a place to settle, whether it happens to be on the beach, in the woods, on a park bench, or in your car along the road. One of the most successful picnics I ever had was in a parking lot on the New Jersey Turnpike, where four of us sat looking out at trees, ignored trucks and cars, and enjoyed champagne, filet of beef, sandwiches, salad, cheese, and fruit. Another time I picnicked with a friend in a car high up on a snowy hill overlooking the mouth of the Columbia River. A view helps, but it isn't necessary.

I probably acquired the picnic mania in my youth. I remember wonderful beach parties on the Oregon shore, which began with clamming and crabbing early in the morning and came to a climax with breakfast by the sea. We ate griddle cakes, eggs, ham, sausages, and fried potatoes—appetites were enormous after all that exercise in the fresh air—and we drank quantities of coffee and tea. Those days must have made their mark: I have

a friend dating from that period who is just as compulsive a pic-
nicker as I am. Whenever we travel together, whether on a
highway from Portland to Seattle, or on a country road in France,
we take along some uncomplicated food and a bottle of wine.

Although a picnic can be an elaborate, planned affair for
thirty or forty people or a whole community, it can also be
quite impromptu, especially if you're driving. It's an easy matter
to gather up a few provisions at a roadside stand or at a shop in
any little town you pass through. Several of my most fanciful
picnics have come straight from a delicatessen, and I recall the
folly of one occasion when I bought a half pound of caviar,
lemons, black bread—lacking toast—and butter. Two friends
and I ate this with a bottle of chilled vodka and finished off the
meal with cheese, more bread, and wine.

In this food-conscious era, picnics offer a wonderful chance
to assemble stylish, imaginative menus. For beginning courses,
you can pack such things as a pâté *en croûte* and hot or cold
soups, according to the weather. Homemade bread and sweet
butter are essential with these. For a main course, I can think of
few things more elegant than a veal or turkey *tonnato,* or cold
chicken roasted with tarragon. The choices of salads are endless. Potato salad is standard picnic fare and always welcome. So
is coleslaw. But you could also have an interesting vegetable
salad with a vinaigrette sauce. Then for a finale you might serve
a selection of cheeses and fresh fruit, or a magnificent homemade cake, or a freezer of rich homemade ice cream. As for
drinks, it is easy nowadays to carry cooled things to the picnic
in portable iceboxes—red wine, slightly cooled if it's a hot day;
or if you really want to be festive, champagne.

If you have children along, naturally you will want simpler
fare. It is no trouble to set up a grill for hamburgers and frankfurters. Have buns, pickles, and mustard on hand, and all of the

items that enhance this sort of food. Also provide a potato salad, carrot sticks, your best cookies, ice cream, and soft drinks.

The picnics I have discussed here are relatively modest compared with those of the Victorian and Edwardian eras that one reads about. In those days, people sent servants ahead to the picnic site with great hampers of food, tables and chairs, fine linen, crystal, and silver. When the guests arrived by carriage, the picnic was already set up in a lovely dell or bosky wood. The servants then brought forth aspics and pâtés, cold salmon bathed in rich mayonnaise and highly decorated, cold birds and champagne, cheese and red wines, and all the things that lend themselves to eating al fresco. Of course, participation in an event like this took a special taste for being luxuriously fed and waited upon. The grand picnic is an art that has been lost, I'm afraid, although a number of years ago *Vogue* revived the idea in an article, with a bit of updating to allow a station wagon, phonographs, and radios.

But there's no reason why a successful picnic can't be had without all the furbelows if everyone grasps the idea that it should be a feast for the senses and the emotions as well as for the palate.

[1978]

Christmas in Provence

Of all the places in the world where I have spent the Christmas holidays, none has touched me more deeply than Provence, that captivating, mystical, sunlit region in the South of France. By day the light is brilliant, and the flowers glow with color. There are lovely skies at night with a gentle chill in the air.

Something about the dry, rugged landscape, dotted with olive trees, suggests the terrain of the original Christmas, and the people of Provence still observe age-old traditions. There are villages around Grasse where the countryfolk carry a live sheep into church at midnight mass to offer to the Christ child, and they sing ancient chants and carols, celebrating the season with a delightful blend of earthiness and naïveté. Food plays an important part in their festivities.

It is a joy simply to walk through the markets of Cannes, Grasse, and nearby villages in the days before Christmas. They are virtually bursting with produce for the holiday table. In the butcher and game shops, you see whole boars, deer, rabbits, pheasants, turkeys, geese, ducks, and quail. The charcuteries are overflowing with special sausages—the *boudin blanc* and the *boudin noire*—pyramids of truffles, and choice pâtés. Pastry shops offer a wealth of petits fours, extravagantly iced, and for those who do not make their own yule log cake, there are wonderfully decorated *bûches de Noël*. One great shop in Cannes, which specializes in candied fruit, displays its wares in such breathtaking arrangements that you can hardly pass its windows without lingering. You see whole peeled candied melons, tiny candied tangerines and oranges, cherries, grapes, figs, prunes. And there are fresh fruits and other delicacies as well from the entire Mediterranean basin and from the Tropics.

I recall wandering through one of the truly super supermarkets in Cannes and finding fresh dates *en branche*, papayas, pineapples, sugarcane, avocados, and mandarins, along with other fruits, all handsomely boxed. Everywhere there are mountains of shining marrons glacés, for no Christmas is complete without them. Many of these treasures will find their way into the traditional Provençal "Thirteen Desserts," the tray of holiday sweets that includes little dishes of dried and fresh fruits, nuts, candies, and cakes. It is a custom that is gradually disappearing, alas, as modern life catches up with this antique land.

There are two main Christmas feasts in this part of France. One, called Reveillon, takes place after midnight mass and may last well into the early morning hours. The other is a baronial Christmas Day dinner. These can be great boisterous family gatherings, or they can be simple, elegant occasions, like those I have enjoyed over many years with my friends Simone Beck and her husband, Jean Fishbacher, at their charming old farmhouse, or *mas*, perched on a hillside near Grasse and surrounded by magnificent olive trees. "Simca," as she is better known, is coauthor with Julia Child of *Mastering the Art of French Cooking*. A warm, individualistic, stylish woman, Simca approaches holiday food with a combination of respect for tradition and her own very imaginative flair. We have shared formal Reveillons, in the French manner, with spectacular foie gras, *boudin* of white sausage, and a fine goose or turkey, and we have had informal Christmas Day dinners, following the American custom, with a few French furbelows.

I particularly recall one Christmas Eve with Simca. There were very few of us present on this occasion, and we had all come from various directions. Simca and her two guests had been to the theater in Cannes, my guests had attended a simple midnight mass in a neighboring village, and I had been resting— I was recovering from an illness. We met at about a quarter to one. I brought some lovely roses I found in Grasse that day, and Simca's friends had brought a number of ravishing potted plants. So while things were brewing in the kitchen, the ladies constructed a Christmas tree with the roses and plants that was ingenious and enchanting. Around it were strewn tiny gifts. We sat down to dine at a low table and toasted each other in pink champagne. Then we ate a delicious fresh foie gras, prepared with fresh truffles and accompanied by piping hot toast, and continued with the champagne. So far, quite proper, but from this point on tradition was abandoned. We had a wonderful soup, thick, rich, and highly flavored, with delicious crusty bread and more champagne. After this came a *salade composé*, made with a number of vegetables, nuts, julienne of meat and chicken, and an excellent dressing. More champagne. We switched to a red wine while we enjoyed a selection of goat cheeses. And finally, with champagne again, we had our dessert, a marvelous *bûche de Noël*, decked with flowers of the season, filled with puréed chestnuts and flavored with liqueur. It was heady and irresistible. We left the table at about a quarter to four that morning, after much gaiety and as exquisite a "simple" Christmas Eve supper as I have ever had.

Just to show that not every Provençal Christmas feast has been perfect, I must tell you about a year when our dinner was ruined because of a crime committed at our favorite local butcher-caterer's shop. We had ordered a fine fat goose for our dinner, along with quail, smoked salmon, caviar, champagne, and Scotch. But two nights before Christmas two thieves—very hungry they must have been—rolled up a truck to the back door of our butcher's and cleaned out everything that was in his refrigerator, cook shop, and storeroom. Gone was our goose, the quail, smoked salmon, and other riches. And, rudest of all, the thieves laid waste to a gorgeously decorated platter of quail and aspic that was to be delivered for someone's luncheon the next day. Though we scurried around and found another goose that looked fat, alas, it was not. We made the best of it and enjoyed a flavorful goose soup the day after Christmas.

New Year's Eve at Simca's can be as great a delight as Christmas, and I remember one party that lasted from nine in the evening until deep in the morning, with course after course, bottle after bottle, and false nose after false nose. At midnight Jeanne, the caretaker of the house, much loved by everyone, appeared in a paper cap and false nose, so overcome with laughter that she set us laughing at and with her throughout the rest of the party.

This meal again started with quantities of foie gras but then went into a Russian theme, with blinis filled with smoked salmon and sour cream, and a borscht with bits of meat and vegetables in it. We proceeded to cold meats, cold chicken and goose, and a sensational variety of salads. On to cheeses. Then came a superb frozen mousse, perfumed with Benedictine and enriched with nuts and fruits. All of this was capped by a large tray of the "Thirteen Desserts"—chocolates, raisins, little Christmas biscuits, glacé fruits, and other sweets. I must confess that we were up the next morning ready to prepare a feast for New Year's Day.

Is it any wonder that I long for this part of the world at holiday time? Not only for the glories of Simca's table but also for the beguiling customs of Provence and the true joy of Christmas.

❧ Simca's Bûche de Noël aux Marrons ☙

1 pound candied chestnuts
  (marrons glacés)
1/3 cup boiling milk
1/3 cup sugar

3 egg yolks
6 ounces butter
Rum

The marrons glacés should be pressed through a fine sieve, if necessary, to a make a smooth purée. In a heavy saucepan, bring the milk and sugar to a boil. Allow to cool slightly, then beat in the yolks, one at a time over low heat, stirring constantly till the custard coats the back of a spoon. Gradually beat in the butter, a tablespoon at a time. Combine the custard with the chestnut purée and flavor with 2 or 3 tablespoons of rum. Place over a large bowl of ice and beat till cold and thick.

Spread over the sponge layer and roll to form a log. Decorate with powdered sugar, meringue mushrooms, and chopped pistachio nuts.

Sponge Layer:

4 eggs	*¹/₄ cup cornstarch*
¹/₄ cup sugar	*¹/₂ teaspoon vanilla*
¹/₃ cup flour	*¹/₂ teaspoon grated lemon rind*

Separate the eggs. Beat the whites to soft peaks, gradually add the sugar, and continue beating until stiff. Beat the egg yolks slightly. Stir 1 cup of the whites into the yolks. Pour over the remaining whites and fold in. Then fold in the flour and cornstarch, which have been sifted together. Finally, fold in the vanilla and lemon rind. Pour into an 11 x 16-inch pan lined with wax paper and buttered. Bake in a 400° oven 10 minutes exactly.

Meringue Mushrooms:

Beat 2 egg whites till they hold soft peaks, then gradually add ¹/₄ cup of sugar and continue to beat until the meringue is shiny and stiff.

Using a pastry bag and plain round tube, pipe meringue into mushroom-cap shapes on a buttered and floured baking sheet. Pipe the stems in straight, rather flat, sections. These can be attached to the caps by brushing the joints with white of egg. Bake 1 hour at 250°. Then turn off the oven, open the door, and leave the meringues to dry out completely.

[1974]

3

*I*n an assortment of pieces, short and long, that begins with soup and ends with garlic, Beard takes a fresh look at foods as familiar as watercress and the hamburger, and encourages a better acquaintance with hominy, quince, and Belgian endive. Many of the shorter pieces were first published in the syndicated column Beard wrote weekly during the seventies and eighties. One of these, "Tabitha Tickletooth's Way with Potatoes," is an example of Beard's habit of poring over old cookbooks, for enlightenment and sometimes for chuckles. The longer treatises on oysters and mustard were written for *Woman's Day* and *Esquire;* the latter was originally accompanied by photographs and ratings of thirty varieties then (1975) on the market.

Two of the articles, published here for the first time, are edited transcriptions of tapes Beard made for his unfinished book of reminiscence and gastronomic highlights. "The Pleasures of

Lobster" tells how he overcame the prejudice of a Pacific Northwest crab lover and learned to love the greatest crustacean of all. It took no effort to enjoy sauerkraut, discussed in the second of the articles, a food identified with Beard throughout his career. He once wrote a booklet of recipes for a commercial food producer, called *Confessions of a Kraut Lover,* and a gargantuan platter of *choucroute garnie* was featured on the initial cover of *The James Beard Cookbook,* along with a beaming Beard.

A Stock Is a Broth Is a Bouillon

The other morning my old friend Helen McCully[1] called me at an early hour and said, "Now that you're revising your fish book, for heaven's sake, define the difference between a stock, a broth, and a bouillon. No book does."

The reason no book does is that they are all the same thing. A stock, which is also known as a broth or a bouillon, is basically some meat, game, poultry, or fish simmered in water with bones, seasonings, and vegetables. Food writers have been known to wax nostalgic about the thrifty French housewife who, according to them, kept a stockpot permanently simmering on the stove, putting in leftovers from various meals. If this ever happened, which I very much doubt, it would have resulted in a ghastly mess of hot garbage. No one in his right mind would throw picked-over chicken and lamb bones, vegetable scraps, and all the other bits and pieces from the dinner table into a pot.

To make a good stock, you have to start with good fresh ingredients. Beef stock is made with beef, beef bones, vegetables, seasonings, and water. For a veal stock, you need veal bones and a bit of meat, especially that from around the neck. Calf's feet, if you can get them, will add a rich, gelatinous quality. A lamb stock is made much the same way. For chicken stock, buy gizzards and bony chicken parts—backs, necks, and wings. A whole chicken poached in this stock will make it even richer and more flavorful. For game stock, you can use the carcasses and tough bits of the game birds. For fish stock, you need heads and bones. A bit of fish flesh (if there is cheap fish on the market) makes the stock even better. For poaching fish,

---

[1]Helen McCully was food editor of *House Beautiful.*

you'd use a fish stock with the flavorings that make it a court bouillon—a carrot, an onion stuck with cloves, a clove or two of garlic, peppercorns, tarragon or thyme, salt, wine, and perhaps a bay leaf.

The purpose of making a stock is to give you the beginnings of a soup or the wherewithal for a brown or white sauce. Beef stock, enriched with marrow bones and cooked down, makes a fine base for onion and other hearty vegetable soups. Chicken stock is good for chicken or cream soups, or a béchamel or velouté sauce; fish stock, for fish soups, poaching, and white sauces for fish.

A *fumet* or *fond*, two words you often find in classic French cooking, is basically just a stock slowly simmered until it is cooked down and full of flavor. Then there is *glace de viande*, which is rich beef stock cooked down, down, down, very slowly until it turns thick and gelatinous, and so solid when chilled that you have to cut into it with a knife or very sharp spoon. Three quarts of beef stock will reduce to a half pint of *glace de viande*, a valuable additive in certain types of cooking.

So now we'll make a good strong chicken stock. Put 2 pounds of chicken gizzards and 2 pounds of chicken backs in a deep pot with 3 quarts of water, 1 onion stuck with 3 cloves, a leek, a carrot, 1 or 2 garlic cloves, a parsley sprig, a bay leaf, 1 teaspoon of thyme, and a few peppercorns. Bring to a boil and, after 5 minutes, skim the scum from the surface. Boil rapidly for 15 minutes, then reduce the heat and simmer, covered, for 2 to $2^1/2$ hours. Do not boil. Season with salt to taste—a tablespoon or more.

For poached chicken, add to the broth a $2^1/2$- to 3-pound chicken, cleaned and tied. Poach for 45 minutes to an hour, or until tender and cooked through but not falling from the bones. Remove the chicken and keep warm. Strain the stock. Melt 3 tablespoons of butter in a small heavy saucepan, blend in 3 tablespoons of flour to make a smooth roux, and simmer 3 to 4 minutes to cook the flour. Stir in 1 1/2 cups hot strained chicken stock, and continue to stir over moderate heat until thickened. Season with salt, pepper, a dash of nutmeg, and, if you like, 2 tablespoons of cognac or Madeira. Simmer a minute or two longer, then add 1 or 2 small pats of butter and stir in thoroughly. Just before serving, mix in 1/2 cup heated heavy cream, correct the seasoning, and add a little chopped parsley. Serve the poached chicken with this velouté sauce, noodles or mashed potatoes, and a green vegetable, such as spinach or broccoli.

The remaining stock—strained, clarified, and cooked down a bit—makes an extremely strong, flavorful consommé or soup base. This stock and any other, after straining and clarifying, will keep for a short time in the refrigerator, longer in the freezer, and it's a boon to have all that good rich stock, broth, or bouillon on hand.

[1974]

*W*hat Is a Salad?

I have been recently judging salad recipes for a contest, and after going through about thirty, I began to wonder what people believe a salad really is.

I grew up thinking of a salad as primarily a mixture of greens with a good vinaigrette dressing; or cold asparagus with a vinaigrette or mayonnaise; or perhaps a Waldorf salad, made with our crisp Oregon apples, walnuts, crunchy celery, and a light mayonnaise. Then, of course, there were such things as the eternally elegant chicken salad with mayonnaise (or half mayonnaise and half sour cream or crème fraiche, which I think makes a better chicken salad); and wonderful seafood salads, like the Louis and the most classic of all the French composed salads, salad Niçoise, which is as universally popular as any, with the possible exception of potato salad.

A Niçoise, that delicious mixture of tuna, anchovies, crisply cooked green beans, potato, tomato, onion, hard-boiled eggs, and a vinaigrette blessed with basil, is never the same twice. Each version has its own quirk. Sometimes the ingredients are put in a bowl with fresh basil and tossed together. At other times, the ingredients are arranged separately on a platter and then dressed.

Another composed salad I am extremely fond of is the one made with cold beef, celery, potatoes, onion, tomato, and hard-boiled eggs, well tossed with a vinaigrette sauce—a full meal and a noble dish for a buffet.

I can't think of any place in the Western world—and even beyond—where a salad of potatoes in one form or another is not part of the cuisine. There is the delicious French *pommes à l'huile,* made with freshly cooked waxy little new potatoes, olive oil, a touch of vinegar, chopped parsley, and perhaps a little chopped onion, served almost warm. For another French potato salad, the potatoes are cut very thin while still warm, placed in a bowl, laved with good olive oil, and allowed to stand for several hours. They are seasoned with vinegar, chopped parsley, onion, salt and pepper, with maybe a little more oil added, and then tossed and garnished with chopped chives or chervil.

The standard American potato salad of diced cold potatoes, chopped onion, chopped celery, and hard-boiled eggs, sometimes dressed with mayonnaise, sometimes with an old-fashioned boiled dressing, is also superb, although completely different. The German hot potato salad, made with pungent smoky bacon, potatoes, onion, parsley, bacon fat, and vinegar, has become part of our heritage, too. The fat replaces oil in the salad, the vinegar and seasonings are blended with the fat, and the whole thing is tossed and served warm, because if it gets cold, it congeals and is not very palatable.

Then there are salads of fruit and seafood. These can be subtle and agreeable. I am particularly fond of a shrimp, orange, and onion salad, where the orange sets off the other flavors. Tossed with romaine or Bibb lettuce and a good rosemary-scented vinaigrette, this is a great combination of textures and tastes, and if you add a diced avocado, you get contrast of another kind. The trouble is, too many people overpower seafood with fruit, and that just doesn't work.

The really sweet salads, mixtures of fruit and marshmallows and other gucky stuff, with a custardy dressing of fruit juices, egg, and whipped cream, topped with nuts and cherries and coyly nestled in a bed of greens, belong in the basement of salad making. I grew up in the days when a popular thing for luncheon was a "Candlelight Salad," a horrible bit of culinary eroticism that consisted of half a banana topped with a cherry and arranged on a slice of pineapple with some coconut and mayonnaise. It wasn't good and it wasn't a salad.

That was bad enough, but the bottom was reached with the gelatin mixtures that in many parts of the South are referred to as "congealed salads." To combine cream cheese or whipped cream and Bing cherries or peaches with fruit-flavored gelatin, pour it into a fancy mold, and serve it unmolded on greens with a salad dressing is nothing short of barbaric. Lovers of congealed salads, if there are any among you, and I sincerely hope not, may write me nasty letters for saying this.

Aspics are another story. A pristine, deliciously flavored jellied broth encasing shrimp, crab, chicken, or vegetables can be a glorious thing. The renowned chef Michel Guérard does exquisite, jewel-like aspics of fresh vegetables that make your mouth water. They could, I grant you, be called congealed salads, but there is all the difference in the world. They have flavor and sub-tlety, the crisp texture of the vegetables contrasting with the velvety softness of the aspic.

The things that have been perpetrated in the name of the salad are unbelievable, but they are fads that come and, we hope, go. Those that endure are the salads worthy of the name. What could be better than a plain green salad? Just rush out to the kitchen and toss yourself a mess of good varied greens with a vinaigrette sauce, eat it quickly while it is crisp, and enjoy something that is all a salad should be.

[1977]

*W*atercress: More Than a Garnish

One of my pleasantest memories, from the days when the great wholesale Paris markets, known as Les Halles, were still flourishing, is of walking through those thronged, clamorous streets at anywhere from one to five in the morning between glistening piles of the freshest, most perfect vegetables. Among the sights that impressed me were the huge baskets of watercress, lovingly arranged, with the bunches spiraled to the sides so the tender leaves would not be crushed and would have plenty of air to keep them crisp. It was such a miraculous display that I always wished I could do something similar, perhaps as an edible centerpiece for a buffet table.

When I see a plate garnished with watercress sprigs, I wonder how many people have the savvy to indulge in their lovely, peppery flavor between bites of roast chicken or steak or lamb chops. I'm afraid most people think that watercress, like parsley, has no function other than providing a punctuation of green on a plate.

Watercress, which those of you who consult nutritional guides will be happy to learn, is a prime source of vitamins A and C, has been used and enjoyed as long as almost any food we know, and has in its time circled the world from east to west. The Chinese use it in a soup that is exquisitely beautiful to the eye and luscious to the palate. Sprigs of watercress are arranged in the bottom of a tureen to form a nest, and poached eggs are carefully arranged on top. The eggs are sprinkled with slivers of water chestnuts and ham, and boiling chicken broth—seasoned with salt, pepper, and a little soy sauce—is gradually poured down the sides of the tureen so as not to disturb the arrangement. Each person gets an egg, some watercress, and broth.

There's a version of that famous and remarkable New Orleans dish oysters Rockefeller in which watercress replaces the usual spinach, giving an entirely different flavor. While no one seems to know which was the original version, the one with watercress has had far less publicity, and I prefer it because the watercress adds a little spiciness that appeals to my palate.

First sauté $1/4$ cup of chopped shallots or green onions, $1/4$ cup of chopped celery, 1 teaspoon of chopped chervil, $1/3$ cup of chopped fennel, and $1/4$ cup of chopped parsley in 4 tablespoons of butter for 3 minutes. Add 2 cups of watercress, trimmed of heavy stems, and just let it wilt. Put this mixture in a blender or food processor with 6 ounces of butter, $1/3$ cup of bread crumbs, and $1/3$ cup of Pernod or anisette. Season to taste with salt, freshly ground black pepper, and a few grains of cayenne pepper. Blend or process to a smooth purée. Have ready 2 dozen raw oysters on the half shell. Put about 1 tablespoon of the purée on each oyster, place the oysters on beds of rock salt in individual containers (tin or aluminum pie plates are excellent), and dampen the salt slightly. Bake in a 450° to 475° oven for about 4 minutes or until the butter is melted and the oysters heated through. Serves 4 to 6.

Watercress is often used in a purée with other greens, such as spinach, and served as a vegetable, and of course it is a natural in salads. A salad of crisp watercress and crumbled hard-boiled egg with a good vinaigrette makes a light, refreshing accompaniment to a hearty or rich entrée. A salad of watercress and thinly sliced raw mushrooms with a well-flavored vinaigrette is excellent, too. You'll also find watercress used extensively in the composed salads that are becoming more and more the vogue on both sides of the Atlantic as first courses or luncheon main courses.

When I'm in England, I always look forward to those delicious watercress sandwiches you find at the tea table or in the picnic hamper. When presliced bread came on the scene, thin, thin watercress tea sandwiches were almost swept out of the door, but thank goodness some people still know how to wield a bread knife and cut the paper-thin slices of white bread within which the watercress sprigs are rolled.

The next time you see watercress on a plate, don't push it aside. Pick up the sprigs, munch them, and see what they can do for your taste buds.

[1978]

*A*ll-American Cheese

Americans have at last developed a palate for cheese. Its growing popularity during the last ten years has been remarkable, and whereas we used to have occasional cheese shops in the larger metropolises, nowadays they are to be found in towns and cities all through the country. Americans are not just eating cheese, they are also becoming more knowledgeable about it. I find it significant that an encyclopedia of cheese written by M. Androuet, one of the leading cheese merchants in the world, and published in France two years ago, has been in sufficient demand here to warrant an English-language edition.

What troubles me, though, is that while French, Italian, Dutch, Scandinavian, and English cheese is consumed enthusiastically, we neglect the excellent cheeses produced right here in the United States. I first discovered them when I was quite young. I can remember eating Brie, Camembert, and little breakfast cheeses from the Rouge et Noir Creameries in Petaluma, California, an enterprise that only a small group of cheese fanciers were in the know about.[1] Today it is a thriving business, and the production of cheese in America has become a national industry. In variety, it is astonishing, and some of it ranks among the world's finest.

There is no doubt that Vermont and New York State cheddars are as good as any to be had. They vary in age and sharpness and are suitable both for a cheese course and for cooking. Few sandwiches are better than a nice sharp cheddar melted on good bread, sometimes combined with a piece of ham or with bacon. One brand that we used to order by mail quite frequently from Sodus, New York, was called Heluva Cheese.[2] It is still an exceptional aged cheddar. There are other aged cheddars to be found in Michigan, and Oregon makes good cheddars, too, but it is sometimes difficult to find aged ones. They are occasionally turned out by the great dairy combine in Tillamook County and are worth ordering by mail if you ever see them advertised.

Another achievement of our cheese industry during the past twenty-five or thirty years is the development of blue cheeses. Blue

---

[1] Now the Marin French Cheese Company; Rouge et Noir is the brand name.

[2] This cheddar can still be ordered by mail from the Heluva Good Cheese Country Store in Sodus, New York.

cheese, as you all know, originated in France. Its unique character is due to an aging process in limestone caves, where the growth of penicillin mold causes streaks of bluish color in the cheese that add great flavor as well as interesting design. The blue cheeses with the oldest history are probably those from the district of the Roquefort caves and have the added distinction of being made with sheep's milk. Other famous blues—Gorgonzola, Stilton, Danish Blue, Bleu d'Auvergne—are all made from cow's milk. After years of experimentation, this country has come up with what not only I but a number of food authorities consider one of the great blue cheeses of the world—Maytag Blue, from the Maytag Dairy Farms in Newton, Iowa.[3] Sold entirely by mail order, it can be ordered in sections or in a whole wheel. It is well made, beautifully aged, and has a flavor that offers much satisfaction to connoisseurs of cheese. We should be very proud of it.

Also from the Midwest comes a Brie that is made in small quantities and, if properly aged and stored, is a match for most of the great French Bries. On a number of occasions, guests of mine have been surprised to find they were eating not a Brie from the environs of Paris but one from Lena, Illinois, with the brand name Kolb.[4] It is an extraordinary cheese.

Swiss cheese—Emmenthaler or Gruyère—has been made in several parts of the country. Unfortunately, very little of it is properly aged, perhaps because most of it is consigned for processing by giant food packagers, and it seldom is allowed to develop the nutty, sweet flavor that one finds in the very well-aged cheeses imported from Switzerland. This is true of the Maytag Swiss and of a number made in Wisconsin. If you find a well-

---

[3]Maytag Blue is also still available by mail order.

[4]From the Lena Cheese Company; the brand name is now Delico. Since this article was written, the number of small, independent American producers of cheese has grown to nearly two hundred.

aged domestic Swiss anywhere in the country, it is likely to come from the Star Valley in Wyoming, where a large colony of Swiss have been making Gruyère and Emmenthaler for years.

Tucked away in northern California around Tomales Bay are several unusual dairies that produce a cheese that is very mild, deliciously creamy in texture, and definitely habit-forming. It is called Teleme. There are shops in San Francisco and Los Angeles where they will ship it for you, often dipping it in paraffin so it will hold its shape during travel. Good with fruit or with toasted crackers or French bread, Teleme is an experience worth seeking out if you haven't already encountered it. Another good cheese produced in California is the mild, pleasantly textured Monterey Jack. Jack is at once a nice plain table cheese and a cheese that is widely used in cooking, especially in Mexican and Southwest dishes and in recipes calling for a melting cheese.

The status of American cheese is similar to that long suffered by American wines, which until quite recently were assumed to be inferior to the wines of France and other European countries. We are now discovering how fine domestic wines can be. Wine and cheese are natural companions, so it would make good sense from time to time to track down the best of American cheese to accompany your American wine.

[1978]

The Delectable Oyster

There is a legend that the first prehistoric eater of oysters got his taste for the bivalve as follows: he was strolling on the shore and spied an oyster, shell open, gaping at the world. On impulse, the caveman stuck his fingers into the opening. As the shell snapped shut he pulled his fingers away and with them, the oyster. Naturally he put his fingers to his mouth and said, Mmm! What flavor!

My own theory is that the Chinese were the first, or surely among the first, oyster eaters. Long ago, they perfected a method of drying the bivalve and stringing it on bamboo sticks to keep for future use. Chinese cuisine includes scores of dishes using oysters and delectable oyster sauces. As for the Romans, we know from Apicius that they cherished the oyster and served it in many ways. One Roman recipe called for stewing oysters in honey. This I don't recommend. The ancient Greeks, who had more conservative tastes than the Romans, were particularly fond of oysters baked in their shells in charcoal or coals just until the shells opened. These they seasoned lightly with lemon and butter. This is still one of the choice ways to cook oysters. Modern cooks sometimes serve baked oysters with béarnaise sauce, a thoroughly delicious combination.

The French, Spanish, and Portuguese, all living near the sea, learned to appreciate oysters in ancient days. The English also loved oysters but, sad to say, served these delicate morsels with vinegar. Dickens, in *Pickwick Papers,* tells how Sam Weller's friend consumed a half-pint of vinegar with a plate of oysters. This mistreatment is doubly horrifying, since English waters produce two of the finest oysters in the world, Colchesters and Whitstables. These, along with the French Marennes, are greatly prized by connoisseurs.

Oysters vary in size, looks, and taste because the water, the climate, and even the exact location of an oyster bed have profound effects on their growth. They range from plump and grayish with a bland taste to greenish or even coppery with a definite metallic taste. Some are as small as your fingernail and others, such as the Japanese or the Malpeques from Prince

Edward Island, as big or bigger than the palm of your hand. The Pacific Northwest, where I grew up, is noted for its tiny Olympia oysters from Puget Sound. These delectable tidbits, not fatty but coppery in flavor, are such midgets that it takes over two thousand of them to make a gallon. An oyster lover can consume at least 250 at a sitting. Olympias command a premium price. Shucking them is a tedious job. Also, as with much of our finest seafood, the harvest grows less each year. We greedy eaters have helped to deplete the beds. The pollution of our waters—a result of our growing population—has also taken its toll.

On the East Coast, the Chincoteagues are the nearest to the Olympias, but the Cape Cod oysters were probably the first to attain popularity in America. They were an important food for the Pilgrims. The small oysters from Delaware Bay pleased William Penn and other Quakers of the Pennsylvania colony. Philadelphians are great oyster fans to this day. Elizabeth Robins Pennell wrote in her delightful book, *A Guide for the Greedy:* "But the glory of Penn's town is the oyster croquette—from Augustine's by preference. A symphony in golden brown and soft fawn gray, it should be crisp without, within of such delicate consistency that it will melt in your mouth like a dream."

The famous Lynnhavens from Virginia are no longer easy to come by. Man has stripped the beds. Nearby are ancient kitchen middens containing over three million shells, a testimonial to the quality of these great bivalves.

When I was young, a family friend in the West transplanted several well-known eastern varieties to the Toke Point area in Washington. We summered at the coast, and each week we received a great sack of these oysters. I can remember the wonderful pyramids of fried oysters my mother used to make with them. This was a breakfast specialty on the mornings when we went clamming and crabbing at dawn. Back we would come, tired, hungry, and cold. My mother was always in the kitchen ready for us. On the stove were two huge iron skillets partly filled with melted sweet butter, bubbling but not the least bit colored. The oysters, about twelve to a person and a few for the pot, were opened and lined up. The moment we came in, the first lot would be quickly rolled in flour, dipped in beaten egg and milk, and then rolled in freshly crushed cracker crumbs. Then the oysters were slowly lowered into the hot butter and allowed to turn a golden brown, no more. They were whisked to the table to be eaten with hot buttered toast and plenty of hot coffee. We bit through the crisp outside of the oysters into the soft, rich center. The coating of crumbs insulated the flesh so that they were always delicate and tender, never tough.

This to me is still a great breakfast dish. Of course, most oyster fans insist that the delicacy is at its best served raw on the half shell. Generally, I agree. And in this form, they need little or no embellishment—a dash of lemon juice and maybe a touch of freshly ground black pepper. But no vinegar, no chili sauce, and no cocktail sauce. With oysters on the half shell, serve thin sandwiches of rye bread lavishly buttered and a good wine or beer or stout. Dry white wines such as Chablis or Pouilly-Fuissé have a strong affinity for oysters.

Here are some ways to vary oysters on the half shell:

1. Serve them with lemon juice and black pepper and piping hot grilled or sautéed pork sausages, or with slices of garlic sausage. Be sure the sausages are hot and served on a hot plate and the oysters freshly opened and well chilled.

2. For a glamorous party dish, serve oysters on a bed of ice with a dab of fresh caviar and a squirt of lemon juice atop each one. Also serve rye bread sandwiches with sweet butter.

3. With the oysters, pass bowls of chopped chives and parsley, along with lemon juice and black pepper. You'll find the tang of these fresh herbs an interesting variation.

4. With cocktails, pass large trays of the oysters, lemon quarters, caviar (if you like), and hot tiny sausages.

⚜ Oyster Stew ⚜

If there is any traditional Christmas Eve dish in this country, I guess it is probably Oyster Stew. Surely it is one of the more delicious dishes when hot and rich and served with piles of crisp buttered toast. You can go as rich as you please here. Try it with milk, with milk and cream, or, to be utterly fabulous, with heavy cream.

5 tablespoons butter
1/2 pint milk
1 pint cream

1 1/2 pints oysters and liquor
Salt, pepper, and cayenne
Chopped parsley or paprika

Heat your bowls first. Add a good pat of butter to each bowl. Keep them hot until ready to serve.

Heat the milk, cream, and oyster liquor to the boiling point. Add the oysters and bring again to the boil. Season with salt, pepper, and cayenne to taste. Ladle into the hot bowls and add a dash of chopped parsley or paprika. Serves 4 to 6.

⚜ Oyster Stew II ⚜

Combine the oysters and butter in a skillet and cook till the edges curl. Add hot cream and heat to the boiling point. Ladle into hot bowls. Season with salt and cayenne and serve with crisp biscuits or buttered toast.

❧ Creamed Oysters ❧

My mother always served oyster patties in season for late supper parties. They were rich and delicious and beautiful to look upon. Serve them with a tossed salad, crisp fresh vegetables, or a cucumber salad, crisp bread, dessert, and coffee.

3 tablespoons flour
3 tablespoons butter
1 pint oysters and their liquor
1 1/2 cups heavy cream

Salt and pepper
2 egg yolks
2 tablespoons dry sherry

Blend the flour and butter well over moderate heat and cook for a few moments before stirring in 1/2 cup of the oyster liquor and 1 cup of the cream. Continue stirring until the sauce is well thickened and smooth. Season with salt and pepper, and then gradually stir in the remaining cream mixed with the egg yolks, and cook just until heated through, but do not let the sauce come to the boiling point.

Heat the oysters in their remaining liquor just until the edges curl. Drain and add the oysters to the sauce along with the sherry. Keep warm over hot (not boiling) water until ready to serve. Ladle into patty shells or bread croustades, or over toast points or steamed rice. Sprinkle with chopped parsley. Makes 4 to 6 servings.

❧ Oyster Pie ❧

Use the recipe for Creamed Oysters and fill a casserole or pie dish with the mixture. Place a small custard cup or support in the center of the dish. Top with a rich pastry that has been rolled and chilled for a half hour or more. Bake at 450° for approximately 15 minutes. Reduce the heat to 350° and continue baking for 5 minutes or until the crust is nicely browned and baked through. Makes 6 servings.

❧ Oysters en Brochette ❧

This is a most picturesque and delicious way to serve oysters. It can be varied in many different ways.

For each brochette or skewer:

1 slice bacon	*Lemon juice*
4 mushroom caps	*Freshly ground pepper*
4 oysters	*Butter*

Precook the bacon for a minute or so and cool it before using. Run the skewer through one end of the bacon, then skewer a mushroom cap, an oyster, and a loop of the bacon. Repeat the sequence until you have the skewer filled with the bacon laced through it. Sprinkle with lemon juice, give the whole thing a grind of pepper, and brush with butter.

Broil over charcoal or in the broiler until the oysters are curled at the edges and the bacon is crisp and done. This is delicious served with a hollandaise sauce.

Variations: Alternate small cubes of beef tenderloin and tiny mushroom caps with the oysters. Brush well with butter, and sprinkle with salt and pepper before broiling.

Alternate small cubes of precooked ham with the oysters. Broil as directed above and serve with a béarnaise sauce.

Alternate oysters, scallops, and chunks of lobster meat laced with bacon strips on skewers and broil. Serve with lemon or with a hollandaise sauce.

❧ Oyster Pan Roast ❧

Pan roasts are particularly popular on the West Coast. They are really oysters poached in butter with high seasoning and look well when served in small copper skillets or in a large oval gratin dish. This is the classic version:

1/2 cup butter   *Cayenne*
1 pint drained oysters   *Lemon juice*
Salt and pepper

Melt the butter in a skillet or in individual skillets, and when it is hot and bubbly, add the oysters. Poach them until they are plumped and curled at the edges. Add salt, pepper, cayenne, and a good squirt of lemon juice. Serve at once on fried toast or on crisp, well-buttered toast with chopped parsley and chives.

Variations: *Piquant.* Poach the oysters in butter. Season to taste and add a good dash of Worcestershire and a dash of ketchup or chili sauce. Serve on buttered toast.

Western. Poach the oysters in butter. Season with salt and a dash of cayenne. Add 1/4 cup of sherry and a little of the oyster liquor, and bring to the boiling point. Serve on buttered toast points with chopped parsley.

⋟ Scalloped Oysters ⋞

This is a traditional New England dish that has somehow or other worked its way into Thanksgiving menus.

Butter   *Salt and pepper*
2 cups coarse, freshly rolled   *Nutmeg*
  cracker crumbs   *1/2 cup cream*
1 pint drained oysters   *1/2 cup buttered bread crumbs*

Butter a baking dish well and cover the bottom with a layer of half of the cracker crumbs. Add a layer of oysters and sprinkle with salt, pepper, a little nutmeg, and 2 tablespoons of the cream. Dot with butter, and sprinkle with the buttered crumbs. Make another layer of oysters, seasonings, and 2 tablespoons of cream. Top with the rest of the cracker crumbs, dot heavily with butter, and sprinkle with seasonings. Add the rest of the cream. Bake at 425° for approximately 20 to 25 minutes. Makes 6 to 8 servings.

⫸ Hangtown Fry ⫷

This is a recipe that supposedly started in the West and for which there seem to be dozens of versions.

6 to 8 oysters
Butter
6 eggs, well beaten with
  2 tablespoons water

Salt and pepper
Crisp bacon

Fry the oysters in plenty of butter according to Harry Hamblet's recipe below. When they are golden brown, pour the well-beaten egg mixture over them, and cook as you would an omelet until done but not dry. Roll it onto a hot platter and garnish with strips of crisp bacon. A perfect Sunday breakfast dish or dinner entrée. Makes 6 servings.

⫸ Harry Hamblet's Golden-Fried Oysters ⫷

Butter
3 eggs
3 tablespoons heavy cream
36 to 48 oysters

Flour
Freshly rolled coarse
  cracker crumbs
Salt and pepper

Melt plenty of butter in a heavy skillet. It should be lavish for this preparation. (You might want to add part oil to the butter to prevent it from burning.) Beat the eggs lightly and combine with the cream. Dust the oysters lightly with flour and dip in the egg mixture. Then roll in the cracker crumbs—soda crackers or saltines are by far the best for this. Let the oysters stand for a few minutes before cooking, then cook quickly in the butter just long enough to brown the oysters nicely on both sides. Salt and pepper to taste and serve on a very hot platter with lemon wedges and coleslaw. Makes 6 servings.

[1964]

The Pleasures of Lobster

I was well past eighteen and had traveled halfway around the world before I ever tasted lobster. We lived on the West Coast, and Dungeness crab was the seafood to cherish. There was no lobster, and there was no langouste (spiny or rock lobster), except in more southern waters. My mother felt that lobster shipped from New England couldn't be good because it had lived through too much on the trip across, which of course was before air travel and overnight shipment of seafood from coast to coast. Other people might buy canned lobster, but not my mother. So we satisfied ourselves with fine Dungeness crab and clams from the Pacific and crayfish from the Necanicum River.

I didn't regret this, because when I finally began to enjoy lobster, at first from the English Channel and later on from Maine and Nova Scotia, I learned that when it is fresh from the sea, it is in another class from lobster preserved in tanks and shipped long distances. I wouldn't think of eating a mature, well-exercised, ready-to-retire Maine lobster on the West Coast any more than I would consider eating an immigrant Dungeness crab in New York. My mother was absolutely right. One ate lobster where it belonged.

Still, when I set out to study voice in England in the twenties, I was embarrassed to admit that I had never tasted lobster.

I considered my palate to be quite sophisticated for my age. My virgin experience with this great seafood came at a favorite restaurant in Soho called Gennaro's. The menu featured an hors d'oeuvre composed of the mother and father of all beefsteak tomatoes, hollowed out and stuffed with a cooled coddled egg, a very large piece of lobster tail, a heavy sprinkling of Italian parsley and tarragon, and an olive oil mayonnaise, served separately. It was not love at first taste, but I liked the dish well enough and ordered it often in the ensuing weeks and months. In the midst of curiosity about other dishes, I eventually forgot about lobster.

It took another event in England to make me a convert. One summer Sunday, my voice teacher, Gaetano Loria (Caruso's former assistant, who had coached many singers of the day), his wife, Mary, and I set off for a garden lunch in Surrey. It was a dreamy day, with blue sky, scattered clouds, trees at their greenest, and flowers everywhere. Our hosts were a family named Liddell. We had a simple but exquisite lunch that did something very special for me, because our main dish was a lobster salad so delicious that it convinced me I had missed a great deal during all those lobsterless years. It was served on a handsome Chinese platter and was composed just of generous pieces of perfectly cooked lobster, a sprinkling of finely diced celery, a fair amount of finely cut fresh tarragon, and some parsley. The whole thing was bound, not flooded, with an excellent olive oil mayonnaise. And it had a border of romaine lettuce, or "cow's lettuce," as the British call it, and a few pieces of lobster claw.

This, with some homemade bread and unsalted butter, was our lunch, and it was ample. And because it was strawberry season, it was followed with luscious English strawberries, with sugar for dipping and clotted cream. We drank a lovely dry German wine—I can't remember which one after all these years—but it had the fruitiness and the tingle of a perfect hock to recommend it. I still dream of that garden and that luncheon. I can almost remember the conversation. It was a milestone in my lobster life, and from there on I began to play with lobster more and more.

Soon after the end of World War II, when I was stationed in Marseilles, I traveled across the Riviera for a weekend in Monte Carlo with friends. After not having seen a lobster or langouste for months, except in the market and at a price beyond belief, I ordered langouste for my lunch. It turned out to be the largest one I had ever encountered. Fortunately, I had three other people to help me eat it. And while langouste is not as delicious in flavor nor as delicate in texture as the lobster from a colder clime, this one seemed ambrosial to me.

Not long after that, I went to Paris for a holiday and was invited to have lunch with Madame Bollinger, a courageous woman, who during the war years had managed to hold on to the family's champagne business and hide away the choicest bottles. She lived in her flat in Paris part of the time and used to bicycle around the city to do her errands. We lunched at a favorite old restaurant of mine called Lucas-Carton, near the Madeleine. The menu offered *les demoiselles de Cherbourg* for a first course. These were young lobsters, about one-pounders, and you were given several of them for an order along with a *rémoulade* sauce or mayonnaise. We both indulged ourselves in these morsels, which were absolutely superb at that point. They were not to be missed on a visit to France, especially if you were traveling through the Champagne country, where you had them with a "black market salad," made with hearts of palm and butter lettuce or romaine.

After the war, when transportation had returned to normal, I traveled on the beloved old *France* for a number of voyages. On the first day out, sailing west, the luncheon menu was very likely to offer a hearty serving of *les demoiselles de Cherbourg*. It was always a pleasant farewell to a dish that was becoming harder and harder to find.

There are two famous ways of preparing lobster that have a close association with America. One is lobster Newburg, a splendid dish first prepared at New York's Delmonico restaurant for a man named Wenburg, according to one story, but when he and the chef had a falling out, the restaurant changed the name of the dish from Wenburg to Newburg. It became popular in both America and France, and the two versions are very similar. The American is simpler, with cooked lobster meat, butter, cream, egg yolks, onions, salt, and pepper. The French uses olive oil, white wine, and a little beurre manié, and is perhaps less delicate. The dish has fallen out of fashion, but it is always a pleasure to find it on a menu, whether for lunch or dinner.

Another classic lobster dish with a close tie to America, at least in name, is lobster *à l'américaine*, which in my opinion is one of the greatest lobster dishes of all. Its origin is still something of a riddle, and no dish in French cuisine has been more controversial. Its very name is in question, as are its birthplace and inventor, to say nothing of the many variations that have been served under its banner. Was it created in a Parisian restaurant in the 1860s and named in honor of American guests? Or—as some authorities maintain—did it originate in Armorique (the ancient name for Brittany) and should thus be called lobster *l'armoricaine?* To deepen the mystery, did the dish have Provençal beginnings, as Escoffier, among others, believed?

A plausible theory attributes the dish to a French chef named Pierre Fraisse, who was born in a Mediterranean port. One night in 1867, so the story goes, when he was chef at Noël and Peter's restaurant in Paris, three Americans arrived very late and demanded dinner. Fraisse had a lobster already cooked, which he heated in a highly seasoned sauce he concocted. The dish was well received, and so he named it in honor of his guests. This theory nicely ties in the American connection with the Provençal accent of the ingredients, which include tomato, olive oil, and garlic.

Whatever its origin, many French chefs have added this recipe to their repertoires, giving it an individual twist here and there. Prosper Montagné's own method calls for a live lobster and is not too far removed from the original, supposedly created by Fraisse, but it differs by the addition of garlic, tarragon, and cognac, which greatly improves the flavor, in my opinion.

Among other good lobster dishes I have known is a variation on lobster à l'américaine in which the lobster is removed from the shell and used hot with pasta. Also, there's a lovely risotto recipe that combines rice, lobster, cream, and Scotch, which I find extraordinarily delicious and far removed from most of the ricey dishes we are usually given with lobster. The guts that the cream and Scotch give this version is something to climb over walls for.

Then there's the wonderful lobster soufflé from the Plaza-Athénée in Paris, which taught me a great deal. I spent one morning with the chef, Lucien Diat (brother of another famous chef, Louis Diat), and learned a secret that few cooks ever know—that a soufflé can be put together and stored in the refrigerator for two to two and a half hours before baking, and it will not fall or be impaired in the least. I had had a great many soufflés in my life, but this never occurred to me. It now seemed so logical.

Another memorable lobster recipe is the consommé prepared by Anton Mossman, chef at the Dorchester in London, which is without question the most exquisitely flavored clear soup I have ever had. I had it in London two years ago, and its bouquet and flavor continue to haunt me.

Of course, I find joy, too, in the simplicity of a freshly cooked lobster, split and served with mayonnaise, toast, maybe a few leaves of salad, and nothing else. This is what I often shared with my late friend and coworker José Wilson. She lived the last years of her life in Rockport, Massachusetts, and would often go shopping for lobsters, cook them quickly, and serve them before they completely cooled or had to be refrigerated. I used to call her "the lobster girl." I can remember going with José and two other friends on a picnic one day in the countryside near her. Each of us had a perfectly beautiful lobster, and there was a very good California chardonnay to drink. We sat under trees by a pond and took absolute hours to eat our lobsters, as we broke off every tiny bit of shell and extracted the goodness from it. I don't think there was one edible fleck of meat left in the carcasses we toted back. Sometimes a dish as simple as cold lobster can be as delectable and as elegant as all the sauced lobster in the world. Our picnic turned into practically a whole day of enjoyment, because we sat long over lunch as we talked and laughed and lobstered.

[1984]

*W*ho Invented the Hamburger?

I read the other day, with some astonishment, that a New Haven man called Kenneth Lassen claims that his grandfather, who opened a small snack bar there, was the first ever to serve a hamburger. That was in 1900. According to Lassen, this was chopped steak between two pieces of toast, with no onion, ketchup, or any kind of trimmings. He is still serving his grandfather's version of hamburger, which has a great following in New Haven, and is trying to get his little restaurant [Louis' Lunch] made a national monument.

Now I'm pretty certain, from what research I have done, that the hamburger was born in Hamburg, Germany. Otherwise, the name wouldn't have stuck all this time. "Hamburg steak" figured in American cookbooks from the 1870s. And in that great reference work, *Larousse Gastronomique, bifteck à la hambourgeoise* is described as chopped steak mixed with chopped onion, egg, and seasonings, sautéed in butter until pink inside, then served with sliced fried onions. What could be more like the hamburger we have today, apart from the fact that it isn't always sautéed?

The hamburger, as we know it, along with the hot dog and the ice cream cone, supposedly came into being at the St. Louis Fair in 1904. Certainly by the time I was growing up, in the early part of the century, we often took chopped meat patties, well seasoned and sometimes mixed with onion, to the beach and either broiled them or cooked them in an iron skillet on a rack over the coals. We served them on the kind of round bun a hamburger goes on, and sometimes we had onion on them. I suppose some of our friends might have had ketchup, too, though our family wasn't too keen on ketchup, nor am I now.

About 1920 or so, places that specialized in the hamburger on a bun, with onions and relish, began to flourish. Great businesses started, building up to the present-day McDonald's. At one point, hamburger was called Salisbury steak. Some say that name came from an imported English machine, the Salisbury chopper. Others believe it was due to anti-German feeling in World War I, which may well be true, because menus did banish German terms. In some places, hamburger was known as liberty steak.

At any rate, the hamburger finally recovered its original name and is now probably the most-ordered food in the world. It appears on the menus of the best American restaurants. There's the super-elegant hamburger served at "21," which reputedly contains a tiny bit of crisp chopped celery and sells for a lordly price; the famous hamburger at the London Chop House in Detroit, done with cognac and freshly ground pepper and flambéed; and the Maxwell's Plum hamburger, rimmed with bacon, topped with cheese, and served in an enormous sesame-seeded bun.[1] At the Four Seasons, the patty of chopped aged beef is called "chopped steak," but it's hamburger nevertheless.

There are many other versions of this American classic. One is the hamburger à cheval, or hamburger on horseback, cooked in butter and topped with a thin slice of onion, two fried eggs, and a few capers. Another consists of two thin broiled patties with a slice of onion in between. As far as I'm concerned, I'll take a good thick hamburger steak.

To serve 4, spread 2 pounds of ground or chopped beef on a board and season with 1 teaspoon of salt, $3/4$ teaspoon of freshly ground black pepper, and 1 tablespoon of grated onion. If garlic is your dish, add 1 or 2 cloves, minced. Form into a large cake about $1^{1}/_{2}$ inches thick, and broil 4 inches from the heat for about 4 minutes on one side. Turn very carefully with two spatulas, brush with melted butter, sprinkle with salt and pepper, and broil until nicely crusted on top and very rare in the middle.

Thinly slice 2 or 3 Spanish onions, sprinkle them with 1 teaspoon of salt and $1/2$ teaspoon of pepper, add vinegar to barely cover them, and let them marinate in the refrigerator for several hours. Serve these piquant sliced onions with your hamburger steak, a green salad, buttered rice or home-fried potatoes, and a glass of red wine. You'll have a magnificent feast.

[1974]

---

[1]Maxwell's Plum, a New York restaurant, and the London Chop House are no longer in business.

$\mathcal{C}$orn It Yourself

I love good corned beef in all its manifestations, whether it be the traditional boiled dinner served with cabbage, onions, carrots, potatoes, and turnips; a succulent hash; or a juicy corned-beef sandwich on rye or pumpernickel, spread with butter and mustard.

Beef brisket or flanken "corned" or cured in a pickling solution is a time-honored American way of preserving meat. Pork and lamb used to be corned just like beef. Though corning seems to have become one of the lost domestic arts, it's easy enough to do. The flavor of home-corned beef is, to me, much better than that of the commercial variety, some of which is pretty poor these days.

If you'd like to try your hand at corning, first of all you'll need a nonmetallic container—glass, enameled metal, or an earthenware crock—big enough to hold the meat and pickling solution, which should come about two or three inches above the meat. Brisket is by far the best cut to buy, as it is thin and well fatted on both sides. It's worth making a batch to last for two or more meals, so I suggest you buy two pieces of fresh beef brisket or about eight to ten pounds in all. Wipe the pieces well with a damp cloth and make several very deep jabs in the meat with a fork so the pickling brine will be absorbed.

Put the meat in the crock. To estimate how much liquid you'll need, measure water into the crock to the necessary level and pour it off. To each gallon of water needed, allow 2 cups of rock salt or curing salt, 2 cups of dark brown sugar, 1½ teaspoons of bicarbonate of soda, and 4 teaspoons of saltpeter (sold in drugstores as potassium nitrate). Add a few crushed peppercorns or allspice, a few blades of mace, and several peeled garlic cloves. Mix these ingredients with 1 quart of lukewarm water, and when well blended and dissolved, mix with the rest of the water. Pour over the beef, making sure it is completely submerged. Let it soak for 8 to 12 days. The longer it is left, the more mature and saltier it will be and the finer the texture and flavor when cooked. You may have to add a little more brine to keep the meat well covered, so check now and then. This corning formula also can be used for pieces of pork or a fresh tongue.

When the beef is cured, remove it from the brine, rinse well in cold water, and cook. After a good deal of experimenting, I have found that corned beef cooks better when steamed in the oven in a flat baking pan with very little water, rather than by the usual method of cooking it on top of the stove in a large pot of water. The steamed beef comes out firmer and easier to slice.

For a corned-beef dinner for 6, allow 4 to 5 pounds of meat, which will give you some leftovers for hash or sandwiches. After washing the meat, trim off excess fat, and place in a flat baking pan with enough water to come almost to the top of the meat, to the fat line. Add half a dozen crushed black peppercorns, a bay leaf, and 3 garlic cloves. Drape a piece of aluminum foil over the pan, and steam-bake slowly in a 325° to 350° oven for about 3 or 3$^1/_2$ hours or until just tender when tested with a large fork. Be careful not to overcook, or it will become dry and stringy; it's important to retain some moisture in the meat. When tested with a meat thermometer, the internal temperature should register 145° to 150°.

For the accompanying vegetables, you'll need 1 onion, 1 carrot, 1 turnip, 1 medium potato, and 1 wedge of cabbage per person. I like to cook the vegetables in separate pots, as they all need different cooking times, but you can cook the onions and carrots together, adding the carrots halfway through the cooking time. Simmer each vegetable for the following times, in salted water to cover: 1 hour for large peeled onions, 30 minutes for scraped carrots, 20 minutes for small turnips (if large, cut them in half). Potatoes should be scrubbed and cooked in their jackets for 30 minutes or until tender. For cabbage, cut a medium head of green or white cabbage into sixths, after removing any discolored outer leaves, put in a pot with salted water to cover, and boil rapidly for 10 to 12 minutes or until just tender, not overcooked. Nothing is more unappetizing than soggy cabbage.

When the corned beef is cooked, remove it to a hot platter and leave in a warm place for 10 minutes, to firm the tissues and make it easier to carve. Surround it with an entourage of the drained vegetables, leaving the potatoes in their jackets. Slice only as much meat as needed, and serve with mustard, horse-radish, and, if you are a pickle fancier, some good homemade pickles. You'll have a lavish and memorable feast that's just right for a cold winter evening.

[1979]

The Wondrous Artichoke

Earlier in the century, Italian and Chinese truck farmers raised great quantities of artichokes in Oregon because they grow extraordinarily well in that temperate part of the country. Our itinerant vegetable man, who came by three or four times a week with horse and wagon, grew some himself and would bring us choice globe artichokes throughout the season. Most of them had been picked the same morning. We took them as a matter of course and ate them in great numbers. In later years, I remember driving from San Francisco down through the countryside around Salinas and Big Sur and seeing acres and acres of this glamorous vegetable, ready for budding and soon to be picked. The plants are stunning, with handsome foliage and, when beyond the edible stages, with extraordinarily beautiful blue flowers.

Once thought to be an oddity, the artichoke has been popularized by French, Italian, and other Continental restaurants to the point where it is now considered as much a part of one's diet as asparagus, green beans, or peas. Thank heaven! Artichokes have been cultivated for centuries and are a kitchen staple in Italy and France. In addition to the large Roman artichoke and the thick globe artichoke, there are two varieties of smaller ones, a long, very thorny one with quite vicious thorns and a tiny purple-tinged one that we sometimes find in our New York markets and in California as well. Years ago, when I was in the hors d'oeuvre business, we used to buy these tiny ones in quantity. After they were properly steamed or boiled, the tops were cut off, the chokes scooped out, and the bottoms filled with foie gras, caviar, and sometimes crabmeat or shrimp. They made an appealing addition to the hors d'oeuvre tray. It is these same miniature artichokes that one finds in the baskets or trays of crudités in Europe. The outside leaves are removed, and the bottom and some of the tender little leaves are eaten raw. They have a special flavor that is enjoyed by many people.

To cook artichokes, they should first be trimmed and the stem cut down to the level of the globe. I usually peel and cook the stems as well. Sometimes I cut the tops off the artichokes completely before I boil them, but at other times it seems more attractive to leave the globes intact. This depends, too, on how they are to be used. They should be boiled in salted water with the addition (to my taste) of several slices of lemon, 2 to 3 garlic cloves, and maybe some crushed peppercorns. In addition, I have been known to add 1 onion stuck with 2 cloves to the water. Artichokes should be cooked until the bottoms are just tender and the leaves come away quite freely when tested. Some people like them cooked to death, till the leaves collapse. I prefer to see a pert artichoke on a plate. When done, cool the artichokes (rather than chill), and serve with mayonnaise, a vinaigrette, or *sauce gribiche*. They make a marvelous first course or luncheon dish, and they complement almost any other food.

An interesting way to handle them, after they are quite cool, is to push the outer leaves slightly away and pull out the center leaves in one conelike piece. You can then scrape out the choke completely from the bottom with a spoon. Some people invert the cone of leaves and put it back in place, so there is a little cup that can be filled with vinaigrette or some other sauce; or it is left just as is. Others push the remaining leaves farther outward to make a larger opening and fill it with a salad—crabmeat, shrimp, lobster, or chicken. It is placed on a bed of greens and served with additional dressing. This makes a substantial luncheon or supper dish.

Hot artichokes are delicious, too. They can be served just as the cold ones are, with a mustard sauce or vinaigrette; and with a hollandaise, they go well with roast or grilled meats. Artichokes prepared for stuffing can be filled with a creamed fish, lobster Newburg, or shrimp Newburg—a very handsome way to serve the vegetable as a first course.

[1978]

Belgian Endive: The Elegant Vegetable

One of the most delicate and delectable vegetables in the Western world, Belgian endive looks rather like an elongated (five- to six-inch) tightly furled bud. The creamy white leaves are tipped with greenish gold and are satiny in texture. Its elegant appearance in produce departments is heightened by the fact that Belgian shippers nearly always pack endive in royal blue tissue paper to shield the pale leaves from light.

Strangely enough, none but the Belgians have been successful in growing this magical vegetable, though horticulturists in France and now California keep trying. Perhaps it's the expertise the Belgians employ in growing the plants in the dark, which thus blanches the leaves. Perhaps it's the careful way the long rows of endives are harvested, packed, and shipped. At any rate, the Belgian product stands supreme.

A member of the chicory or curly lettuce family, Belgian endive (the Flemish name is *witloof,* which means "white leaf") was created by accident in 1843, when a gardener inadvertently left some chicory roots in his moist, dark cellar. Sometime later he found that the plant, deprived of sunshine, had put forth fragile white leaves that tasted absolutely delicious—tangy and crisp, with an elusive hint of bitterness.

Belgian endive is, strictly speaking, a winter vegetable, but it is now available from September through May, with the height of the season from December until February. Alas, it is never really cheap. But then, it's not your ordinary lettuce. It requires pampering in special heated trenches of sandy soil.

I recently received a formal invitation from the Belgian consul-general in New York to attend a luncheon at the famed Palace Restaurant, which was organized by the National Office for the Promotion of Agriculture and the Belgian Endive Marketing Board. The Belgian government even sent over one of the finest chefs from Brussels to participate in the occasion. I could hardly believe my eyes when I noted that the luncheon was scheduled to last from noon until four o'clock. No luncheon in creation should take that long, except perhaps a wedding celebration. It turned out that I could arrive late, but I was still not prepared for a menu such as the one presented. It was far too long and complicated, and I failed to see the advantage of offering three fish courses at a luncheon supposed to be featuring endive. What's more, the fish was overcooked. The poor endives were quite lost in the gastronomic excess.

To my mind, endive is at its best when raw. It needs only a few shreds of brilliant rosy beets and a fine vinaigrette sauce to set it off. The beets add color and sweetness, tempering the endive's slight bitterness. Braised endive is next in line for the most distinctive treatment.

Choose 6 full heads of endive. Trim the root ends, and wipe with a damp cloth. Melt 6 tablespoons of unsalted butter in a skillet. Add the endives in a single layer, and sauté on all sides over medium-high heat until lightly colored. Reduce the heat, cover the pan, and simmer until the endives are just tender and pierceable. Season with salt and freshly ground black pepper, and remove to a hot platter. Heat 4 tablespoons of butter over medium heat, shaking the pan from time to time, until it turns a deep golden color, but do not let it burn. Pour over the endives, garnish with chopped parsley, and serve.

Alternatively, sauté the endive as above and then add $1/2$ cup or more of well-seasoned beef or chicken stock to the pan. Cover and simmer until the endive is tender. Remove to a platter. Cook down the broth a little, add a few drops of lemon juice and some chopped parsley, and pour over the endive. Either dish makes a delicious vegetable or first course.

[1981]

Tabitha Tickletooth's Way with Potatoes

If you collect old cookbooks, as I do, every once in a while you fall upon a real treasure. Recently I was dining with an old friend, a former governor of Oregon, who loves to cook, and he gave me a little volume of cookery by a Miss Tabitha Tickletooth, published in London in 1872. I don't know whether Miss Tickletooth dreamed up her name as a pseudonym or whether she came from a line of early dentists, but she wrote a most amusing and opinionated cookbook.

Miss Tickletooth lived about the time of Alexis Soyer, the great French chef, who is noted for having masterminded field cooking for armies, field hospitals, and hospitals generally, and for redesigning restaurant and club kitchens, the most famous of which was that of the Reform Club in London. This was considered a model, and it completely revolutionized kitchen design. Like many ladies of her era, Miss Tickletooth was a snob and a believer in class distinction. In her opinion, it was not fitting for the middle classes to attempt to ape the aristocracy by serving seven or eight courses for dinner, with two or three items for each course. This excerpt from her book gives a clear indication of what she thought a middle-class dinner party should be: "If you will imitate your superiors and ask persons to dinner, attend to the following things. Always invite the wives of your male friends. These women will much abridge the evening, being desirous to get home to their children and they will, in some measure, be able to check intemperate habits. Give your meal at six, as persons of your class are unaccustomed to wait so long and will have lunched, whereby you will save."

Despite her rampant snobbery, Miss Tickletooth does know what she is about in the kitchen. She likes potatoes, as I do, and she has a recipe for boiling potatoes in their jackets that she claims is absolutely foolproof. I tried it, and it really is a surprisingly good way to do potatoes. With her method, some very mediocre potatoes I had been using came forth firm, waxy, and just as I wanted them for the beef hash I was making, so I thought I'd pass her secret on, in her own words.

"Carefully select potatoes of an equal size and put them into a saucepan with a tablespoon of salt and just sufficient cold water to cover them, for if there be too large a quantity they must remain in the water a long time before they boil and, consequently, break before they are done. When they have boiled five minutes, pour off the hot water and replace it with cold, and a half tablespoon of salt. Neither simmer nor gallop, but boil steadily, with the cover on, for three-quarters of an hour." Some of our potatoes, of course—and this is Beard speaking—require no more than twenty minutes. "When you are sure they must be done—and if you are in doubt, probe them with a fork—drain them dry, put them in a clean cloth kept for that purpose, cover closely with a lid and let the saucepan stand on the hob or the back of the stove until you are ready to serve your dinner. Then you must take them out with a spoon. If you use a fork for that purpose, you will in all probability break them, if they are floury." She adds, "Cooking and serving in the skin is unquestionably the best method if the quality of the vegetable will warrant, but when peeling is necessary, on the Irish principle of killing the sick pig to save its life, you must make the most of it."

So for my beef hash, having boiled 4 medium potatoes by Miss Tickletooth's method, I peeled and cubed them, cubed 2 cups of leftover roast beef, and coarsely chopped 1 large sweet Walla Walla onion (you can substitute a yellow onion). I cut off and rendered 3 or 4 tablespoons of fat from the roast, in which

I sautéed the onion until lightly colored. I added the potatoes and pressed them down, seasoning them with salt and freshly ground pepper and adding some of the juices from the roast beef. Then I put in the cubed beef, pressed this down also, poured on a little bit of red wine, and let this cook down quite well. I then turned the hash over with a spatula so the crusty bottom bits got mixed in with the rest, pressed it down again, and repeated the process. It took just about 15 minutes of cooking, and it was one of the best justifications for having roast beef that I know, because the hash alone was almost worth the price of the beef. I served this with crisp bread and a salad, with fruit and cheese to follow, and it made a thoroughly enjoyable meal. I'm sure that Tabitha Tickletooth would have approved of having her potatoes used in such a savory dish.

[1974]

Baked Potatoes

In my youth, I used to travel back and forth between Oregon and New York. I had the choice of the Great Northern or Northern Pacific, the Milwaukee Line or the Union Pacific. Being a great eater, I almost always took the Northern Pacific because it had a reputation for extraordinarily good food and was known as "the line of the great big baked potato." The potatoes, specially grown for the Northern Pacific, were huge, weighing over a pound each, and they were always perfectly baked, no small feat in the galley of a dining car, you must admit. They came from the kitchen split and dripping with butter, and one ate them with steak or chops or fried chicken, sometimes with fresh trout, put aboard at one of the station stops. They had a quality one seldom finds nowadays, and I have never forgotten how good they were.

There is something very satisfying about a perfectly baked potato. Its delicious floury lightness and the earthy flavor of the crisp, chewy skin, intensified by the baking process, needs no dressing up. I prefer to savor that wonderful earthiness with just freshly ground black pepper and a touch of salt—no butter, no sour cream, no chives. Well, maybe a little bit of butter with the skin, but more often just pepper and salt.

So many people who are dieting say they love potatoes but wouldn't dare to eat them because they are fattening. That's hogwash. A plain baked potato without butter or trimmings has only about ninety calories, and it's full of riboflavin, iron, thiamine, niacin, and vitamin C. According to the research department of the Department of Agriculture, a diet of whole milk and potatoes supplies almost all the food elements necessary for the maintenance of the human body. Ounce for ounce, a baked potato has about the same number of calories as a banana, apple, or pear, and it is certainly more filling, satisfying the craving for something different in taste and texture from the usual diet foods. Of course, if calories don't matter to you, you can load your baked potato with good sweet butter, salt, and pepper; with yogurt, sour cream, or crème fraiche; or maybe with some chopped chives, crumbled bacon, or finely cut green onions.

Or you can stuff your baked potatoes. When done, cut off about 1/4 inch across the top, scoop out the pulp, and mix it with butter, bacon bits, chopped onion, parsley, and shredded Gruyère cheese. Return the mixture to the shell, dot with butter, sprinkle with Parmesan cheese, and pop into a 350° oven for 15 minutes to reheat and blend the flavors.

Or you can have baked potatoes with caviar. That was first served, if I remember rightly, on the Hamburg-America Line and then taken up by other steamship lines. For this, you bake the potatoes in a 400° oven until tender, then break them open and add a large spoonful of caviar and a spoonful of sour cream. Serve at once as a first course or luncheon dish. You can sprinkle the sour cream with chopped chives or scallions if you like, but it is not really necessary. Just the combination of the hot, fluffy potato and the delicious cold caviar, with the benison of sour cream, makes this a never-to-be-forgotten experience.

There's another, completely different way of treating baked potatoes that gets twice the mileage out of them. The dish is called Lord Byron's potatoes, and why they were named for Lord Byron I have never been able to discover. Anyway, they are delicious and disgustingly rich. You bake 6 large potatoes, split them, and scoop out all the pulp into a bowl—saving the skins for later. Mix into the potato pulp 8 tablespoons of sweet butter, 1 teaspoon or more of salt, 1 teaspoon of freshly ground black pepper, and about 4 tablespoons of freshly grated Parmesan cheese. Toss well with a fork, then arrange in a large, shallow baking dish (a quiche dish is perfect, or a pie pan will do), and let stand for a few minutes. Then pour over the potatoes a good $1/2$ to $3/4$ cup of heavy cream. Sprinkle with more grated Parmesan, and return to a 400° oven until heated through, with delicately browned edges.

Now for the skins. After removing all the pulp, cut them into strips about an inch wide with scissors, and place them on a baking sheet. Brush generously with melted butter, season with salt, pepper, and a dash or two of Tabasco, and put either in a 475° oven or under the broiler until they become brown and crisp. If you use the broiler, make sure they don't burn. Serve these hot with drinks. They are far better than any potato chip. If you get them crisp enough, they can be stored in an airtight tin and reheated slightly before serving.

I also happen to like overbaked potatoes—potatoes baked at 400° for 2 hours instead of 1, which gives a thicker, crisper skin and an entirely different flavor. Or you can, if you are in a hurry, slice the potatoes in thirds, straight across, arrange them on a lightly buttered baking sheet, and bake at 450° for about half an hour, until crisp, brown, and slightly puffed on the surface and moist and tender inside. There are more ways than one to bake a potato, and no matter how you do them, they are one of our greatest gastronomic delights.

[1977]

*H*ominy

During my boyhood in Oregon, I would wait eagerly for the sound of the hominy man, who came by our house twice a week in his horse-drawn cart selling fresh hominy and fresh horseradish. While that, alas, is a custom that has long since vanished from the domestic scene, fresh hominy remains one of my favorite foods, with an enduring place among my food memories.

I'm often surprised to find how few people are familiar with hominy. One of our oldest indigenous foods (the name comes from the Algonquin Indian word for parched corn), it is made from dried corn—not the sweet corn we eat on the cob, but field or Indian corn. The New England settlers ground the parched Indian corn into samp, a coarse meal that they made into hasty pudding, a sustaining porridgelike mush.

Our hominy today comes from kernels of hulled, dried white or yellow corn, which have been treated with a lye solution that dissolves the skins and makes the kernels puff up. After the kernels have been thoroughly washed, they are boiled for several hours and become fresh hominy, which looks a lot like popcorn.

Hominy has been used for generations in the South and Southwest, although these days it is more readily available in the form of hominy grits—dried, ground hominy, which is *not* one of my favorite foods, although I know southerners who dote on it. The good old-fashioned fresh hominy once sold in bulk in many shops is hard to come by. Usually you have to buy the dried whole hominy, soak it yourself, and boil it for a long time; or use the ready-cooked canned variety, which only needs heating.

At home we would wash and drain the fresh hominy, sauté it in butter, adding a little cream, salt, and plenty of freshly ground pepper, and have it with fried chicken and cream gravy. Or we would steam it in the top of a double boiler with a little chicken broth, top it with grated Gruyère cheese, and serve it with pork chops. It made an appetizing change from the usual starchy vegetable.

Recently, when I was planning a party menu with ham as the main dish, I suddenly thought, "Why not combine hominy with sweet corn?" I played around with the idea and came up with the following two-corn casserole, which I think you will find a pleasant introduction to hominy if you've never had it before.

For this I used three 1-pound cans of whole hominy and two 12-ounce cans of whole-kernel corn (if you were to use fresh corn cut from the cob, that would be about 6 ears). Wash the hominy before you use it, and drain. Butter a 2-quart baking dish or casserole. Put in a layer of a third of the hominy and a third of the sweet corn. Add a good grind of black pepper, a touch of salt, and 3 tablespoons of finely chopped canned peeled green chilies. Dot very lightly with butter, add about 4 tablespoons of sour cream and 1/2 cup of shredded Monterey Jack cheese. Repeat the layers of hominy and corn, seasonings, chilies, sour cream, and cheese, ending with the final third of the hominy and corn.

Top with a few dabs of butter, freshly ground pepper, and more shredded cheese.

Bake the casserole in a 350° oven for 35 to 40 minutes or until the hominy and corn are piping hot and the cheese melted. This is a perfect foil for ham, roast chicken, roast turkey, or even cold meats.

If you have trouble finding whole canned hominy in your local market, ask if it can be ordered for you. Should you have a Mexican or Latin American store nearby, you'll be sure to find it there, for the Mexicans are also very fond of hominy, which they use in delicious soup-stews like *pozole* and *menudo. Menudo,* a glorious mélange of hominy, tripe, calf's foot, and other tasty bits and pieces, is a real one-dish meal, which, served with side dishes of chopped green onions and chilies, has become a classic hangover cure after the New Year's Eve bash.

Hominy is a vegetable—or maybe we should call it a cereal—that deserves to be revived and used more often. Not only does it have an extraordinarily good corn flavor, but it is uniquely American, something you won't find outside the Western Hemisphere.

[1974]

Chess Pie

We Americans undoubtedly eat more kinds of pie than any other country—not just fruit pies, but also lemon meringue pie, cream pie, sugar pie, pumpkin pie, shoofly pie, pecan pie, and Boston cream pie; the list seems endless. One of the oldest of our pies is the chess pie, and lately, while delving into early American traditions, I've come up with some interesting bits of lore about this pie, which has cropped up in various parts of the country and in sundry guises.

The very earliest chess pies I could trace appeared in Virginia and Tennessee, relics of the English heritage in those parts of the country. The word *chess* is actually a bastardization of *cheese,* and the cheese pie—which, interestingly enough, contained no cheese— was very popular in England for many years as a tea or supper dainty, in the form of little tarts.

One of the most delicious recipes I have come across for the English cheese pie comes from Eliza Acton, a great food authority in nineteenth-century England. Many people, including Elizabeth David, believe Eliza Acton to have been the finest food writer in the English language. That is a matter of opinion, but certainly her works show her to have been scholarly, brilliant, and creative, and her reputation has withstood the test of time. This recipe of Eliza Acton's came from Christ Church College, which I think makes it even more interesting.

Grate the rind of 1 large lemon. Mix it with $1/2$ cup of sugar. Add the well-beaten yolks of 3 eggs and the well-beaten whites of 2 eggs. Beat together thoroughly. Add 4 tablespoons of cream, $1/2$ cup of melted butter, and the strained juice of the lemon (this should be stirred in rather quickly). Add a touch of orange-flower water or, if you find this difficult to get, a little grated orange rind. Line 8 or 10 small tartlet pans with flaky pastry, and half fill them with the mixture. Bake for 30 minutes in a 350° oven.

Looking through my old cookbooks, I found an early American recipe that was very similar, except that it contained cornmeal, which to my mind would absolutely ruin anything as delicate as this.

How "cheese pie" became "chess pie" no one seems to know. One story goes that a lady asked her cook what she was making and was told, "It's jes' pie," which she mistook for "chess pie," but I don't place much credence in that version. More likely the name just got corrupted along the way, as so often happens.

When chess pie started a trek to the West, people began adding other ingredients, such as nuts and dried fruits. The following version is one I remember from my childhood, when we took it on picnics.

Cream 8 tablespoons of butter with 1 cup of light brown sugar. Beat in 2 eggs. Stir in $1/4$ cup of thin cream or evaporated milk, 1 cup of chopped walnuts, 1 cup of raisins (or raisins and currants, or chopped dates), $1/3$ teaspoon of vanilla, and $1/3$ cup of orange juice, grape juice, or sherry. Spoon the mixture into 8 or 12 pattypans or a 9-inch pie pan lined with pastry, made with butter or half butter and half shortening. Bake the pie in a 450° oven for 15 minutes, then reduce the heat to 325° and bake about 20 minutes longer. For individual tarts, bake at 450° for 5 to 6 minutes, then at 300° for 7 to 10 minutes longer, depending on the thickness of the filling. Cool on a rack and serve slightly warm.

This is the kind of chess pie made in New England and the Virginias. Much later came a southern version known as Jefferson Davis pie, which in addition to the cream, eggs, and sugar, included flour and spices—cinnamon, allspice, nutmeg, and sometimes powdered cloves—and sometimes raisins or chopped dates. The chief difference, though, was that the filling was cooked over direct heat until thickened, and then it was poured into a baked pie shell or crumb crust, topped with a meringue, and browned in the oven, which would give a rather more elegant and spicy variation.

[1979]

$\mathcal{A}$pple Pie

On their trek from East to West, far from any orchard, our pioneers longed for their apple pies. They had to improvise. Between two crusts they baked a filling of soda crackers, syrup, butter, and spices, with a bit of vinegar to simulate the tartness of apple. A modern-day version of this idea continues to circulate, promoted by one of the major manufacturers of crackers, and is trotted out from time to time by housewives as a fool-the-tongue recipe for company. Who knows, judging by the apple pie we put up with today, the mock might be better than the real.

Although Americans are not as apple pie crazy as they were a couple of generations ago, they are still apt to become rapturous over the great national dessert. I find this hard to understand. I've probably sampled as many different apple pies as anyone alive, in restaurants and homes and at official pie tastings. I have been offered the best damned apple pie ever baked. But thinking back over the last fifty years, I conclude that where the marriage of apples and crust is concerned, my taste is decidedly un-American.

If I am to enjoy apple pie at all, it must be made with juice-laden apples of good flavor and crunchy fresh texture, preferably left in their natural state, apart from sugaring, and it must have a fine, crisp crust. Simple enough, but these qualifications are rarely achieved by the standard two-crust pie served in this country, which is generally nutmeged and cinnamoned to the point where the fruit hardly matters, and it invariably has a soggy bottom.

As for the major ingredient, apples, they are selected from the three or four varieties put on the market for long shelf life rather than for excellence in cooking. After withstanding a long period of refrigeration, they often reach us musty and mushy. By the time they are baked, they are practically without flavor. Occasionally, we are lucky enough to find nice tart greenings or Granny Smiths.

I'm spoiled, of course, because I grew up in apple country: Oregon. We had a succession of superb cooking apples through the year—Gravensteins, transparents, waxens, pippins, greenings; round ones, fat ones, yellow, red, russet; each having a distinctive character. How long since you smelled a really fragrant apple, if you don't have your own apple tree or live near a farmer's market? When did you last slice an apple and find that it was crisp and juicy? or that it cooked to a tender, translucent state, soothing to the tongue?

Probably the worst apple pies to be found in the country are those in restaurants and bake shops turned out in assembly-line quantities. The leathery crusts are a far cry from the fragile, flaky produce of a skilled pastry maker's hand. And the filling is made with either a packaged apple pie mix or with those omnipresent "good keepers." Yet there was a time when one could get an acceptable commercial pie. The late Clementine Paddleford, who for many years wrote a food column for the *New York Herald Tribune,* had an annual apple pie contest for professional bakers, and almost without exception, Schrafft's won the prize. In its day, that organization did put forth a very fine apple pie. It was a two-crust pie, naturally. The crust was crisp, short, and well flavored, the apples were ripe, and the spicing was subtle. Eaten slightly warm or with a large scoop of ice cream, which was to become an American addiction, it was for many years the best that the city of New York could offer.

I can remember one other restaurant pie, perhaps more distinguished in some ways, that had a reputation in Seattle. It was served at an amusing place called the American Oyster

House, operated by a somewhat eccentric restaurateur who served just the things he really liked. He thought the only dessert in the world worth having was apple pie. His ideal version was made by a fine pastry cook, a woman he had discovered. It had a beautiful hand-hewn crust that was rich and flaky. The apples were the choicest the state of Washington could produce, and they varied with the seasons, starting with very young green Gravensteins and transparents, and rotating to the pippins. When apples were not in season, neither was apple pie.

My memory also goes back to one of the early chains of hamburger stands, called the White Spot, that spread throughout Los Angeles many years ago. They made quite a decent apple pie that was served warm, with melted sharp cheddar cheese poured over it at the last minute—not processed cheese, but a good natural cheddar. It had the customers nearly fainting. As we all know, the pairing of cheddar and apple pie has long been a peculiarly American favorite, although it is less popular than it once was.

Among the chains of restaurants in operation today, one offers an apple pie of sorts that is surprisingly passable. This is the glorified turnover sold by McDonald's, which I have eaten two or three times around New York. It is served warm and seems to be far above the average commercial concoction. There may be other examples around the country, but I confess that my sharpened prejudice keeps me from tracking them down.

To go even further, let me say that I believe the English have come closer to perfecting the combination of apples and crust than we have. After all, they have had a longer time to practice. Even though apple pie is regarded as an American institution, it was part of English cookery at least two centuries before we took it up. The English version has one crust, usually made of puff paste or rough puff paste, that is placed over cooled, lightly precooked apples, seasoned with butter, sugar, and a bit of lemon. The shape is apt to be oval. During the baking, the crust rises and becomes crisp and dry. And if one obeys the rule, he removes the crust after baking and cuts it into "sippets"—little triangular pieces—before serving. One helps himself to a sippet and some of the apple mixture. No bottom crust, no sog.

In the eighteenth century, the English varied this idea by adding a mixture of egg yolk and cream to the pie after the crust had been removed and the minute it came from the oven. The heat of the apples cooked this into a delicate, custardy cream. I find such a recipe in Mary Ann Carter's book *The Frugal Housewife, or Complete Woman Cook*, first published in London about 1770 and issued in Boston in 1771, making it one of the earliest publications in American culinary history. So we can assume that Mary Ann Carter's recipe was a model for many American cooks. Here it is in full, worth quoting because of its charm:

"Make a good puff paste crust. [To the English, a three-turn puff paste would be more familiar than the six-turn for this type of pie.] Lay some around the sides of the dish. Pare and quarter your apples and take out the cores and lay a row of apples, thick. Throw in half the sugar you designed for your pie. Mince a little lemon peel fine. Throw over and squeeze a little lemon over them, then a few cloves, then the rest of your apples and the cores in fair water with a blade of mace till it is very good. Pour it into your pie, put on your upper crust and bake it. You may put in a little quince marmalade if you so please. You may butter them when they come out of the oven or beat up the yolks of two eggs and half pint of cream with a little nutmeg sweetened with sugar. Take off the lid and pour in the cream. Cut the crust in little three-corner pieces. Flick about the pie and send it to the table."

Well, that's not a bad idea for a pie. Boiling a syrup with skins and cores is a very intelligent way to sweeten the pie and give it body. And there is little enough mace, so I would endorse that, too. The quince marmalade, though, is rather unnecessary.

The French also approach apple pie with wisdom, it seems to me, in their famous *tarte Tatin.* This again is a one-crust pie, but it is inverted at the finish to make an upside-down pie. There are many ways of preparing it, but I prefer to start it off in a heavy skillet that can go into the oven. I caramelize some sugar in the skillet, then arrange layers of sliced apple over that, sprinkled with sugar and dotted generously with butter. A crust is fitted over the apples, and the pie is baked until most of the juices have evaporated and the crust is golden. The tart is then turned out onto a serving plate—a tricky bit of work until you've had practice—revealing beautifully glazed apples. In this case, too, the crust stays crisp, and the apples melt into a luscious consistency.

[1975]

*C*ream and Schlag

My mother had a dear friend—a stately, aristocratic woman with a Viennese background—who was exceedingly hospitable and enjoyed giving teas. I remember, as a very young child, being taken there and being enchanted by the whipped cream that was served with tea and had something wonderful in it, which I found out later was praline. It was homemade, crushed, and then folded into the whipped cream or *schlag*. There was also plain *schlag* if you wanted coffee. So, you departed really creamed to the hilt.

Schlag or *schlagobers* means a great deal to Central Europeans. In Hungary and Austria, it is a way of life. No one would dream of not having *schlag* in coffee, on desserts, and sometimes in soup. I grew up with *schlag* in coffee and hot chocolate. How good it was on a wintry day to have a tall, rich cup of well-made chocolate, with cinnamon overtones and topped with *schlag*.

In former times, if your dairy had Guernsey or Jersey cows, you could use cream from the tops of the milk bottles, thick enough to be whipped. In winter, the milk on the doorstep would freeze in the bottle, and you'd find a little cylinder of icy cream pushing up the cap. It would soon melt down into the bottle again and become its normal self. If you bought heavy cream, it was 40 percent butterfat. Today, the richest cream you can get, called heavy whipping cream, is about 36 percent butterfat. It is super-pasteurized, whereas other creams are merely pasteurized. One also finds in some localities "coffee cream" or light cream, which has less butterfat, will not whip, and is not any more desirable than half-and-half, easily available everywhere in the country. Half-and-half, as its name indicates, contains roughly equal quantities of cream and milk and has a butterfat content of not more than 18 percent. It's perfectly good for coffee, for fruit, and for various soups— unless, as I do, you occasionally have that desire to be totally luxurious and use heavy cream for everything. I recently had a Northwest clam chowder, with heavy cream abounding, that was one of the finest I have ever had in my life, because time, effort, and love went into it. It was hot, pungent, and everything that clam chowder should be and often isn't. The cream helped to make it so.

When you're whipping cream to make *schlag*, it's vitally important to have both cream and utensils cold. Putting whisk and bowl in the refrigerator for half an hour or an hour is sufficient.

This will reduce the whipping process by three or four minutes. When you have nearly achieved the texture you want, add confectioners' sugar if it's for a dessert, or a little salt or other seasoning if it's for a soup.

Kirsch goes beautifully in whipped cream that is to be served with strawberries or raspberries; rum goes well with pineapple; bourbon, with peaches; apricot brandy or cognac, with many other fruit dishes. If you are making a sponge cake or layer cake and want to decorate it with whipped cream, it's a good idea to add a bit of gelatin. For each cup of cream, dissolve 1 teaspoon of unflavored gelatin in $1/4$ cup of cold water. Place it on very low heat, and let it simmer until the gelatin is completely melted. Cool it and stir it into your whipped cream. This will stabilize it and give it a longer life, and it does not affect the flavor at all.

If you want to make a chocolate whipped cream, combine 2 tablespoons of confectioners' sugar with 2 tablespoons of cocoa and 1 cup of whipping cream. Refrigerate for about 30 minutes before whipping. For a mocha-flavored cream, add 1 tablespoon of instant coffee along with the cocoa. You may also add a bit of vanilla, some shavings of chocolate, or a dusting of cinnamon to give it a little class. This can be used for cakes or pastries or just by itself.

People are often confused about another class of creams—Devonshire cream, Cornish cream, and crème fraiche. These are not *schlag*, although Devonshire and Cornish creams can be whipped lightly to form a different texture, and some people do the same thing with crème fraiche. Devonshire cream is made with raw milk, which is allowed to sit until the cream rises. Then it's placed over very low heat and left for a considerable length of time until the cream becomes "clotted" and forms sort of rolls on the surface. This is skimmed off very carefully into jars or pots and has now become Devonshire cream. Much the same process is followed for Cornish cream. These creams are usually served with fruit and, in England and Wales, with hot scones or muffins and preserves for tea.

True crème fraiche is very mature cream, rich in butterfat—much more so than our whipping cream—that has been allowed to sit atop milk until it develops a slight, distinctive acidity. This may be used with fruits, with pastry, or with almost any kind of dessert, and it is extremely effective in sauces, because good, honest crème fraiche is a liaison and thickener.

You can make a substitute crème fraiche in your own kitchen by combining 1 or 2 tablespoons of buttermilk, sour cream, or yogurt with a pint of heavy cream, shaking it vigorously, and then letting it stand for several hours before refrigerating it. This will serve most purposes except that of thickening a sauce. So, be guided accordingly.

[1983]

Quince, a Forgotten Fruit

It's really too bad that the quince is now relatively unknown and unappreciated in this country. At one time, it was quite as popular as the apple and the pear. In fact, quince seeds were among those listed as being wanted from England in the Massachusetts Bay Colony's Memorandum of March 16, 1629. By 1720, the quince was reported to be growing abundantly in New England. Today you are lucky if you can find any in the markets.

When I was a boy in Oregon, the most magnificent quince tree grew near the edge of our property. In spring, the pinkish blossoms were like lace against the sky. Their scent gave promise of what was to come. In the fall, as the fruit began to mature, the perfume was much more noticeable and the color of the fruit a beautiful gold.

I remember the kitchen of our house being piled high with quince. They were a great favorite of my mother's. To have sixty or eighty fuzzy, delicately colored quince massed on a big table or in a basket was a wondrous sight. I loved to watch the peeled fruit turn from ivory to a somewhat golden peach when it was cooked with sugar. We used to have, at least once or twice a season, a superb quince tart, equaled only in later years by that served by my friend Leon Lianides at his famous restaurant, the Coach House. (His recipe is given below.)

Then there was quince honey—in reality a fine-textured marmalade of quince cooked down until it formed an almost solid preserve, akin to the quince paste of the Middle East, Spain, and South America—which you can buy in tins. If well made, it is exquisite served with a little bland cheese and a morsel of bread.

I once heard from a Chinese friend that quince seeds, which contain enormous amounts of pectin, were cooked and strained by Chinese women to make a natural hair fixative. When perfumed and applied, it kept their elegant coiffures in place. I wouldn't know about that, but I do know that just one quince added to apple jelly or strawberry jam improves both the flavor and the jelling.

Quince are much too astringent to eat raw, but they have a wonderful honeylike taste when cooked with sugar. Baked quince is an exquisitely simple dessert that should not be missed. If the fruit are the old-fashioned type with the delicate fuzz, be sure to wipe it off before you peel; it's easier that way. Peel and split 3 large ripe quince, and cut into eighths. Arrange in a $1^{1}/_{2}$-quart baking dish. In a separate pan, combine 2 cups of sugar, $^{3}/_{4}$ cup of water, and a pinch of salt, and bring to a boil. Simmer for 3 to 4 minutes, then pour over the quince. Bake in a preheated 325° oven for about 45 minutes, or until the fruit is tender but not mushy. Cool but do not chill, and serve with heavy cream or sour cream.

❦ The Coach House Quince Tart ❧

Place 2½ cups of flour in a large bowl. Make a well, and add ½ pound of unsalted butter, softened and cut in pieces; 2 tablespoons of sugar; 3 egg yolks; ½ teaspoon of cinnamon; and the grated zest of 1 lemon. Knead until it is well mixed and forms a ball. Chill until firm.

Peel and core 6 large quince, saving the seeds. Cut the fruit into julienne strips. In a heavy skillet or enamel pan, boil together 3 cups of water, 3 cups of sugar, and the juice of 1 lemon, strained. Then add the strips of quince and a cheese-cloth bag containing the quince seeds, a stick of cinnamon, and 2 whole cloves. Bring the mixture to a boil, lower the heat, and simmer for 1½ hours or until thickened. Stir from time to time to keep the mixture from sticking and burning.

Discard the bag of seeds and spices, and let the mixture cool. At this point, it can be poured into sterilized glass jars and sealed with paraffin if you want to use it for preserves rather than for a tart filling.

Preheat the oven to 375°. Roll out two-thirds of the pastry between two pieces of wax paper, and fit it into a 12-inch cake or quiche pan with a removable bottom. Bake for 10 minutes. Remove from the oven, and fill the shell with the quince mixture. Use the remaining pastry to make a latticework top. Bake for 20 to 30 minutes, or until the pastry is golden brown and the filling is bubbling. Remove from the oven and sprinkle with

2 tablespoons of lightly roasted chopped almonds. Let cool at least 2 to 3 hours or overnight, but do not refrigerate. Serve with whipped cream, crème fraiche, sour cream, or vanilla ice cream.

[1982]

*R*hubarb, American "Pie Plant"

Rhubarb grew in so many gardens in nineteenth-century America and found its way into so many puddings and pies that it came to be known as "pie plant." It wasn't admired by all Americans, however. Miss Eliza Leslie, a rather starchy lady and a prolific writer of cookery books between 1828 and about 1858, observed: "This [rhubarb] is sometimes called spring fruit or pie plant. It comes early but is by no means as good as gooseberries. We do not think it worth preserving or making into a sweet." Maria Parloa, redoubtable principal of the Boston Cooking School, ignored rhubarb completely in her *New Cook Book* of 1880, but then she disapproved of fruit-and-pastry desserts altogether. She heralded the advent of family-sized ice cream freezers with joy, "as they will soon do away with that unhealthy dish—pie." Well, unhealthy or not, I'd say that pies are here to stay.

Technically a vegetable, rhubarb is used mainly as a fruit and turns up in puddings, pies, tarts, and preserves on both sides of the Atlantic. As long ago as 1760, the famous English cookery writer Hannah Glasse gave a recipe for rhubarb tarts, commenting that they might be thought odd but were actually very fine, with a pretty flavor. (Then she went on to recommend rhubarb leaves as a fine thing to eat for a pain in the stomach, which is rather unfortunate, because the leaves—though not the fleshy stalks—contain oxalic acid and are, in fact, poisonous.)

The Polish people treat rhubarb as the vegetable it is. They combine it with new potatoes and flavorful dried wild mushrooms and herbs and use it as an accompaniment to pork and chicken. Here, in this country, I've been served a very tasty side dish with venison that consists of rhubarb cooked with fatback, raisins, onions, a touch of vinegar, and a little brown sugar. Like applesauce with pork, the contrast in flavors is a delight to the palate.

Some years ago, a friend cooked a wonderfully spicy and aromatic dish for me that one might almost term a Middle Eastern version of sweet and sour, using lamb instead of pork. I obtained the recipe, of course, and make the dish when spring rhubarb first comes into the markets. If you want to try it, get cherry red rhubarb (rather than the green) if you can. It has an excellent flavor.

✒ Persian Lamb with Rhubarb ✒

Put $2^1/_2$ cups of sliced fresh rhubarb in a bowl with $^3/_4$ cup of sugar and $^3/_4$ cup of water, and let stand for 30 minutes. Peel and chop 1 large onion. In a large heavy skillet, melt 4 tablespoons of butter. Sauté the onion until transparent, then transfer it to a heavy casserole. In the same skillet, sauté 1 pound of lean lamb, cut into 1-inch cubes, until brown on all sides. Season with 1 teaspoon of salt, $^1/_2$ teaspoon of freshly ground black pepper, $^1/_2$ teaspoon of ground cinnamon, and $^1/_2$ teaspoon of ground nutmeg. Stir in 1 cup of chopped parsley, and continue cooking for another 2 minutes. Add the syrup from the rhubarb.

Transfer the meat mixture to the casserole. Cover with a circle of wax paper cut to the same diameter as the casserole. Put on the lid, and simmer very gently for 30 minutes. Stir in the rhubarb, and continue simmering for another 20 to 30 minutes or until the meat is very tender. Taste for seasoning. Combine 1 tablespoon of cornstarch with 1 tablespoon of cold water, and stir into the meat mixture. Cook gently for another 2 or 3 minutes or until the sauce thickens, by which time the rhubarb and onions will have melted down. Serve over hot cooked rice. Serves 4.

I've noticed that rhubarb is turning up in nouvelle cuisine entrées these days. Its tart, sweet-sharp quality makes a fine foil for duck's fatty richness, for example. For all that, I still have a sneaking fondness for a traditional rhubarb pie or perhaps a creamy fruit fool. Unlike Miss Leslie, I *do* think rhubarb worth preserving and making into a sweet. Or a sweet and sour.

❧ Rhubarb Fool ❧

Cut 1 1/2 pounds of rhubarb into 2-inch lengths, and combine with 1 to 1 1/2 cups of sugar and 1/4 cup of water in a heavy 2-quart saucepan. Cover, and simmer until the fruit is very tender, about 20 minutes. Allow to cool, then chill in the refrigerator. Force the rhubarb through a food mill or sieve, and fold into approximately 1 1/2 cups of slightly sweetened whipped cream or a rich boiled custard. For a different taste, fold the rhubarb into a half-and-half combination of sour cream and plain yogurt, sweetened to taste with brown sugar. Serve any of these very cold. Serves 4 to 6.

[1982]

*M*armalade, Bittersweet Treat

While marmalade brings to mind visions of golden citrus fruit, the original version was made from a totally different fruit, the quince. The word is an anglicization of *marmelada*, a paste or jam made by the Portuguese from the *marmelo*, or quince.

To those of us who were brought up with some British background, the epitome of marmalade is the dark, tart kind made from Seville oranges, which have a bitter tang like that of wild oranges. No self-respecting British breakfast could be considered complete without a nice pot of Seville orange marmalade, to be enjoyed with some toast and butter and a final cup of tea after finishing your bacon and eggs, or kidneys, or kippers.

Seville oranges have always been much sought after by professional and amateur marmalade makers. At one time, fancy grocery stores and fruiterers would send out an annual mailing to their regular customers, advising them of the approach of the Seville orange season so they could reserve a share of the limited supply. People prided themselves on their marmalade, putting up large batches that they would give away as birthday and Christmas gifts.

As an alternative to the hard-to-get Seville oranges, I find that a combination of citrus fruits—orange, lemon, and grapefruit—is the next best thing. The sweetness of the oranges, the acidity of the lemons, and the slightly bitter taste of the grapefruit blend into a pleasantly bittersweet overall flavor, while the juices turn the jelly an attractive delicate amber. The fruits should be peeled rather thin and the peel cut into fine shreds or chunks, according to your preference. I favor little shreds myself. They give the marmalade a pleasing texture, and if the jelly is nice and clear, the suspended shreds form a lovely pattern. The white pith and seeds contain a good deal of pectin, so I tie them in a cheesecloth bag and put them in with the marmalade rather than using commercial pectin to bring the mixture to the jelly stage.

For my three-fruit marmalade, you will need 3 pounds of mixed citrus fruit—about 3 grapefruit, 3 oranges, and 3 lemons—and, of course, granulated sugar (to be measured later).

Wash the fruit well. Dry it, and peel off very thin layers of the rind, without the pith, and cut this into shreds. Holding the fruit over a bowl to catch the juice, cut off the pith and remove the seeds. Tie pith and seeds in a cheesecloth bag. Cut the fruit into very thin slices. Measure the fruit and juice, and put in a large bowl with three times the quantity of cold water. Add the bag of pith and seeds and the shredded rind. Let this stand for 24 hours.

Pour the contents of the bowl into a preserving kettle and bring to a boil. Cook uncovered over low heat, stirring occasionally, for about 2 hours. Remove and discard the cheesecloth bag. Measure the fruit and juice, and for each cup, add 1 cup of sugar. Stir back into the kettle until the sugar is dissolved. Bring to a boil again, watching carefully to prevent its boiling over, and cook until it reaches the jelling stage— 220° on a candy thermometer. Another test for jelling is to spoon a small amount on a cold plate and see if it forms a sort of wrinkly skin.

Ladle the marmalade into hot sterilized jars, and top with a thin layer of melted paraffin. Let the paraffin cool and set, then put lids on the jars. Store the marmalade for about 2 weeks to settle down before you eat it.

Mrs. Fiske, one of the famous actresses of the past, loved marmalade with toast and heavy cream for tea, which to my mind would be a pretty rich combination. I like mine with nothing more than buttered toast, or perhaps in a dessert— either in little tartlets, to which the pungent juices and chewy shreds give a marvelous quality, or in a steamed soufflé, an ethereal puff of egg whites, sugar, and marmalade.

[1979]

$\mathcal{P}$raline Puzzle

Praline is one of those terms about which there seems to be a certain amount of confusion. To the French it is one thing, to Americans in the South quite another. In classic French cooking, *pralin*, also known as *nougatine*, is a mixture of toasted nuts (usually almonds, although hazelnuts or a mixture of hazelnuts and almonds may be used) and sugar cooked to a rich caramel. This is cooled on an oiled surface until hard, then broken up and reduced to a powder, which is used to flavor butter creams, soufflés, ice cream, pastry cream, and sauces. Like many other French cooking terms, it has quite a history, originating with the cook of a seventeenth-century French nobleman, the Maréchal du Plessis-Praslin, after whom it was named. Just to complicate things further, there is also a French candy called praline, a sugar-coated almond, which is something else again.

As for the American praline, it is a round, thin, brittle, cookie-shaped candy made with a brown sugar penoche base and pecan halves, which is a specialty of New Orleans and other parts of the South. These New Orleans or Creole pralines, with their lovely alliance of burnt-sugar flavor and rich, crunchy nuts, are irresistible to the bite and the palate. Many mail-order companies sell these regional confections, and they are shipped all over the world.

The French *pralin*, or praline powder, as we call it, is not difficult to make, especially if you have a food processor to grind it, and it is an excellent thing to have on hand. Stored in a screw-top jar or a can with a tight-fitting cover, it will keep almost indefinitely, so it's only sensible to make it in a fairly large quantity. The powder is extremely good mixed with or sprinkled over ice cream. If mixed in, allow about a half cup of praline powder to a quart of ice cream. You can use about the same amount to flavor a soufflé, in which case you should reduce the sugar in the recipe. Or you might try tossing a little praline powder into whipped cream during the beating. Put this on an ice cream sundae with perhaps a little caramel syrup, and you'll have something utterly ambrosial.

Praline powder is also good for flavoring a butter-cream filling for cakes, such as this glorious Austrian chocolate confection, *délice au chocolat.*

First, make the praline powder. The following recipe makes about 3 cups, of which you'll need 1 cup for the butter cream.

Put 2 cups of granulated sugar in a heavy pan with 2 tablespoons of lemon juice, and let it melt over very low heat. Stir from time to time with a metal spoon until it caramelizes and turns a deep golden color. Immediately stir in $^3/_4$ cup of coarsely chopped toasted blanched almonds and $^3/_4$ cup of coarsely chopped toasted hazelnuts (or, if you prefer, use only almonds). Bring just to the boiling point—the caramel must not get too dark or it will turn bitter—and then pour onto a well-oiled marble slab or cookie sheet, spreading it in a thin layer with an oiled metal spatula. Be sure to oil the slab or sheet or the praline will stick. Leave until cool and completely hard, about 10 to 15 minutes. Break into pieces, and pulverize in a food processor or electric blender. If you don't have an electrical aid, you can also crush the praline in a mortar or with a rolling pin, which requires some muscle. After using the amount of powder required in the recipe, store the rest in a tightly sealed can.

For the cake, combine in a pan 1 pint of milk, $1^1/_2$ cups of sugar, $^1/_2$ pound of unsalted butter, and $^1/_2$ pound of unsweetened chocolate. Bring to the boiling point over medium heat. Remove from the heat and cool slightly. Separate 4 eggs. Beat the yolks into the slightly cooled chocolate mixture, then beat in $2^1/_3$ cups of sifted cake flour, sifted again with 2 teaspoons of baking powder. Beat by hand for 5 minutes or in an electric mixer for 2 minutes at medium speed. Beat the egg whites until stiff but not dry, as for a soufflé, and fold gently into the chocolate mixture.

Pour the batter into a well-buttered 10-inch ring mold, and bake in a preheated 325° oven for 50 minutes. The cake should not be baked until firm; the center should still be moist and soft when it is removed from the oven. Cool the cake while making the butter cream.

Cream $^1/_4$ pound of softened unsalted butter in the bowl of an electric mixer. Gradually beat in 1 cup of praline powder and $^1/_4$ cup of sugar, and continue beating until creamy. Cut the cooled cake in half horizontally, and fill with the praline butter cream. Put the halves together, and decorate the top of the cake with toasted almond halves.

[1979]

$\mathcal{T}$alk About Bread

Homemade bread seems to be the hottest topic around, with everyone sounding off in print about how it should be made and what should go into it. For instance, John Hess of the *New York Times* and his wife, Karen, who lived for many years in France, regard the addition of sugar to bread as a despicable practice.

It's true that the great breads of France and many other countries are made without sugar (although they have a proper amount of salt, which most American breads lack), but much of this inveighing against sugar arises from a misconception of its role in bread making, a question I played around with quite a lot while writing *Beard on Bread.* The addition of a small amount of sugar speeds the action of the yeast by supplying something for it to feed on, and I think it gives bread a more balanced flavor and, to some extent, a better color. Since the amount varies from a teaspoon to a tablespoon, there is hardly any discernible sweetness.

Most American bread recipes, dating back to those given by such famous cooks as Mrs. Lincoln and Miss Leslie, do use sugar in varying quantities, and traditionally, we Americans have a sweet tooth. Otherwise there wouldn't be all those sticky buns, sweet muffins, and fruit and nut breads on our bread trays, a practice to which I have never been able to accustom myself. Even today's so-called "health" breads are heavy on raw sugar, molasses, and honey.

If I'm not mistaken, it was honey that gave the sweetish overtone to Margaret Rudkin's Pepperidge Farm bread, the famous loaf that grew into a multimillion-dollar industry. Mrs. Rudkin started by making batches of bread in her Connecticut kitchen, which her husband would drop off with her customers in New York on his way to the office. Her bread proved so much to the American taste that it became distributed throughout the country and was eventually taken over by a large food corporation.

Another controversial ingredient in bread making is yeast, with many people insisting that fresh or compressed yeast does a better job than active dry yeast. I don't agree. I, too, favored fresh yeast for years, but I have changed my opinion. If you treat dry yeast with care and use your sense of timing, it will produce as good a loaf with as great volume as the fresh. It is certainly more dependable if, like me, you find yourself baking in different parts of the country. All too often the cake yeast I bought in a supermarket turned out to be moldy and unpleasant, so these days I pretty well stick with the dry.

To get back to the sugar question, I'm going to give a recipe for one of my favorite breads, Sally Lunn, and I suggest that those of you who are antisugar make it first with sugar and then without, and see how you feel. To my mind, the sugar makes the bread taste better, but I may be wrong.

Sally Lunn stirred up a bit of a gastronomic brouhaha in its time. It seems that the bread was originated by an Englishwoman, a pastry cook in Bath, and copied by Carême, the great French chef who cooked for the Prince Regent at the Brighton Pavillion. He so admired Sally Lunn's bread that he took it back to France as his own creation, which the British regarded as hardly cricket.

Combine in a mixing bowl 1 package of active dry yeast, $1/3$ cup of sugar, and $1/2$ cup of warm water (110° to 115°), and let the yeast proof. Add $1/2$ cup of lukewarm milk, in which you have melted $1/4$ pound of butter together with 1 teaspoon of salt. Stir well, then add 3 eggs, one by one, beating thoroughly after each addition. Beat in $3^{1}/2$ to 4 cups of all-purpose flour in small amounts, again beating after each addition, until you have a stiff but workable batter. You may need all 4 cups and slightly more. Cover the bowl with a cloth, and let the batter rise slowly until doubled in bulk. Beat it down with a wooden spoon for about a minute, then scrape it into a well-buttered 9-inch tube pan. Let the batter rise again, this time to the top of the pan.

Bake in a preheated 375° oven for 45 to 50 minutes or until the bread is golden on top and sounds slightly hollow when rapped with the knuckles. Turn out on a rack and serve warm. Instead of cutting this bread, break it apart with two forks. The English sometimes serve Sally Lunn with clotted cream, but I like sweet butter better.

[1974]

$\mathcal{P}$ickling Time

I have always been a pickle boy. I can remember when I was young that one of the joys of going to the local grocery store at the beach in Oregon was the huge barrel of dill pickles that stood just inside the door. You could buy one for a nickel, and if you didn't have any change with you, you could always put it on the bill. They were wonderful crunchy pickles, with juice that ran at the first bite. If I was feeling especially self-indulgent, I would follow this treat with an ice cream cone (and quite often, a bilious attack), but usually the lovely fat dill pickle was enough—my idea of heaven.

While pickles are, of course, international, they have always been part of America's eating habits and must have originated very early in our culinary history, when people hungered for something tart, green, and appetizing to enhance the sparse winter foods—mostly cured and smoked meats and fish, dried beans, and perhaps a few root vegetables. Our ancestors put up dozens of varieties of pickles in crocks, barrels, gallon jars, and smaller containers that filled the shelves of their larders and cellars. In the nineteenth century, relish dishes of pickles were put on the table for nearly every lunch and dinner. Very often there would be a silver tray loaded with pickles, olives, and sticks of celery and carrot to munch on while waiting for the first course, a habit that still persists in many of our restaurants. Pickles have also been associated with picnics and cold suppers, with sandwiches and hamburgers. When I was a schoolboy, there would always be two or three pickles in my lunch box. They are just about as American as anything I can think of in the food world.

Many of our most popular pickles came over from Europe with the different immigrant groups. The English, for one, had a great many pickles to offer, some of which have become classics—notably the chowchows and chutneys, which were a development of the ones they found in India. The famous chowchow made by Crosse & Blackwell has been a standard in English households for as long as I can remember, along with Major Grey's chutney, sour gherkins, pickled walnuts, and the tiny, crisp, spicy pickled onions one finds in many English bars—a delightful bite with a glass of beer and maybe some bread and cheese.

While the French don't go in as much for pickles, they do produce excellent *cornichons,* those inch-long crisp little gherkins that accompany pâtés and terrines and other cold meat dishes, where their brisk, vinegary sharpness is almost a necessity. These minute cucumbers are pickled with vinegar and sometimes a sprig of tarragon or other herbs and spices, such as coriander seed. Occasionally, you will find a jar that contains part tiny onions and part *cornichons,* a combination I am particularly fond of.

Germany, as you might expect, has an enormous variety of pickles. Dill pickles, sweet gherkins, sweet-and-sour cucumber pickles, and a number of others are served with cold meats and with sauerkraut dishes. They are also very common in Austria. The Russians, too, use dill pickles and cured cucumbers in various and sundry ways, one being a famous cold soup with a base of salmon or salmon broth with finely chopped dill pickles.

In this country, we have a staggering range of dill pickles, including those you find in good Jewish delicatessens, redolent of dill (although I am afraid that all too often dill oil is used nowadays instead of fresh dill branches, and the difference is unbelievable). Then there is a Polish type made with smaller cucumbers and highly garlicked.

I am fond of the fresh dill pickles that my housekeeper, Clayton Triplette, makes. They can be done very quickly and easily and are extraordinarily good. For Clay's dill pickles, wash and dry 3 pounds of small pickling cucumbers, the unwaxed kind, about $2^1/_2$ to 3 inches long, that are in the markets in summer and early fall. Pierce each end of the cucumbers with a good-sized needle. This lets the pickling solution seep in and makes the pickles much crisper to the bite. Pack the cucumbers into a 2-quart jar with 1 teaspoon of salt, 3 unpeeled garlic cloves, $1^1/_2$ tablespoons of pickling spice, and 3 sprigs of fresh dill, arranging them neatly to make what Clay calls "a fine picture jar." Bring to a boil 5 cups of water with 1 cup of white wine vinegar, and pour this over the cucumbers. Leave for 15 minutes before putting the lid on the jar. Store for 4 to 5 weeks before using.

Dill pickles are good to munch as a snack with cold foods and wonderful with *choucroute garnie* or any hot sauerkraut dish, to which they give a pleasant zest. Thinly sliced dill pickles are marvelous tucked into a hamburger, and I also like to serve them, thinly sliced, with cold salmon or halibut or any other cold fish with which I'm serving a mayonnaise or dill sauce. You can make a quick tartar sauce for fish by chopping the pickles or putting them into the food processor with a little onion, garlic, parsley, and mayonnaise. In fact, you can make your mayonnaise in the food processor, then switch over from the blade to the shredder and shred the onion and dill pickle right into the mayonnaise.

One of my all-time favorites is oil pickles, thinly sliced cucumber pickles that are perfect with fish or cold meats. They make fabulous sandwiches, too. Put a little heavy mayonnaise or sweet butter, a slice of onion and tomato, and some of the oil pickles on rye bread or coarse-grain bread, and you will have something very special in the sandwich world. These oil pickles are so delicious that I used to make them in vast quantities and pack them in pint jars to give to my friends.

To make about 5 pints of oil pickles, take 10 cucumbers about 4 inches long, wash them well, and remove any wax with hot water and vigorous rubbing. Cut into thin slices not more than $1/4$ inch thick. Peel and slice paper-thin 4 medium onions. Mix the cucumbers and onions in a large bowl, and sprinkle with a mixture of $1/2$ cup of salt and 1 teaspoon of powdered alum (the alum keeps them very crisp). Let stand in a cool place overnight. Next morning, drain and rinse well. Also rinse the bowl. Put the vegetables back in the bowl, and pour over them enough wine vinegar to just cover. Let stand 1 to 4 hours. Drain, saving the vinegar. Measure the vinegar into a pot, and for each cup of vinegar, add 2 tablespoons of olive oil or salad oil. Mix in 2 tablespoons of celery seed and 2 tablespoons of mustard seed. Bring to a boil and pour over the cucumber-onion mixture. Pack into hot sterilized jars and seal. These should stand for a week before they are eaten.

Earlier I mentioned the pickled onions one eats in English bars. You can provide a big bowl of them with cocktails or serve them with cold meats. They are spicy, crunchy, sweet and sour, and thoroughly delicious. The onions you should use for this are the little pearl or pickling kind that are less than an inch in diameter. You have to look around for them, because they are rather hard to find.

First bring a gallon of water to a boil in a large pot. Drop in 4 quarts of small white pickling onions, and let stand (off the heat) 5 to 10 minutes. Test occasionally to see if the skin will slip from an onion. When it does, immediately drain the onions and pour cold water on them. Slip off the skins and trim the root ends, but be sure to leave enough so the onions will not fall apart. Place them in a large bowl, sprinkle with 1 cup of salt, and cover with cold water. Let stand overnight. Next day, drain and rinse very well with cold water. Bring to a boil 6 cups of white wine vinegar (or 4 cups of vinegar and 2 cups of dry white wine) and 2 cups of sugar. You may also add, if you like, 1/4 cup of pickling spices tied in a cheesecloth bag. If spices are used, simmer them in the mixture for about 10 minutes. Have ready 5 or 6 sterilized pint jars or 10 to 12 half-pint jars. Add the onions to the vinegar-sugar mixture, and bring just to a simmer—do not boil; they should remain crunchy. Pack the onions in the jars and fill to within 1/4 inch of the top with the hot vinegar solution, then seal.

Last year my secretary, Richard Nimmo, made a pumpkin pickle that we all declared to be extraordinarily good. It is as beautiful to look at as it is to eat and makes a great little gift if packed in half-pint jars.

Peel and seed a 4- to 5-pound pumpkin and cut into 1/2- to 1-inch cubes. Soak in water to cover, adding 4 tablespoons of salt for each quart of water. Let stand 4 hours or overnight. Drain and rinse well. Boil together for 5 minutes 1 quart of water, 2 cups of sugar, 1 cup of vinegar, 1 tablespoon of whole cloves, 1 stick of cinnamon, and 1 tablespoon of whole allspice. Remove from the heat and pour over the drained pumpkin. Let stand overnight. Next day, add 3 cups of sugar and 3 cups of vinegar to the syrup, and bring to a boil. Pack in hot sterilized jars, adding a pinch (about 1/8 teaspoon) of powdered alum to each jar. Seal and leave for 1 week before using. This makes about 4 pints.

I think most pickles are mellower and more delicious to the palate if they are aged for two or three months before being eaten. Store them in a cool, dark place (not the refrigerator) until you are ready to use them. If you already have favorite pickle recipes, experiment with them. Add a few cloves of garlic, a sprig of parsley, or a sprig of mint to the jars, to give another flavor.

If you like garlic as much as I do (it is the breath of life to me), you might make yourself some garlic pickles. While not generally known, this is a very old pickle the Chinese have used for centuries and very simple to make. All you do is peel perfect, unblemished garlic cloves, put them in pint jars, and add some salt and vinegar—wine vinegar, rice wine vinegar, malt vinegar, or cider vinegar. Fill the jars to the brim with the garlic and vinegar, seal them tightly, and store for at least a year. You can use this delicious pickled garlic with hot or cold meats, toss it in a salad, or nibble it with drinks. The aroma and flavor are breathtaking.

[1977]

ℐ Taste for Sauerkraut

Sauerkraut is more or less neglected in this country. One place you can be sure of finding it is on hot dog stands, where, after standing and steaming for hours, sometimes for days, it gets forked onto a frankfurter. This has little resemblance to sauerkraut as it should be. However, a very few fine French restaurants in New York do a brilliant job with it, and occasionally it's treated well in Pennsylvania Dutch restaurants. Also, as you traverse the country, you'll find German restaurants where they really pay some attention to sauerkraut. But this is not the average diner's experience.

In Europe, it's quite a different matter. In France, and especially in Alsace and in Paris, they make a great production of a sauerkraut dish called a *choucroute* (the word for sauerkraut). It's a habit-forming meal that people seek out more often than you might think. Somehow, it's a very good antidote if you've been eating copiously of rich French cuisine and come to a place where you think you've had too much, which I experienced a number of years ago when I felt that every meal in Paris might be my last. As far as I'm concerned, there's nothing better for settling the tummy and adjusting the interior workings than a fine *choucroute.* You search out a good one in a favorite restaurant, take your time over it, and enjoy it with some good beer or white wine. It is so satisfying and replenishing, it's almost like a spa treatment.

Not only the French and Germans respect sauerkraut. I remember being very surprised on a cruise I took from Venice to Turkey on an Italian ship, when, the second or third day out, the steward suggested I have a sauerkraut-sausage dish for lunch. It was an Italian-Austrian version of *choucroute,* quite different from any other I ever had, and it was not the last time that I ate sauerkraut Italian style. Russian cuisine, too, includes sauerkraut, and we know the Poles revel in it. *Bigos,* which is almost the national dish of Poland, is very much like an Alsatian *choucroute.*

Reading Jane Grigson's book on European cookery the other day, I happened to find an interesting mention of sauerkraut. Mrs. Grigson, who is British and appreciates the fact that her countrymen are not sauerkraut fanciers, suggests that if people are presenting sauerkraut to their friends for the first time, they should add some pineapple juice or bits of sweet pineapple, which is an old German custom. The fruit cuts the rather startling flavor of the sauerkraut and smooths it out nicely. This brought back to me the days when I was in the catering business with Bill Rhode and his sister, Irma. We were often asked to design a special party for someone, and for one holiday gathering, goose was to be the featured dish. While searching out contrasting flavors to go with the goose, we found tiny Puerto Rican pineapples that were beautifully ripe and very sweet. We scooped out the pineapples—one per person—cut the flesh in small bits and combined it with sauerkraut while it was cooking, then warmed the pineapples and filled them with the pineapple-*choucroute* mixture. It was a sensation. I often served it after that but had forgotten about it until Mrs. Grigson jogged my memory.

Some people have nursed the idea that sauerkraut came from the Orient via caravans and other treks across Asia, which I'm doubtful of for several reasons. I once thought that *kimchi*—the staple of Korean cooking—might be *choucroute*'s ancestor, but I soon gave this up as well. Although both are fermented (sauerkraut, made with cabbage, and *kimchi*, with practically any vegetable), the flavor of sauerkraut is gentle, while the flavor of *kimchi* is intense and absolutely soul searing in its heat. Also, unlike *choucroute*, which is taken in small doses and from time to time, *kimchi* is more of a fetish. For some Koreans, it's as necessary to a meal as coffee is to most Americans. After spending a number of days in Korea, tasting and eating *kimchi*, I decided it was altogether a far cry from sauerkraut; but so exciting to the palate is it, I believe that if it had ever spread from its native land, we might never have heard of sauerkraut.

Nowhere but nowhere has the art of fermented cabbage reached the level that it has reached in Alsace. If I were going to introduce anyone to *choucroute*, I would certainly lead them to a source in, say, Strasbourg or Riquewihr, a little country town that has carried on the tradition for years, almost centuries. Here, *choucroute* is even more classic than the French and far more varied in its appeal than the average version eaten away from Paris.

I have a favorite menu that I indulge in very often with guests. I'm very lucky in New York. While I can't make crocks of sauerkraut or store a barrel of it in the garden, I have a choice of about three places where it is almost family made. So I make a *choucroute garnie* of sorts, not as copious as the Alsatian dish and not as difficult to prepare, but quite satisfying. I try to start this meal, which is not the lightest, with something seasonal. My favorite is artichokes, when they are at their best, served with a good vinaigrette sauce. Guests can take their time eating and talking, because nothing is going to come to a climax in the oven and spoil. It's the kind of dinner where you want everyone to relax. Freshly cooked corn makes another wonderful first course—not too heavy, not too light.

As for the sauerkraut, I cook it with chicken broth, a few juniper berries, freshly ground black pepper, and 2 or 3 garlic cloves for 3 to 4 hours. Potatoes in their jackets are a must with this, and as a change from the usual meat, I roast a loin of pork, basting it with juices from the sauerkraut or with some apple purée or honey. And I usually have a kielbasa, made by a Polish butcher in the neighborhood whose sausages are remarkably good. All this is served with good mustard and followed with a tossed salad—or sometimes with just a small plate of cheese and crisp bread—and finished off with a seasonal fruit. It can be strawberries or raspberries, peaches or pears. It's about the only dessert I can think of that goes well with a meal as substantial as this.

Our household in Oregon, in earlier days, was always blessed with a plentitude of pheasants, and when we acquired some that were past their tender youth, my mother would set them aside and prepare them in her favorite way, braised with sauerkraut. She made plenty, because we liked leftover pheasant in a salad or tossed into a soup of some kind. First she plucked the pheasants and rubbed them inside and out with lemon, then attended to the rest of the recipe, which used white wine as well as chicken broth for the braising liquid and was finished off with a bit of calvados or cognac.

This is the version I have adapted and used through the years. Thoroughly wash and drain 5 to 6 pounds of fresh sauerkraut. Line a large braising kettle with thin slices of salt pork, about $^1/_2$ pound. Arrange a layer of the sauerkraut on the salt pork, and add 2 finely chopped garlic cloves, 1 teaspoon of freshly ground black pepper, and about 12 juniper berries. Rub the cavities of 2 mature pheasants with a cut lemon, and in each put an onion stuck with 2 cloves and a sprig or two of parsley. Truss the birds.

Heat 4 tablespoons of butter and 5 of oil in a large skillet, and brown the birds on all sides. Arrange on the bed of sauerkraut, and cover with the rest of the sauerkraut. Add 6 more juniper berries, another grind or two of pepper, and $2^1/_2$ cups of chicken or veal stock. Bring to a boil, cover tightly, and transfer to a 300° oven to continue cooking for $1^1/_2$ hours or until the birds are tender. After the first 45 minutes, add a large kielbasa or 2 French garlic sausages or an Italian *cotechino* sausage, and press down into the sauerkraut. Also add additional broth, if needed.

Remove the pheasants, let them rest for a few minutes, and then carve them into serving pieces. Mound the sauerkraut at one end of a large platter, and arrange the pheasant pieces on top. At the other end, heap potatoes boiled in their jackets. Garnish the platter with sliced sausage and salt pork. This will serve six rather well, and here I think you can drink a pleasant light red wine, although you might prefer a more traditional Alsatian Riesling or Gewürztraminer.

[1983?]

*E*ven Vinegar Has a Mother

The recent vogue for flavored vinegars in nouvelle cuisine dishes is, to my mind, more a matter of fashion than of taste. Some of the flavor combinations are so bizarre I cannot imagine how one might be expected to use the stuff. I tasted a French white wine vinegar the other day with bright red chili peppers in it. The pale gold vinegar was a lovely color, as were the red peppers, but it tasted awful. What salad greens could possibly stand up to that kind of competition?

And I can't help chuckling to myself over the raspberry vinegar craze. Country folk have been making raspberry vinegar for generations, but it was never intended to go in sauces for defenseless little quail or in salads. It's a drink—not to be imbibed neat, of course, but mixed with ice and lots of sparkling water it's very refreshing on a hot day. Raspberry vinegar is made by steeping the equivalent of twenty-four baskets of ripe raspberries in a gallon of cider vinegar or malt vinegar, then clearing off the fruit and repeating with another tray of raspberries. These steps are continued until you achieve a really aromatic brew.

Not too very long ago, you could buy a vinegar "mother," the natural yeast culture that, put into wine, turns wine into vinegar. It was sold for a few cents in a little glass jar and looked somewhat like a jellyfish. Contrary to popular belief, old wine will not turn into vinegar if simply left in the bottle; it will merely die. To make vinegar, you need a mother.

I remember buying some in Lancaster or Reading, in Pennsylvania Dutch country. I took this culture back to New York and put it into a five-gallon jar. For years, I made my own vinegar by adding my leftover wine to it. The ground-glass stopper was left very loose to allow essential air circulation. My vinegar contained some pretty fine vintages, I can tell you. Well, I went off to Europe on a trip and someone rammed the stopper down while I was gone, with lamentable results. It smothered mother.

People have made their own vinegar for centuries, and before the days when citrus fruit was common, cooks would use a few drops of vinegar instead of a squeeze of lemon to point up the flavors in a dish. Of course, vinegar has always been used in pickling. And in Colonial times, cider vinegar was used in folk medicine for an extraordinary assortment of ills as well as in cooking. I know people who still swear by cider vinegar and honey to cure a cough.

The English have always been partial to malt vinegar, a predilection that spread to Canada. Canadians automatically sprinkle malt vinegar on their french fries (whereas Americans favor sweet tomato ketchup, and the Dutch like mustard mayonnaise).

Verjuice—literally, "green juice"—is an earlier type of cider vinegar distilled from crab apples, and it was used in cookery right up until the nineteenth century, especially in meat and game pies. Verjuice, or *verjus,* is still made in France—I tried a French mustard the other day that is flavored with it—but the French use the *verjus* grape rather than crab apples.

The Italians made verjuice or *agresto* from acid grapes grown for that purpose, and in fact, *agresto* was one of the most widely used condiments in medieval and Renaissance cookery. In modern times, Italians—or more specifically, the Venetians—use vinegar with calf's liver. It's a classic dish that has been known to turn liver haters into liver lovers.

❦ Fegato Veneziana ❦

Have your butcher slice 1 pound of choice calf's liver ¼ inch thick. Cut it into strips about 1 inch wide. Discard any skin or gristly bits. Heat 3 tablespoons of olive oil in a large skillet, add 2 cups of thinly sliced onions, and sauté gently until limp and delicately browned. Remove and keep warm. Increase the heat to high, add more oil to the pan if the onions have absorbed most of it, and when the oil is very hot, sauté the liver strips very quickly for about 1 minute. The reason most people think they dislike liver is because it's overcooked. Liver requires minimal cooking to be delicious. Season with salt and freshly ground black pepper to taste. Return the onions to the pan, and toss with the liver just long enough to reheat, then stir in 1 tablespoon of wine vinegar. Serve at once. Serves 4.

Another classic recipe that employs vinegar is this French chicken dish.

❦ Poulet au Vinaigre ❦

Melt 6 tablespoons of unsalted butter in a large heavy skillet with a tight-fitting lid. Add 2 frying chickens (2 to $2^1/_2$ pounds each), cut in quarters, and brown on all sides. Lower the heat, and season the chicken to taste with salt and freshly ground black pepper. Add $^1/_2$ cup of water, and simmer over low heat, covered, for 15 minutes. Add 2 finely chopped green onions and 1 tablespoon of chopped parsley. Move the pieces of white meat to the top so the dark meat, which takes longer to cook, can get more heat. Cover and cook until just tender but still juicy, about 10 minutes.

Remove the chicken, and add $^1/_4$ cup of wine vinegar to the pan. Bring to a boil and continue to cook, scraping up the brown residue in the pan, until the vinegar has reduced to a bubbly consistency. Then add $^1/_4$ cup of water and mix until smooth. Add $^1/_4$ cup of chopped parsley, and pour over the chicken. Serves 4.

[1981]

𝒥 Love Mustard

I recently sampled thirty or so of the mustards now on the American market. At no time in history have we had such a wealth available to us—French, English, German, Polish, and domestic mustards, ranging from velvety mixtures of mustard flour, white wine or vinegar, salt, and herbs, to crunchy blends made with unsifted seeds crushed to varying degrees of coarseness; mustards dark brown to bright yellow; fiery hot to sweet. We are the inheritors of a condiment that has evolved since prehistoric times. The Chinese grew mustard plants three thousand years ago, and in Europe, mustard has been used for at least two thousand years. The Greeks and Romans, who knew it as *sinapis,* used it in powdered form to flavor meats and also prepared it as a paste in recipes remarkably close to those of the present day. It is said that the taste-corrupted Romans included it as an ingredient in the fishy, half-putrified, highly prized sauce called *garum.* And we know from biblical references that mustard was used in the Near East before the time of Christ.

Modern mustard did not come into general use until as late as the thirteenth or fourteenth century, when the ground seeds were mixed with unfermented wine or "must." Our word *mustard* comes from this root, just as the French *moutarde* comes from their word for must, *moût.* Yet there is a legend that *moutarde* came about in quite a different way. As the story goes, in 1382, the Duke of Burgundy was so grateful to the city of Dijon for supplying him with soldiers in a successful military campaign that he granted it armorial bearings with the motto *Moult Me Tarde*— "I ardently desire." This was carved on the principal gate of Dijon, but the middle word was accidentally destroyed, leaving only *Moult Tarde*—"to burn much"—which was a source of amusement among visitors to the city. Since the people of Dijon were, and are still, the greatest traders in what was called *sénevé,* this seed was nicknamed *moultarde* whenever it hailed from Dijon.

The importance of mustard in French history cannot be overestimated. One of the popes at the court of Avignon appointed a nephew Chief Mustard Maker. Louis XIV gave mustard a coat of arms, a silver funnel on a blue ground. And that elegant woman Madame Pompadour, at the height of her power, named Maille, one of the famous mustard makers, Vinegar Distiller and Mustarder to the King of France. Maille was also engaged by the rulers of Germany and Russia and eventually turned out twenty-four mustards, along with ninety-two toilet vinegars, very much like our cologne waters, which became highly fashionable. Parisian mustard makers began to compete with the Dijon group and put out exquisite formulas of their own, including a health mustard, a mustard flavored with rose petals, and another with vanilla.

Dijon, dear to the hearts of all gastronomes as the gateway to Burgundy, survives as the mustard capital of the world, producing some eighty or ninety varieties. Some of the old mustard firms—Grey Poupon, Maille, Bornibus—have remained in business, and the shop of Grey Poupon is a curiosity to all visitors because of its incredible display of old mustard pots and its many pots for sale. In passing, let me say that people *collect* mustard pots. I know of two private collections that number into the hundreds, some of the pots exquisitely decorated and ranging in size from minuscule to several gallons in capacity. Who would need a five-gallon mustard pot, you might ask. Well, people used to consume mustard in greater quantity than they do nowadays. In the accounts of a thirteenth-century Tudor household, we find listed seven to ten gallons of mustard monthly, and we have a record of a dinner served by a Duke of Burgundy in honor of a visiting king at which one hundred gallons of mustard were eaten.

One of the most interesting episodes in the history of mustard, and in the history of advertising, occurred when Alexandre Dumas' *Grand Dictionnaire de Cuisine* was published in 1873. Mustard is not listed in the body of the dictionary but is discussed in a long treatise following the text. At its conclusion, Dumas endorses a brand of mustard. This is what he wrote: "I have been asked which mustard I prefer above all. Until I tasted and appreciated the mustard made by Alexandre Bornibus, I preferred the aromatic mustards of Maille and Bordin to all others, but when by chance I tasted Bornibus' mustard, I knew at once it was the best of all." Dumas then goes on to tell that he made his discovery because he got off the train at Dijon by mistake on one occasion and was obliged to spend the night there. He had supper at the Hôtel du Parc, where he ordered two chops in mustard and half a cold fowl.

"What mustard do you want?" the waiter asked him.

"Why, Dijon mustard, of course," said Dumas.

"I know that," said the waiter, "but what I'm asking is whether you want men's mustard or ladies' mustard."

"Oh," said Dumas, "so there's a difference between mustard for men and mustard for women?"

"For ladies."

"All right, for ladies."

"Yes, sir, since a lady's palate is more delicate than a man's, ordinary Dijon mustard is too strong and sharp for them, so Monsieur Bornibus has invented a special mustard."

After a further exchange Dumas ended up having both men's and ladies' mustard. "I am no great expert on the subject of mustard," he continues. "I've always had a fine stomach and never made any great use of this 'preface to appetite,' as Grimod de la Reynière calls it. But on this occasion, at the sight of the fine canary yellow color, I plunged in the wooden spoon and made two pyramids, one of men's mustard and one of ladies,' on my plate. I must say that from that moment I made a turnabout and developed an enthusiasm for Bornibus mustard."

There aren't many food manufacturers lucky enough to have so distinguished an ad writer.

At an earlier date, a significant event in mustardry occurred in Durham, England, when a woman named Mrs. Clements found she could grind mustard seeds in a mill and sift them to make a powder or flour. Her mixture of black and white seeds prepared in this way was called "Durham Mustard," and she traveled through England taking orders for it. Its usage spread across the United Kingdom and to other parts of the world.

The English, of course, have been the hardiest of mustard eaters, and the pot of "made-mustard" or commercial mustard is a staple of English tables. Salt and pepper casters include a holder for the mustard pot, and one finds it on hand at breakfast, lunch, tea, dinner, and supper. I have never been won over to the English system of applying mustard to bacon or sausages in the morning, but if you have a taste for it, why not?

The Germans, also great consumers of the condiment, like their mustards darker in hue than either the French or English and also less piquant, sometimes tending to a sweet quality. German mustards come mainly from the famous mustard city of Düsseldorf, and they lend themselves to the wursts, Westphalian hams, and other typical German fare. The Poles, both in their native land and in the United States, make a fairly good selection of mustards, too. Theirs are closer to the German mustards than to the French, and again, they seem to go well with cured sausages and hams.

Italy has a unique approach to mustard, using it in a distinctive mixture called *mostarda di Cremona*, which consists of beautiful whole miniature fruits—pears, plums, cherries, figs—preserved, almost candied, in a clear mustard syrup. When I first tasted them, they came packed in cans that were an absolute horror to open but well worth the struggle. Now they are usually sold in jars, and, strangely enough—whether because of the container or a trick of memory—they do not seem to have the fiery piquance they once had. *Mostarda di Cremona* is a traditional accompaniment to *bollito misto,* the Italian equivalent of pot-au-feu, which includes beef, veal, pork, chicken, sometimes calf's head, and the pungent Italian sausage *cotechino.* This is all served forth with vegetables and a green sauce as well as the mustard fruits. The fruits are served with other Italian dishes, too, and they go well with cold meats for a buffet, but with bollito misto they make a classic marriage.

The Chinese and other Orientals are great mustard users, as we know. Like the English, they prepare a simple, rather hot mixture of mustard powder and water or other liquid, which they use alone or in barbecue sauces (not to be confused with the American kind), tomato sauces, or plum sauces. And the blending of mustard and soy is a common dip for many Chinese dishes.

If you are making your own mustard, by the way, be sure to let the mixture mellow for ten to fifteen minutes before serving or it will be bitter—a chemical action is really taking place.

Here in the United States, in addition to the array of imported mustards on the market, a large quantity is produced domestically. A number of these I classify as "ballpark" or "delicatessen" mustards. You will also probably find them in those little squeeze bags on your tray the next time you eat airline food. These mustards are bland and nondescript, really a form of salad dressing, with a closer resemblance to German mustard than any other. The most famous one in this country, French's, is produced by the R. T. French Company, which is owned by the people who make Colman's mustard. It is particularly high in vinegar content and low in distinctive flavor. The same can be said for most of the Heinz mustards and the Gulden's, save for one, Spicy Brown, which is a fairly honest reproduction of a German recipe. Though they do not excite the palate and can never be considered prize condiments, these American mustards will fill the need of many people, and you'll be faced with them the rest of your life wherever there are hamburgers, frankfurters, and pastrami or corned-beef sandwiches—unless you carry your own little pot of mustard with you, which isn't such a bad idea.

I think we have learned from the French as well as from the English to increase our appetite for mustard. New brands are constantly appearing on the market. Many come from Dijon, some from Paris. Those from London, I note, stick closely to the original English formula for a hot mustard and are made with mustard, flour, salt, either wine or water, and perhaps a little oil. This is the mustard made famous by Colman's, who have long packaged mustard flour and prepared mustard under their name. An American firm has the rights to Grey Poupon, the famous Dijon mustard, which is made in Hartford, Connecticut. It is not as expensive as the French product and, to my palate, not quite as good, but it is used widely and seems to be available in supermarkets throughout the country.

Some of the more attractive forms of mustard you'll find on restaurant menus and in people's homes nowadays are mustard sauces. There's one, often called *sauce Dijonnaise*, which is used with fish dishes. It is basically a rich béchamel or velouté to which several tablespoons of Grey Poupon mustard have been added, followed by a pat or two of butter to enrich it. The piquant but delicate mustard flavor in the creamy béchamel or velouté makes it an ideal addition to a sauce for fish.

A mustard mayonnaise is frequently served with seafood. It is extraordinarily good with crab legs, crabmeat, lobster, shrimp, or scallops. It is also excellent with that unusual Italian dish called carpaccio, which consists of slices of raw beef pounded paper-thin and served as an hors d'oeuvre. Mustard mayonnaise is made simply by adding mustard to taste to a good olive oil mayonnaise. The proportions can range from one tablespoon of mustard per cup of mayonnaise to equal quantities of each. Some chopped parsley or a few chopped chives give it added flavor.

In Scandinavian countries, they make a sauce with mayonnaise, mustard, sugar, and dill, which sounds like a ghastly combination but is intriguing when eaten with gravlax. The sauce is made with about three parts of mayonnaise to two parts of Dijon mustard, a tablespoon of sugar to sweeten it slightly, and a tablespoon of freshly chopped dill.

Another interesting sauce that takes time and care is a type of mayonnaise made with hard-boiled egg yolks. For it, you'll need about six to eight yolks, mashed well with a fork. To the yolks add perhaps one to two tablespoons of Dijon mustard, and stir until it becomes a paste. Then, drop by drop, add good olive oil until the mixture emulsifies, very much like a mayonnaise. This makes a fascinating sauce for a beet salad, a chicken salad, or a hearty fish salad.

There are many dishes in which mustard, preferably Grey Poupon or Pommery, is an essential ingredient. It is commonly used in game cookery, especially with rabbit, or with pheasant, duck, and partridge, used as a coating after the birds have been subjected to a spell of hanging to ripen.

A famous French dish called *lapin à la moutarde* is made with domestic rabbit, which is seared and browned, painted well with a rather sharp Dijon mustard, then placed on a *mirepoix* of vegetables and herbs. Cream is added to the dish, and it is baked until the rabbit is tender and the cream and mustard have blended together into a luscious sauce, which absorbs the flavors from the *mirepoix*. The same dish is often made with a plump chicken.

It has long been a practice to coat veal kidneys with mustard before grilling them, sometimes with strips of bacon. This makes an exciting dish for those who love the innards of animals as much as I do. It calls for a Dijon or a hot mustard such as Colman's made-mustard.

One of the most satisfying salads in the world is a beef salad Parisienne, which can be served as an hors d'oeuvre or a main course. It's made with the boiled beef from a pot-au-feu, cut into dice and blended with potatoes, celery, onion, and various other vegetables. The mixture is bound with a highly mustardized dressing—either a vinaigrette with a great deal of Dijon mustard added to it or the form of mayonnaise made with hard-boiled egg yolks. The dressing is poured over the salad long enough before eating to let it marinate slightly.

Mustard plays an important part in old English cookery books and in some of the early American books. It entered untold bean pots in New England, usually the dry variety or the dry mixed with water, along with salt pork, molasses, maple syrup, and onion. It was also added to cream, along with salt and pepper, for various fish dishes. I recently found a finnan haddie recipe from an early English book in which the fish was given a brushing of dry mustard mixed with water and then cooked in cream and milk until it was heated through. Just before serving, it was anointed with butter. This, with crisp toast and perhaps a boiled potato, must have been an exciting breakfast dish when people ate breakfasts of that caliber. There are numerous recipes, too, that call for brushing fish with a little made-mustard before broiling.

Of course, our enjoyment of Smithfield and Kentucky hams and other country hams has always been enhanced by mustard. The glaze I recommend for baking hams, which have first been boiled, is dry mustard and brown sugar. Other glazes can be made with apricot jam or currant jelly and mustard. Often crumbs are sprinkled on the glazed ham, and sometimes it is basted with Madeira or sherry or other wine as it bakes. A ham prepared with untold numbers of cloves, a rather ruinous practice, will never have the flavor and éclat of one done with a mustard glaze.

Mustard has a definite place in barbecue sauces and marinades, adding great character when stirred in with the usual additives, which can include ketchup, Worcestershire sauce, Tabasco, garlic, soy, and sometimes fruit juices or preserves. Very often you will find recipes for spareribs, chops, or steaks glazed with a sauce of hot prepared mustard and ketchup, and there's one widely used dressing for steak that is made with blue or Roquefort cheese, cognac, butter, and dry or Dijon mustard, blended together into a paste, which is rubbed on the meat for the last few minutes of broiling and forms a crusty coating.

In England and America, mustard pickle has been a standard for generations. There are hot mustard pickles (sometimes called chowchow), sweet mustard pickles, or just mustard pickles. Unfortunately, most of these have become turmeric pickles. There may be a little mustard flour mixed with the other ingredients, but it's the turmeric and vinegar that dominate. The good mustard pickles I fondly remember had plenty of hot, dry mustard to give them dash and could only be compared with the mustard fruit of pre–World War II vintage.

A rather severe canapé was created by Prosper Montagné for a gathering in France at the beginning of the century. It was made with squares of rye bread, or what is known in France as *pain de seigle*, spread with very hot prepared mustard and then with freshly grated horseradish. I have served this with drinks in the past, and it was considered a smashing combination with martinis. But it is strictly for the flame eaters.

For a more modern French experiment with mustard, I turn to Simone Beck, coauthor with Julia Child of the two volumes of *Mastering the Art of French Cooking* and author of a brilliant book of her own called *Simca's Cuisine.* One time when Simca was teaching a class of mine on how to make a quiche, she came up with the idea of brushing the partially baked pastry shell with Dijon mustard before adding the filling. Not only did this help to keep the shell from becoming soggy, but it added an intriguing, unidentifiable flavor to the quiche. It is an invention that all of Simca's students eagerly adopted and that I have, too.

I would be remiss not to speak of the medicinal value of mustard through the centuries—as a liniment, emetic, and stomach stimulant. I can remember when it used to be quite common to apply a mustard plaster to the skin for anything from a chest cold to a stomachache or backache. This supposedly burned out the malady or soothed the muscles, but it often had the effect of simply blistering the patient.

And that reminds me of an incident I witnessed in my youth when I was on a cross-country train journey. In those days, I used to travel in an upper berth because it saved money, and, once installed, I seemed to have more freedom than in the lower and a better view of what went on in the car. I had been observing a man and woman across from me who had spurned the then fabulously good dining services of the Chicago, Milwaukee, St. Paul and Pacific Railroad and brought hampers of their own food. They ate heartily, and the second night out I was awakened at two o'clock in the morning by a man's groans. Peeping through my curtains, I saw madam, my neighbor, heading for the ladies' room to prepare (it turned out later) a mustard plaster for her husband's indigestion. She tiptoed back, drew the curtains, and applied the paster. Then back she went to the ladies' room, no doubt to collect her first-aid kit and wash her hands. Suddenly there was a piercing cry. I knew what had happened. Madam had gone to the wrong berth and slapped her mustard plaster on the back of a stranger. The poor man had just come into a state of consciousness. Well, there was no more sleep in the car that night. There were apologies, explanations, arguments. The entire crew of the train came forth. The sick husband, I might add, recovered almost from the moment of his neighbor's scream. All of which proves that if you are traveling in an old-fashioned Pullman, you better know how to count.

There are still English and French firms that produce ready-to-go mustard plasters. So, if you would like to take a few on your next trip, it's a sensational way to get acquainted with a stranger.

[1975]

Garlic

Garlic is something that few of us can cook without, although there are still those who look down their noses and consider it vulgar. As a flavoring additive, it is as old as time. The ancient Chinese were perhaps its first cultivators and users. In today's Chinese restaurants, where there is still some tradition in the kitchen, one occasionally finds pickled garlic, one of its oldest known uses. The cloves are put in a strong vinegar and kept as much as one or two years before being eaten, by which time the pickling has tamed the strong flavor. The Russians also have a version of pickled garlic, only they use whole heads, rather than cloves, pickle them in red wine vinegar, and serve them with lamb, along with tomatoes, cucumbers, and greens. We all know that roast lamb and garlic are intimate companions.

I don't think you'll find a country along the Mediterranean where garlic is not a predominant flavoring agent in cooking. The Greek historian Herodotus wrote about the Egyptians using it, and from Egypt it spread to Greece, Rome, and all through the Mediterranean basin. Undoubtedly it was Mediterranean people—the French who came to Louisiana, and later, Italian immigrants—who introduced cultivated garlic to this country, although we have always had wild garlic growing in our fields and meadows, a source of great fascination for cows in the spring. Many a dairy has a problem during that season because the copious quantities of wild garlic eaten by the cows flavor their milk. Anyone pouring a glass of milk in the morning or putting cream in their coffee will encounter a strong and totally unexpected taste of garlic.

I remember once arriving in Marseilles during the summer and being delightfully assaulted, as I leaned from my hotel window, by the aroma of garlic, garlic, garlic. I was across the street from the annual garlic fair, where various and sundry garlics, dried and braided into long festoons, were being sold over several days. This was originally started to attract restaurateurs, housewives, and others who did not grow their own garlic, and it had become a pretty remarkable gathering. People were there in throngs, shopping around for the small-cloved white garlic, the slightly larger one with a pink scale, and one with a purple scale, all with different degrees of pungency and hotness.

Garlic comes in more than one form. Tender young green garlic, pulled from the garden with the tops on, before it has started to dry, is sometimes referred to as "milk garlic" because of the milky white fluid inside. Peeled and spread on crusty French bread with sweet butter, it makes a great lunch, followed by a glass of wine and cheese. One year, when I was living in Provence and garlic happened to be at its prime, this was my supper for two or three nights in a row. It was sheer heaven.

In the region around Nîmes, Arles, Avignon, and Marseilles, as far as Toulon, the typical Friday midday meal is salt codfish, or sometimes fresh fish, with boiled potatoes, carrots, and hard-boiled eggs, served with aïoli, which has been called "the butter of Provence." Aïoli is a form of mayonnaise, made with crushed garlic, egg yolks, and olive oil, and worked by hand in a big marble mortar until it comes forth thick, stiff, yellow, overpowering to the nose, and absolutely hypnotizing to the palate. In the Catalan section of Spain you find *ailloli*, their version of the sauce. I remember having it one New Year's Day with crisp, luscious suckling pig. Then there's the Greek *skordalia*, which is much the same except that it may include bread crumbs or ground almonds, customarily served with fish, vegetables, and sometimes chicken.

For years, one of my favorite dishes has been chicken with forty cloves of garlic—chicken sealed in a pot and braised with the garlic. The cloves cook slowly to a butter-soft smoothness and delicacy of flavor. Then they are spread on pieces of bread and eaten along with the chicken. No one can ever believe there are really forty cloves of garlic in the dish. In fact, several times when the recipe appeared in print, skeptical food editors had changed the amount to four.

One day it occurred to me that it might be a smart idea to make and keep a garlic purée, which I have done with great success, storing it in a screw-top jar in the refrigerator, where it keeps for several weeks. I add it to stews and sautés as a seasoning, mix it into salad dressings, flavor vegetables with it, or spread it on toast as an hors d'oeuvre. It's a highly versatile mixture with no resemblance to raw garlic in flavor, and it's certainly simple enough to make.

Take 2 dozen heads of firm garlic (and I do mean heads), separate them into cloves, and peel the cloves or leave them in their papery shells. Put them in a pan of boiling water with a teaspoon of salt, and simmer over medium heat for 30 to 45 minutes, depending on the size of the cloves, until very, very soft. Drain well. If you peeled the cloves, now put them in a food processor or blender and purée. If you left the shells on, rub the cloves through a food mill to leave the husks behind. Add a touch of salt and 2 to 3 tablespoons of olive oil to the purée, put it in a jar, and refrigerate until needed. If you try this, I can guarantee you'll never want to be without it. Mixed into crème fraiche, for instance, it makes a glorious sauce for roast lamb.

Another thing that a lot of cooks don't know about garlic is that it doesn't need to be peeled to add flavor. If you are sautéing something like chicken or a pork or veal chop and want garlic flavor, throw in a few unpeeled cloves. You'll find that the garlic flavor permeates its skin and extends into whatever you are cooking. You also save time by not peeling the cloves.

When you buy garlic, it should be very fresh and firm, not soft, marred with brown spots, or sprouting. It's well worth shopping around to find a place that sells good garlic and has a quick turnover. Better vegetable markets, Italian and Chinese markets, and Korean vegetable stores are preferable to supermarkets, where the garlic—the small white California type—usually comes sealed in little boxes and is often overage. The larger white or red Italian garlic is a better buy.

Lately a new strain of garlic has become rather common on the West Coast, although it has yet to take over the East. This is elephant garlic, so called because the cloves are gigantic, at least four times the size of an ordinary garlic clove, and the heads are as big as an apple or large orange. Elephant garlic has a more delicate and balanced flavor than the other varieties. Some seed companies and West Coast vegetable farmers sell the bulbs by mail for planting in home gardens.

For centuries, garlic was regarded as a highly useful medicine. It was thought to be a cure for leprosy, good for the liver, and a diuretic. At one time there was a theory, which I'm told is still prevalent among certain groups, that one way to treat a cold was to rub the soles of your feet with garlic. Well, that may not help you recover from the cold, but it will almost certainly keep other people from catching it by driving them away.

[1977]

$\mathcal{B}$eard was one of the few food writers who could also speak with authority about wines and spirits. He educated himself with forays to the vineyards of France and Germany, as well as to the sherry country of Spain. He talked and ate with producers and grape pickers alike. For many years, he was a consultant to the Madison Avenue firm of Sherry Wine & Spirits (now Sherry-Lehmann) and was often on the road for Edward Gottlieb Associates to promote champagne and cognac, flambéing his way across the country. (He once wrote to his friend Philip Brown, "I have to take the gospel of cognac to Texas again next week and show Houston how to burn up a lot of good food.") When Restaurant Associates was creating its jewel in the crown, the Four Seasons, Beard assembled the wine list and for several years gave weekly classes on wine and wine service for all the captains.

Meanwhile, he was writing his monthly "Corkscrew" column on wine and spirits for *House & Garden*, which advised on such matters as choosing the right glass, decanting wine, drinks that go with Chinese food, and nearly a hundred other alcoholic topics. The sampling here gives minicourses on vodka, gin, white brandies, and champagne. The more informal pieces on mint julep—singular, please—and restoratives for the morning after were first published in Beard's weekly column.

The Vogue for Vodka

Vodka has been a pleasant influence in my life ever since the day in my flask-carrying, party-going youth when my father presented me with a large, mysterious package wrapped in plain paper. "Drink this," he said, "instead of bootleg whiskey." The package contained dozens of flat tin cans of vodka, colorfully labeled in Russian characters. It was smuggled vodka, of course, brought in by ships that touched China's ports. My first taste of it was very tentative. I expected it to be fiery, and I half thought it might have the flavor of potatoes. It packed a wallop, yes, but it was by no means lethal, and I was delighted with its clean flavor—or lack of flavor. So I began as a pre-repeal vodka fan.

Now, of course, there are millions of other enthusiasts to help me protest the myth that vodka is a dangerously potent brew of fermented potatoes. Like gin, rye, and Scotch, vodka is a grain distillation, and its alcoholic strength is not startlingly high. Most vodka is eighty proof, or milder than most gins and whiskeys. Only a few distillers offer hundred-proof vodka.

It was three years after the Congress of Vienna in 1815 that the firm of Smirnoff in Russia began the distillation of vodka from grain and soon became official purveyors to the royal house. A hundred years later, the Smirnoff secret fled the revolution to France, and production went on there. After the repeal of Prohibition in the United States, the firm moved to Connecticut and was the first in the American vodka market. They have been followed by such other fine old Russian names as Romanoff, Orloff, and Hiram Walker.

One type of vodka, called *dubrowka*, has a blade of sweet grass in each bottle that gives the liquor a somewhat sweetish herb flavor. But other vodkas contain no aromatics and are practically flavorless. It is one of the few spirits—cognac and Armagnac are others—that do not ruffle your taste buds so you miss the true flavor of wines served at the dinner. However, I am of the opinion that a moderate amount of any spirit really doesn't kill the taste for wine.

Generations of Muscovites have drunk their vodka neat. Neat or not, it should be served well iced. A famous Russian restaurant in Paris—Dominique—serves vodka in a cooler, like champagne or white wine. You are expected to drink it right through the meal because it "cuts" the heaviness of the rich dishes of Russian and Polish cuisine. I do not recommend this custom to Americans, who sensibly prefer wine, not spirits, during dinner.

Vodka is ideal accompaniment for caviar. It should be iced and drunk in small glasses—one full glass at a gulp after a hearty partaking of caviar. With the exception of champagne, it is the only drink for which caviar has a strong affinity.

In recent years, the popularity of vodka has grown spectacularly. The producer who uses the phrase "It leaves you breathless" attributes the rise in consumption to an American fondness for discovery and novelty. Women like vodka because it is a relatively low-calorie drink.

The vodka martini is the current rage. It is drier than its ancestor, the gin martini. To make it, combine 4 parts of vodka to 1 part dry vermouth. Always pour the liquor over cracked ice. Stir well—one of the great faults of martini mixing is too little stirring. Strain the martini into chilled glasses and add a twist of lemon peel. It's best to serve each martini in a freshly chilled glass, even seconds and thirds. Keep several glasses in the refrigerator for constant martini drinkers and you will win their praise.

For a Gibson with vodka, pour 8 parts of vodka to 1 part of French vermouth over cracked ice, and stir well. Strain into chilled glasses, and add pickled onions. The original addition for a Gibson was a pickled hazelnut, but unfortunately, these no longer can be bought on the market. If you want to make them for yourself, it is not a hard job. Merely cover blanched hazelnuts with white wine vinegar and a touch of tarragon. Let them stand for about 2 weeks before using.

A Bloody Mary is recommended as a morning-after drink, but it also stands on its own as a refreshing lunchtime cocktail. Combine in a cocktail shaker 2 ounces of vodka, 3 ounces of tomato juice, $1/2$ ounce of fresh lemon juice, a dash of Worcestershire sauce, salt, pepper, and, if you like, a dash of Tabasco. Add cracked ice, shake very well, and strain into a chilled glass. Serve with a dusting of paprika.

The screwdriver has become the most popular drink the West Coast has seen in years. Merely add 2 ounces of vodka to a tall glass of orange juice with ice. This is ideal for a Sunday brunch in that it combines the cocktail and first course.

A vodka daiquiri appeals to those who love the flavor of lime. Pour the juice of 1 large or 2 small limes over ice in a shaker. Add a barspoon of finely granulated sugar and $1^{1}/2$ to 2 ounces of vodka. Shake furiously, and strain into chilled cocktail glasses.

Vodka gimlets are favorites with people who are loyal to the flavor of Rose's Lime Juice, and there are many. Combine 3 parts vodka to 1 part of Rose's lime juice, and pour over ice in a shaker. Shake well, strain into a large cocktail glass, and add a splash of soda.

Some years back, a great Hollywood restaurant perfected the Moscow mule and used it to publicize not only the restaurant but also a copper mug. So traditionally, it is served in a copper mug, but it tastes just as good in pewter or glass. Pour 2 ounces of vodka over several ice cubes in a tall glass. Add a squeeze of half of a lime and the lime itself. Fill the glass with ginger beer (not ginger ale). This is refreshing and bitey.

A vodka collins of course resembles other collinses, but I think most people make a very bad collins. To make a good one, combine in a shaker the juice of a large ripe lemon (or 1½ less juicy ones) with a small barspoon of sugar, 3 ounces of vodka, and ice cubes. Shake well. Pour ice and all into a tall glass. Add soda to taste, a strip of lemon peel, and a long slice of cucumber peel.

[1956]

*G*in

Wherever the cocktail crowd gathers, the great gin controversy rages. One contingent advocates only the driest of the drys, while another avows a taste for the aromatic or flavored gins. More than any other liquor, gin has throughout the centuries been a cause of contention—except in Holland, where for four hundred years it has maintained a position as stable and respectable as whiskey in Scotland or bourbon in Kentucky.

Originally, the gin produced in Holland, called Holland or Genever gin, was a distillation of juniper berries. These gave the gin its distinctive flavor and the fine clean feel to mouth and palate. It is a gin that has little or no kinship to any other drink of the same name. Holland gin should be drunk neat. To my taste, it is best when chilled, although I have known many people in Europe who could drink vast quantities at room temperature.

Holland gin arrived in England when there was rum and a good deal of cognac but as yet no whiskey. This new spirit caught the public's fancy right off. By 1736, Lord Hervey had published a complaint that all of London and much of the hinterland was drunk twenty-four hours a day. He said the country resembled more a scene of bacchanalian revels than "the residence of civil society." Gin shops in those times offered far more than our modern bars. They advertised that one could get drunk for a penny and promised clean straw in the cellars for those who could not make their way home.

With the beginning of illegal distilling in England and the development of legal distilling, the flavor of Holland gin changed. Aromatics like coriander, orris, pepper, and ginger came to be an integral part of the brew until the taste altered completely from that of good gin from Schiedam to a more refined English version. About this time, a shop became famous for a drink made with gin, soda water, lemon juice, and sugar. Its bartender was named John Collins, and he called his drink a "sling." But it has come down to us as a "collins," with the "John" changed to "Tom" in most parts of the drinking world.

English gin became more and more highly competitive, evolving from a messy distillation to a fine-flavored alcohol that was purified and redistilled several times. When it started to be used in mixed drinks, it was made less aromatic and more delicate in taste. As people grew to know the pleasures of iced potions, in summer, and particularly in the Tropics, gin and its compatible flavorings offered a variety of delicious drinks.

Before Prohibition, America used many fine English gins. The martini, the Bronx, and the Tom Collins became a part of our daily drinking pattern. The term *London Dry Gin* or *London Club Gin* gave gin added distinction. It was definitely a snob drink on the one hand, but at the same time, it was a drink of, shall we say, less wholesome groups. To a certain part of our population it was what absinthe was in France—an escape.

Then came Prohibition. Gin, being a white *eau-de-vie*, was found to be one of the easiest liquors to prepare at home from alcohol, a few aromatics, and distilled water. Thus "bathtub gin" came into our lives. And it literally was made in the bathtub, as I can testify. The mother of two girls I knew decided she would rather go into bathtub gin production herself than worry about the safety of bootleg gin for her daughters and their friends. She enlisted the services of some of us, and Sunday afternoons were spent making gin in the bathtub, then rolling it around the floor in a wooden cask to "age." Several hours later it was served in our Sunday night's cocktails. I may say that after two years of this, I became quite deft as a gin maker.

After Prohibition left us, there were more gin drinkers in America than there were wine drinkers in France. The English gins, which were of lower proof than most of the gins we were accustomed to during the drought, seemed tasteless and kickless. Consequently, all the great producers started making gins in the American idiom, and the difference in flavors between English and U.S. gin became very marked. Proof varied, too. We now had English gins at seventy proof and American gins at ninety and ninety-four. Some houses made both an American and an English gin, and there were gins so aromatic that you could smell them across the bar or from the other side of a room.

With this shift in taste came a change in making drinks. It became impossible to get a martini dry enough to suit anyone. The on-the-rocks school came into being. Soon people seemed to be rinsing a glass with vermouth, then adding gin and ice. Books were written on the martini. One person even published a cookbook with recipes and menus geared to the varying numbers of martinis one might consume.

The martini has come a long way since the 1880s and 1890s when it was made with Old Tom gin, which is slightly sweetened. In those days, one used a great deal of vermouth, and in some cases, two kinds, Italian and French. From the rather gooey mess originally called "Martinez," the martini has evolved to the potion we treasure today.

A good martini is an achievement, and when I say it is the perfect cocktail, I mean it wholeheartedly. Its success depends on the gin one uses, but also on the care in its preparation. During the last decade, the debate about this drink could lead one to believe it is deadlier than absinthe. Most of this talk is folly. There is no drink so brisk and so palate-cleansing if taken in moderation. When one gulps quantities of martinis in a short time—what is known as the great American lunch— the effect can, of course, be paralyzing.

Let's ignore all the old wives' tales about "Mother's ruin" or "Annie's ruin." Gin is a spirit that is beautifully purified and not at all disagreeably inclined toward your stomach. The martini, if properly consumed, is the appetite's great ally. Drink one or two before dinner for a lift. Two will pique your palate; more will dull it.

Europe, where the martini has been practically all vermouth, has begun to cater to the American taste in recent years. And the search for a good "dry" is now international. European gins vary a good deal because some of the local ones are made with cane alcohol instead of grain alcohol. Also, the aromatics are as variable as perfumes. But there are bars where visitors can drink as many drys as they do in their own favorite spot in the United States. The French and Italians have gingerly delved into this experience, and the dry martini is becoming as typical a part of European eating and drinking as a famous soft drink of American origin.

Now it seems to me that the trend is changing again. English gins are becoming increasingly popular here—for example, Beefeater. Because of the vogue a restaurant called Whytes created for the Beefeater martini, this comparatively unknown gin has skyrocketed to national success. Other English firms—and American ones, too—have since developed vigorous campaigns to win consumers.

The end result has been that the standard of the average martini served in bars has improved immensely. Even the more conscientious home bartenders are making a far better martini than they used to. They ice the glasses well before serving. After pouring a drink, they are more apt to drain off the remainder and refrigerate it, rather than leave it to cool in a slushy soup. And the selection of excellent vermouths and gins now available has done much to abolish that horrid stale vermouthy flavor one found in the early years.

Although the martini is the undisputed classic in the home bartender's lexicon, there are many other excellent gin drinks that cannot be overlooked. Gin and tonic and the Tom Collins are perennial summer favorites, and a taste is developing for the gimlet, that importation from the Orient by way of the West Coast. It is made with half English gin and half Rose's Lime Juice, which you stir with crushed ice, then strain into a cocktail glass. Another recommendation for those who like to keep their gin drinks dry is gin and bitters (the "pink gin" beloved of the British navy), in which a hint of Angostura bitters—some advise just swirling it around the glass and then discarding it—fulfills the same purpose as vermouth in a martini.

Here is the classic recipe for the dry martini, in case there is anyone who does not know it.

Place a tall beaker or pitcher filled with ice cubes in the refrigerator, and let it chill thoroughly. Put cocktail glasses to chill also. When you are ready to mix the drinks, remove the beaker and pour out the ice. Put in a few cubes of fresh ice and, for each drink, add 4 or 5 parts of gin to 1 part dry vermouth. Stir quickly until thoroughly blended, but not to the point where the ice melts and dilutes the drink. Strain immediately into the chilled glasses, and add a twist of lemon peel or an olive, according to taste. If there is any martini left in the beaker, remove the ice and place the beaker in the refrigerator to keep cold.

Gibsons are made in the same way, increasing the proportions to 6 or more parts of gin to 1 of dry vermouth. Add a pickled onion or pickled hazelnut to each glass.

[1960]

The Rare White Brandies

When you hold a chilled glass of *eau-de-vie de framboise* in your fingers, you may find it hard to believe that the colorless liquid is the very essence of pounds of ripe red raspberries. Other white alcohols bring you the concentrated flavor of wild black cherries, strawberries, or plums. All these white alcohols (there are about a dozen that are becoming well known in this country) have a pleasing delicacy. This is apt to be deceptive, for they are exceedingly potent; their alcoholic content may be higher than that of gin or Scotch. They are best taken in small quantities and are at their finest when served cold. I always think of them as small potions of summer magic. They conjure up bowls of ripe summer fruit, refreshingly chilled.

Besides being colorless, the white alcohols are completely dry—that is, unsweet. They are so dry that the first sip startles your tongue. To go about this correctly, bury your nose in the glass and breathe in the aroma of the fruit. Then take a mere sip, let the liquid trickle down your throat, and wait for the aftertaste. As soon as the tang of alcohol dies away, you will savor the rich fruit flavor.

Why are the white alcohols colorless? Because no coloring is added to the distilled liquid, and they are stored in paraffin-lined casks or earthenware crocks. All brandies are *eaux-de-vie*, distilled from wine or from fermented mash of fruit, and all, in the original state, are colorless. The famous cognacs, the most elegant of grape brandies, start out pale as water, but while aging in oak casks acquire their color from the wood. The popular sorts of sweet fruit brandies, such as apricot, blackberry, and peach, take some color from the casks in which they are stored, and coloring matter and sweet flavoring are usually added.

The main sources of white *eaux-de-vie* are Switzerland, Germany, and the French provinces of Alsace and Lorraine. For generations, the fruit growers in these regions have made their own white brandies in small pot stills, mostly for their own pleasure. The Alsatian fruit growers do sell some home-made brandies to good restaurants and inns in France. During visits to France, I have often searched the countryside for bottles of white *eaux-de-vie*, crudely labeled in the handwriting of the grower-distiller. The hunt takes you on back roads, and the bottles you find are usually superior to the commercial brands shipped to this country. However, the commercial white alcohols now available in our leading liquor and wine shops are generally excellent, and in recent years, the choice has become more varied.

Kirsch or kirschwasser is the best-known white alcohol and the most easily obtained. It is made from the small wild black cherry native to the Black Forest region of Germany and to nearby Switzerland. The fruit and its pits are crushed and allowed to ferment. Then the whole fermented mash goes into the pot still.

Long a standard household liquor in West Central Europe, kirsch is an important ingredient in a number of classic recipes.

Swiss cheese fondue calls for liberal amounts of kirsch, some elegant German dessert pancakes are flamed with it, and it is used all through Western Europe to flavor ice cream. Most kirsch comes from Germany or Switzerland, and some from Alsace, and there is now an American kirsch on the market, made in the Hood River Valley of Oregon. The different brands vary considerably in flavor and in price. After you've tried several, there will probably be one that pleases you most.

Eau-de-vie de framboise, the distilled essence of raspberries, is the most glamorous of white alcohols and far rarer than kirsch. It takes about forty pounds of this delicate fruit to make one quart of the *eau-de-vie,* so it will not surprise you to know that it is very expensive. The best is found in France's great restaurants, but a small amount is shipped to this country. If you find a bottle, buy it promptly and treat it with respect. Though *framboise* is unbelievably good with fruit desserts, my inclination is to save it for drinking straight. It seems too precious to lose one drop of the full flavor. Sip it from a chilled glass and enjoy the rich aroma of ripe raspberries.

Himbeergeist is the German version of *framboise* and not so costly as the French. It, too, is rich with the odor and subtle flavor of the raspberry.

Mirabelle, not so well known in this country, is the essence of the small yellow plums of the same name and deserves to be more popular. It's dry, of course, with a soft, delicate flavor similar to that of poached plums. I like it straight and as a delicious addition to plum and other fruit tarts.

Quetsch is made from purple plums and has a quite different flavor from *Mirabelle.* Some people prefer one, some the other.

Pruna is the white alcohol of the prune plum, with a more pronounced flavor than other plum brandies. I grew fond of it during a stay in France with friends who own a large distillery and produce white alcohols. This was their favorite after-dinner drink. At first I thought it had a strange aftertaste, but soon I found the flavor compelling.

Fraise, the essence of strawberries, is probably the scarcest of white alcohols. Rich with the aroma and taste of ripe red strawberries, yet dry and tingling, it should be carefully husbanded and sipped chilled.

Myrtille is a white alcohol distilled from wild blueberries and huckleberries, and it possesses their unusual, gamy flavor. You will find your introductory sip more of a surprise than your first taste of any of the other white brandies. It is scarce.

Serve white alcohols in tulip-shaped glasses or, to capture their full fragrance, in large brandy goblets. First fill the glasses with cracked ice, and swirl the ice to chill the glasses thoroughly. When they are frosty, pour out the ice and pour in a small amount of white alcohol. Sniff, swirl, and sip. You may chill the brandy slightly in the refrigerator if you wish, but be careful not to let it get icy cold. When too chilled, it loses some of its aroma and flavor.

As with other brandies, white alcohols keep well after the bottle is opened. Simply cork it up and put it back on the shelf.

Kirsch is more widely used with fruit than any other white *eau-de-vie*, mainly because it is easy to find. You may substitute any white alcohol for the kirsch suggested in the following combinations:

Pour kirsch over sugared fresh strawberries or raspberries.

Peel a fresh pineapple and cut it into thin slices. Sugar to taste and add kirsch.

Peel fresh figs, sugar lightly, and add kirsch.

Select a ripe cantaloupe, casaba, or Persian melon, and cut a slice off the top. Scoop out the seeds, and fill with kirsch. Put the top slice back on the melon, and place it in the refrigerator to chill for several hours. Serve sliced with some of the kirsch spooned over each serving.

Combine sliced fresh peaches and apricots, sugar to taste, and add kirsch.

Combine fresh strawberries, fresh pineapple chunks, and preserved ginger. Sweeten with a little of the ginger syrup and add kirsch.

Peel oranges and cut them into thin slices. Sugar to taste and add kirsch.

Poach fresh pears, peaches, or plums in syrup. Add kirsch just before serving.

Cook dried prunes, apricots, pears, and peaches in syrup flavored with lemon and orange peel. When they are cooked, add kirsch, and let stand in the refrigerator for one or two days.

For cherries jubilee, poach fresh black cherries in a little syrup until just tender (or heat canned black cherries). Flame the hot cherries with kirsch, and spoon over vanilla ice cream.

Add kirsch to cherry pie, tarts, or puddings, or to other cooked fruit pies and tarts.

Bake bananas in their skins, split them, sugar lightly, and flame with kirsch.

Mirabelle is especially good with fresh pineapple, poached or stewed plums, plum tarts, and either fresh or cooked peaches.

And finally, for those elegant moments when you want to be generous with *eau-de-vie de framboise:* splash it liberally over fresh red raspberries; or over raspberries and fresh pineapple; or over ripe fresh peaches, plain or combined with raspberries; or over fresh peach halves, broiled with a brown sugar and butter topping.

[1957]

Champagne: Bottled Gaiety

Not all light sparkling wine is champagne. The correct general term for wines that sparkle is *vins mousseux,* and they are made in many wine areas. *Champagne* refers only to the sparkling wine from a tiny region, the Champagne district of France. The word is exclusive, just as *Bordeaux* refers only to wine from Bordeaux, and *cognac* only to brandy from Cognac.

The Champagne district has a rather severe climate for growing wine grapes. Autumn may be cold there; the spring frosts bite. Under the thin soil lies a vast deposit of chalk. Yet these apparent drawbacks have been used as assets. The vineyards face the sun from the slopes of a low, hilly plateau—not too high because they would be exposed, not too low because the frost collects in the valleys. The chalk of the soil reflects the sun, and its rays shed a whitish glare over the slopes.

The growers of Champagne are proud of a planting system that has evolved over hundreds of years. Some vines are planted well up on the slopes, others in more sheltered positions; some bask in a glare of sun, others have less. Grapes from the various vineyards contribute different qualities: roundness, bouquet, delicacy. It is the carefully calculated blending of these qualities that makes a fine champagne.

The wine of Champagne has a long history. Roman legionnaires found vineyards when they first marched into Gaul, and the Romans who settled in Champagne made wine themselves. Old Roman wine cellars are still there. The Champagne wine of two thousand years ago was a red wine, not the golden glory we know, but it must have been good. When it threatened to put the wines of Roman Italy to shame, the Emperor Domitian ordered the vines of Champagne to be destroyed. Two hundred years later, they were replanted, and Champagne has flourished ever since as a wine region.

Beginning with the crowning of King Clovis in the year 496, Reims, the capital of Champagne, became the scene of French coronations and champagne the coronation wine. In fact, champagne became so important at royal affairs that both French and English kings owned vineyards just to be sure of a regular supply. England's King Henry VIII, a historic gourmand, owned a Champagne vineyard and drank huge amounts of the wine. Even then, the wine was not today's golden magic. It was an excellent light red, probably similar to Bordeaux.

Yet there was something strange about this wine that caused local peasants to call it bewitched. During the spring in some years, there would be an unexplained stirring in the wine. It would bubble up vigorously and spill out over the cellar floors. Those who sampled it found it unbelievably delicious. How could it be saved? How could it be kept in the bottles?

Tradition gives credit for capturing the magic fizz to a Benedictine monk, Dom Perignon, who in 1670 became cellarer of the monastery at Hautvilliers, in the heart of Champagne. Probably from itinerant Spanish monks, Dom Perignon learned about corks made from the bark of a tree in Spain. He introduced their use and devised a way to anchor the corks firmly in the bottles. He may have been the one to discover that an early cold spell stopped the first fermentation of the wine and that it resumed in the spring. He laid down rules concerning temperature, and he devised the art of blending grapes from different vineyards to produce a balanced wine. Today Dom Perignon's statue looks down from pedestals throughout the Champagne district. He stands in stone, clutching a glass filled with his own concoction. He beams with satisfaction.

Already the favorite wine of royalty, champagne now became sought after by all who could afford it. In fashionable circles in every European capital, and across the sea in Boston, New York, and Philadelphia, champagne became the wine of wines. Elegant ladies sipped it with delight and confidence. Madame Pompadour had said, "Champagne is the sole wine a woman who is careful of her beauty can drink. You can drink it all evening and still be beautiful when you wake the next morning."

In the Gay Nineties and the Edwardian period, champagne became the symbol of success. Newly arrived millionaires tried to outdo one another giving champagne parties. At one lavish affair, the majolica fountain in the courtyard of the famous Savoy Hotel in London spouted champagne all evening. Another magnate had the same courtyard flooded so he could serve a champagne dinner to guests in a floating gondola.

Always in demand, champagne is of course expensive, and it will never be cheap. Machines offer no shortcuts that might replace the years of care that go into the production of each bottle. The wonder is that it costs so little.

The *vendange* or grape harvest in Champagne begins a cycle that will not be finished for seven or eight years. Harvesttime is determined by the weather. At the crucial moment, the call goes out for the pickers. All over the district, men and women swarm along the roads and lanes to the vineyards.

Meanwhile, the growers are quickly getting huge dormitories ready and stacking baskets in the courtyards. Although everyone works hard long hours, there is a festive air about the harvest. Many grape pickers may not have seen one another for a year, and there's much news to be exchanged. The food that the growers give the *vendangeurs* is abundant and delicious, and each worker receives a daily ration of wine. I have had some memorable meals with grape harvesters in Champagne.

Grapes from different vineyards are pressed separately. Most people are surprised to hear that both red and white grapes are used in champagne. The red grapes are run through the presses very quickly to prevent the skins from coloring the wine. Only a very small amount of champagne is made from white grapes alone. It is generally known as blanc de blancs and is liked by people who prefer an exceedingly light wine.

From the press houses, the juice is carted in barrels to the cellars of the champagne firms. Here it rests for twenty to thirty days while the first fermentation takes place. After this step, the cellar master faces the most important task in the making of champagne—blending the *cuvée*. He tastes and mixes the various wines until he finds just the right combination of body, bouquet, and delicacy of flavor. He must be able to imagine how the green wine will taste when it is mature and mellow. Each great champagne firm has its own standard in blending. If the cellar master finds the wine is not up to the usual quality, the firm will not bottle it as vintage champagne. Instead, it will be blended with wine reserved from a previous vintage. This blend must also meet a high standard, but the wine will be sold at a lower price as nonvintage champagne. Such a wine from a reputable firm often equals or even surpasses a vintage wine from an obscure house. This is an important point to keep in mind when you shop for champagne.

Early in spring, the wine is bottled, the corks are fixed with steel clamps, and the bottles are stacked like piles of cordwood in the deepest part of the cellar. Some enormous cellars hold millions of bottles arranged in seemingly endless rows. I once lost my way in such a cellar, walking a twisting, turning path through the maze. Just as I had decided to drink my way out, I was rescued by one of the cellar master's assistants.

When the warm spring comes and the sap begins to rise in the vines, the bottled champagne becomes "bewitched" and ferments a second time. This intermittent fermentation continues sometimes for as long as four years, and during this period the bottles are not disturbed.

Fermentation develops a sediment in the wine. To remove it, the bottles are placed in special racks, their necks slanted toward the floor. Each day skilled workmen go along the rows, twisting and jiggling each bottle to loosen the deposit and force it toward the neck. When I watch these men, I am reminded of a ballet of automatons, deftly twisting a bottle, moving a step, twisting, and on again. Day after day, week after week, they repeat this, gradually tilting the bottles farther forward until the sediment is trapped in the necks of the bottles.

How do they get the sediment out of the bottles? First of all, the necks are frozen to hold the sediment together. Then a trained workman removes the cork with a twist of the hand. The gas inside pushes out the sediment. The workman rapidly adds wine to fill the space, plus a slight dose of cane sugar dissolved in champagne. The amount of sugar added governs the sweetness of the wine. Now the wine is corked, wired, and sealed. All this is done with the utmost speed so that none of the fizz of the champagne is lost.

Altogether, the creation of champagne is time-consuming and costly, and it requires years of skill. How could it be cheap?

It is well worth an occasional splurge. There are twelve to fifteen great champagne firms. Go to a reputable wine dealer and trust his judgment. Remember, nonvintage champagne from a fine firm is a good buy and the nearest thing to a bargain in champagnes. They range from very dry to very sweet, and the designations on labels are confusing. Here is what they mean:

Brut or English Market and English Cuvée: This is the driest and, in my opinion, the finest. It is the best choice for an apéritif and for drinking throughout a meal.

Extra dry: Actually, this type of champagne has as much as 2 percent additional sugar and is noticeably sweeter than brut.

Sec: Although this is the French word for dry, the wine contains as much as 6 percent additional sugar and is definitely sweet.

Demi sec and Doux: Both are exceptionally sweet. No leading champagne producer would waste good wine on these. They are always made of champagne too poor in quality to stand by itself.

The regular champagne bottle holds four-fifths of a quart and will give you about six to eight glasses of wine, but few people are satisfied with only one glassful. Order generously for a party. It is better to serve a good still wine and have enough than to be skimpy with champagne and run out. Other bottle sizes in champagne are:

Magnum—equals two bottles

Jeroboam—equals four bottles

Rehoboam—equals six bottles

Methuselah—equals eight bottles

Salmanasar—equals twelve bottles

Balthazar—equals sixteen bottles

Nebuchadnezzar—equals twenty bottles

Some of these larger sizes are sensible buys for big parties, and they certainly look dramatic. Champagne also comes in half bottles and splits. Wine bottled in such small amounts does not keep well and is more expensive in the long run. Splits and half bottles do, however, make excellent gifts for friends in the hospital.

Champagne adapts to any occasion. It is right for the formal dinner party and for the informal cold buffet supper; it's the best choice for Sunday brunch and for midnight supper; it's the perfect touch at a picnic. It goes with all foods, from appetizers to desserts, from hearty roast beef to delicate shellfish. It has a particular affinity for caviar, oysters, and foie gras, and it enhances ham, chicken, and summer fruits. Sauerkraut, simmered for hours in bubbling champagne, becomes a classic dish.

Champagne should be served at 45° to 50°. If it is too warm, it will be flat; if too cold, it loses flavor. Chill it in a wine bucket or cooler filled with ice and water, or for several hours in the refrigerator. If you chill more than you use, leave it in the refrigerator, and it will keep for weeks. Returning it to room temperature and then rechilling it robs it of some of its flavor.

Contrary to popular custom, the cork should not explode from the bottle. Uncork it carefully to avoid losing any of the precious liquid. Loosen the wires, slant the bottle slightly away from you, and gently twist and ease out the cork. If the champagne bubbles up out of the bottle, it may mean you have not chilled it thoroughly or you have jiggled it too much. Wrapping the champagne bottle in a napkin is an affectation, which, incidentally, conceals the label.

The best glass for champagne is the tulip-shaped wineglass. This shape allows the bouquet to accumulate, which the old-fashioned flared champagne glass does not do. (The hollow-stemmed version—not too sanitary and not too efficient—has mercifully all but disappeared.) If you haven't all-purpose wineglasses, any similar tulip or balloon glass will do. Actually, champagne is superb drunk from any container. I have enjoyed it from a paper cup. Do not put ice in the glass. This is heresy. And above all, avoid the swizzle stick. Swirling the wine only dissipates the bubbles, the product of years of hard work and the very thing you paid for.

Finally, sip it slowly and savor every drop.

[1956]

ℳint Julep

The season of the Kentucky Derby and the spring greening of the countryside always brings forth memories of mint julep. (By the way, a treatise on whiskey I read years ago stated there was no plural for the word *julep.* You did not make "four mint juleps," you made "julep for four," and you didn't drink "three juleps," you drank "julep thrice." This neglected bit of usage needs more investigation.)

My old and wonderful friend Mary Hamblet, who is almost my contemporary and whom I have known for well over seventy years, has always been a remarkable julep maker. Her version is powerful, pungent, pleasant to nose and palate, and disastrous if more than three are consumed. When we were younger and perhaps braver, we would very often gather of a Sunday afternoon and have a julep festival. Occasionally, we included our mothers, whom we knew would provide entertainment, because after two juleps (with added sugar for them), they became red cheeked, reminiscent, and extremely amusing. What else should a julep do if not exhilarate and refresh?

Mary's theory has always been that you use—and sometimes they're hard to find—14-ounce glasses, and failing those, you use 12-ounce. I agree with her, except that it's even better if they have handles. The next thing is ice. It must be very, very fine. In the days before processors and electric ice crushers, we filled a canvas bag with ice, placed it on the floor, and beat it with a mallet until the ice was finer than fine, almost powdery. Next in importance is good fresh mint, and if you like your mint crushed, as we do, you will place 6 or 7 leaves in the bottom of the glass with 1 to 2 teaspoons of sugar and crush sugar and mint together. A long barspoon is good for that. Spread the mixture around the glass so that it trickles down and perfumes the inner surface. Then add 2 jiggers, and I mean 2 jiggers, of the best bourbon. Fill the glass with crushed ice, insert a barspoon, and, without touching the sides, stir madly until you begin to get a frost on the glass and the drink has as much coolth as you want. If there's room, you can add a little more ice and more bourbon. Finally, and this is very important, take a generous sprig of mint, dip it lightly in powdered sugar, and place it in the glass—so that the olfactory senses are stimulated before the julep touches your lips.

For an even chillier drink, place the glasses on a tray in the refrigerator—again, without touching the sides—for about ten minutes, by which time they will have frosted beautifully. The first sip will be pungent and blissful. Sip slowly, and if you feel up to it, try a second. If you are still steady on your feet, you might possibly try a third, but I don't advise going beyond that.

Now, mind you, this is Mary Hamblet's and my version of a mint julep, so if you have your favorite recipe, don't bother to write and say, "You're wrong. Mint juleps should be made thus and so . . ." We don't care. We like it our way. If we do not conform to the tradition of the first mint julep made in Kentucky or Virginia, that's quite all right.

The other day I received a message from a Scotch whiskey firm that rather shocked me at first and then made me say, Well, why not? They were proposing a version of mint julep that, of course, used Scotch. I have a great love of Scotch. As a matter of fact, it's my tipple, but I had never considered it as julep fuel before. The Scotch julep was different from the classic one in another respect in that it used a small amount of the liqueur made from Scotch—Drambuie—instead of sugar. I tried this, using the same method I would use for a bourbon julep, stirring 3/4 ounce of Drambuie into the crushed mint leaves, dribbling the mixture along the sides of the glass, then filling the glass with fine ice and 1½ ounces of good Scotch. After stirring, I placed it in the refrigerator for 10 minutes or so, and it developed a beautiful frost. I plunged a sprig of mint into it and tasted. The first sip was extraordinarily interesting, not nearly as sweet as some julep drinks, and as I continued to taste and consider, I decided the results were really quite pleasing, and there was no reason why a julep had to be made with bourbon alone. A bourbon julep might be good for one occasion, and a Scotch julep for another. I could have my pick of two whiskeys for my spring and summer pleasures.

[1983?]

New Year Remedies

One doesn't read as much about the New Year's drinking as one used to, perhaps because people have become saner in their consumption of alcohol. It used to be that the restorative was as necessary as the imbibing the night before. Having known some pretty heavy imbibers in my long and varied career, I've always been amazed at the varying customs for keeping the pains of what I prefer calling a holdover—as opposed to a hangover—at bay.

One year, in my theatrical days, I traveled with one of the greatest actresses I have ever known. She should have been very famous, and would have been but for her slavery to alcohol. She was a champion at holdover remedies. I remember her rushing into a restaurant or hotel dining room and ordering a large soup plate of canned tomatoes, cold. This made her feel she was back in the land of the living. She took great comfort in the soothing quality of the tomato and the bright briskness of the acidity. This was before the days of various and sundry tomato drinks for the same purpose. I am sure that if she had added a dash of vodka, the remedy would have been even better.

The original Bloody Mary, which was made with gin and shaken in a cocktail shaker, had a wondrous restorative effect on those who overindulged the night before. It was not as long and as hearty a drink as it is now, but brief, ginny, spicy, and toma-toey. It did seem to revive one's spirits and suddenly make the sun break through the clouds that encircled a heavy head. It was made with about two ounces of tomato juice, the same of gin, the juice of half a lemon, and a dash of Tabasco or Worcestershire sauce, shaken vigorously with ice, then poured into a chilled glass. A good brisk drink it was, and if you didn't go on and have a couple more, it did restore you.

Shepherd's Hotel in Cairo was famous for its restorative drink, known far and wide as a Suffering Bastard. It was only equaled by an American slug called the Prairie Oyster. So popular was this drink that two versions existed, both authentic. One was more western than the other; the eastern version was more, shall we say, refined. The western contained as its basic ingredient a raw egg. This was administered to the victim with a jigger of brandy, a healthy dash of Worcestershire sauce, and salt, if desired. The egg was very carefully broken into a 6-ounce glass, then the Worcestershire sauce and brandy were added. They were lightly blended with the egg white; the yolk was kept whole and untouched. This recipe was in Patrick Gavin Duffy's great *Standard Bartender's Guide*. It was followed by the rather grim instruction: "Take!"

The other Prairie Oyster was nonalcoholic but had its power. It was made with 1 egg yolk, carefully slipped into a small glass, with 2 dashes of vinegar, 1 teaspoon of Worcestershire sauce, 1 large dash of Tabasco, and a pinch of salt. Again, the trick was to not break the yolk before swallowing.

I remember a German friend, a brilliant boulevardier, whose thirst knew no bounds. He indulged it to the hilt and had his own method for restoring the status quo. No drink for him but an enormous helping of freshly mixed steak tartare, made with a raw egg, onion, mustard, Tabasco, and Worcestershire, all blended together and served with toast. This really delicious restorative did wonders for his constitution and is one of the most sophisticated remedies I know of, though not everyone can face raw meat for breakfast.

I have also known those who would reach for, and heavily indulge in, good cold beer. It would make me feel infinitely worse, but it is nevertheless an extremely popular remedy, frequently known as "the hair of the dog that bit you." Another, more friendly draft is milk punch, which can be made with cognac, Scotch, or bourbon. It's a wonderful potion to offer New Year's Day guests, and even though you are not deep in the throes of a holdover, it makes a refreshing start for the new year. I make it as follows:

I have both the milk and glasses very well chilled. I pour in about two jiggers of milk and add a touch of sugar, a dash of nutmeg, and as much bourbon, brandy, or Scotch as the palate dictates. Stir and imbibe slowly.

This drink is exciting, it's deliciously restorative, and it's a nice alcoholic baptism for the year to come. Of course, let us not forget champagne. It's just the thing to have on hand for your holiday visitors. It dispels any lingering holdovers, and nothing could be more festive. Offer some chicken sandwiches and cucumber sandwiches with it, and have a happy New Year.

[1982]

5

*A*nother of the roles Beard played was that of restaurant reviewer. He wrote about restaurants throughout his career but functioned as a regular critic just twice—for *Gourmet*, in 1949 and 1950, and for *Town & Country*, in 1966 and 1967. Unlike other critics, Beard could never enter a restaurant incognito, hiding behind dark glasses or under a broad-brimmed hat. He was eminently visible. The welcome carpet was rolled out, the check torn up—which sometimes meant he couldn't be as unkind as he needed to be.

In the beginning of his stint for *Town & Country*, I collaborated with him on a monthly roundup of New York restaurants. He soon found that boring, bowed out, and turned the job over to me, while he went on to write far-ranging pieces that covered restaurant eating on the West Coast and in Europe as well as in New York. Three of them are reprinted here. They are no longer useful as guides, to be sure—some restaurants have folded, some may be better or worse than in Beard's day—but the pieces are worth preserving for his general observations on Irish food, the drama of Michelin ratings, and the vanished glories of hotel dining.

The two brief columns on shipboard and train meals are also, to some extent, about vanished glories, while "Send It Back" tells the timid American consumer how to cope with restaurant trauma. It includes Beard's account of a nasty episode in Carpentras, in the South of France, over a bad bottle of wine. I was there and can testify to the nastiness of the wine and the encounter. Even Beard's bellowing baritone, which was awesome, could not convince the patronne that her wine was over the hill. Anonymity has its disadvantages. In Carpentras, James Beard was just another customer.

*H*otel Dining in the Grand Manner

Time was when the hotels in this country, and especially the luxury hotels, were gastronomic centers, attracting every traveler who cherished good food. The same was true in Europe. Escoffier himself spent many of his active years in hotels, and the culinary traditions of the Savoy, the Ritz, and the Carlton in London were all founded on his genius. From those kitchens came Pêche Melba, Poire Mary Garden, Soufflé Sarah Bernhardt, and many other dishes named for the renowned of the era. One of Escoffier's most celebrated patrons was the Prince of Wales, later Edward VII.

The famous Hôtel de Paris, in Monte Carlo, had none other than Prosper Montagné as chef for several years at the turn of the century. Indeed, it was there this incredibly gifted man collaborated with Prosper Salles to create the first volume of *La Grande Livre de la Cuisine*—the 1929 edition possibly being the greatest achievement in the literature of cookery.

The Ritz in Paris, the Danieli in Venice, Raffles in Singapore, and the Peninsula in Hong Kong were also known for exquisite food and fine wines, and in New York there were Holland House and the old Waldorf, to say nothing of the superb food at the Lafayette and the Brevoort. The first luxury hotel I ever knew was the Palace, in San Francisco, which used to be a paradise for food. As late as the thirties, it was still excellent, and even in the early fifties there were traces of Chef Lucien's reign.

Alas, much of the glory of hotel dining seems to have gone forever. But fortunately, a number of hotels that serve food in the grand old manner have survived. A few have lost none of their original quality, and others, though a bit tarnished, are notable by today's standards.

Of all the hotels in Europe, probably the Ritz in Paris has best maintained the quality of its food and service. Both the restaurant and L'Espadon (the innovation of Charles Ritz when the old Grill had had its day) do a remarkable job of following in the footsteps of César and Marie Louise Ritz. One finds the same smooth service and the same knowledgeable staff—with some retirements and new faces, of course; and the menu in the restaurant perpetuates favorite dishes dating from the time when the dining room was established. If L'Espadon was a break with the history of the Ritz, it has brought new interest to the hotel's cuisine by offering excellent fish and seafood in season as well as some of the dishes for which the old Grill was famous. One still finds the delicious *pieds de mouton* and the soufflé surprise, with poached eggs tucked into the *appareil.* It is possible to dine sumptuously at L'Espadon or with relative simplicity.

If there are fine vegetables available in the market, they are sure to turn up at the Ritz, properly prepared and served. The cheese is specially chosen by one of the captains every morning on his way to work. Thus the board presents only the best of cheeses in their absolute prime. The wine list, too, is excellent in its scope. International epicures are eminently well served here. Yet each is served as though his taste were supreme. Let us hope the Ritz continues for our lifetime.

Another Paris hotel that serves some of the best food in town is Le Berkeley.[1] It is small but luxurious, with the rooms nicely planned and well appointed, and the service is delightful. The clientele is about as impressive as that of the Ritz, and the regulars are ardently faithful. The *écrevisse à la nage, ballotine* of

---

[1] Le Berkeley's hotel rooms have been converted into apartments, and its restaurant is now a modest brasserie.

duckling, *jambon à la crème*, and certainly the strawberry soufflé are all top attractions.

One of the most famous dishes in Paris is the soufflé of lobster at the Plaza-Athénée. This was a creation of Lucien Diat, brother of Louis Diat, former chef of the Ritz in New York. When I was gathering recipes for my book *Paris Cuisine*, I had the privilege of observing M. Diat prepare this famous dish as well as his wonderful *crêpes Montagné*. Although he has long since been gone from the hotel, his imprint has lingered, and I find the food exceptionally good.

The Relais Plaza also pleases me for late supper or dinner or for a light lunch. The ambience is enjoyable, and one never lacks a pageant of interesting people.

London's posh hotels have kept up the Edwardian custom of fine food more consistently than those of any other city. Unhappily, the Carlton is only a memory—and the Victoria and the Metropole—but the Savoy lives on and is still one of the great restaurants to be found anywhere in the world. The grill is continually satisfying, giving one the feeling of dining in another era. The service is attentive, and you have the impression that the freshest salmon or the best sole or the newest potatoes have been kept just for you, as though the management knew all the while you'd turn up and request those particular delights. The passing parade here, too, adds to the excitement for anyone seeking London's pleasures.

The Connaught is laden with traditions similar to those of the Savoy. The food is excellent, and the hotel itself is no less luxurious, although more intimate. One has the illusion of staying in a huge town house with perfect service.

Claridge's has maintained quite another tradition—one of elegance and mysterious glamour, which has been enhanced through the years by the presence of Oriental potentates traveling with entourages of fabled proportions, who have been known to occupy whole floors, complete with private kitchens and staff. The dining room in Claridge's has always offered a heavy-damask, heavy-silver style seldom equaled in hotel experience. In fact, the grand manner may frighten those who are not able to recall the splendors of prewar living. The food is soigné and quite impeccable.

If you are unacquainted with the Ritz in London, go to have a breath of its fast-fading past while the handsome dining room is still there. The gastronomic attractions have long since gone, but it is pleasant to go for tea and imagine what it once was and perhaps catch sight of the old-timers who pass through every so often.

There are many who will dispute me, but I am convinced that the only city left in Italy where the grand old traditions are intact is Venice. First among its hotels and surely the ultimate in grand luxe is the Gritti Palace, which has kept its traditions, superb service, and a high standard of food. It is a joy just to sit at one's table on the terrace, watching the traffic float by and inhaling the mixture of Venetian smells and the culinary perfumes of one's food.

The Danieli Hotel is also luxurious and beautiful, and the view from its roof is as magnificent as any in Venice. The food is extremely good, and one might think it was perfection if one didn't already know the Gritti. The elusive factor known as personality or charm can be overpowering where it exists to any degree. The Gritti has it, and while I salute both hotels, the one has a stronger hold on my heart and palate.

Fine food traditions still obtain at the Hôtel de Paris in Monte Carlo, and the dining room atop the hotel is spectacularly situated, overlooking the storybook harbor and countryside. One dines exceedingly well while taking in the view. Some of the famous old dishes of the Montagné-Salles era crop up on the menu, and there are other great specialties of haute cuisine along with the fruits of the sea. On a gala night, it can be a stunning experience to dine here.

One can name many other luxury hotels, but most of them are luxurious in everything but food. Those palaces I have singled out are to be treasured by the world traveler. They are the last stand of culinary grandeur.

[1966]

*E*ating and Drinking in Ireland

One searches in vain in Ireland for the dishes that might constitute a national cuisine, but, save for the famous stew, the fine ham and bacon, and one or two native dishes like colcannon and boxty, there are few things that can be called Irish. In fact, if the cuisine can be characterized at all, it is French with local modifications. There are, however, wonderful raw materials, especially from the sea, that should have been the inspiration for a creative cuisine—the Dublin Bay prawns, similar to langoustines and scampi; the salmon; and the Galway Bay oysters. And I must concede that the bread of Ireland would tempt the most rigid dieter. After the first day of my visit, I found that I could be more than content to make a meal of bread—whole meal, soda, or any of the many other types—good Irish butter, and the excellent smoked salmon or prawns. I cannot recall a country where bread is so universally delicious and in such variety.

Whatever its national origins, the food can be quite good in the restaurants of Ireland. I think the spot that pleased me most was not a converted castle or an elegant dining room but a simple pub with enormous personality. There are more pubs per square mile in Ireland than anywhere I have been. Some are fascinating, some are merely good, and many are without merit. A few, like Paddy Burke's [Oyster Tavern], are worth the trip to Ireland. It is located on the Galway-to-Limerick road in a village called Clarinbridge. Don't expect luxury, and don't bother with the formality of a reservation. Just drop by. You'll soon fall under the spell of Paddy and the air of good fellowship that permeates the premises. Villagers, visitors, and perhaps a celebrity or two mingle here happily. There is an appreciative representation from New York, and from time to time Burl Ives, Burgess Meredith, and John Huston turn up.

In September, the Mayor of Galway eats the first oyster of the season on the pier of Clarinbridge, and this is the signal for a splendid bash at Paddy Burke's, with the heartiest patrons trying to outdo each other in the consumption of oysters and libations. On the last day of April this year, we ate not the first but the final oysters of the season, along with good brown bread and Guinness, and had several portions of smoked salmon as well.

Nearby is Dromoland Castle. This beautiful structure, like many another castle, has been turned into a handsome hotel. The interiors are grand luxe indeed, and the service is well managed and elegant. The food, however, is as disappointing as any I have ever had in a place of this caliber. Even breakfast, which is hard to ruin, was largely inedible. However, you might still wish to visit it for the pleasure of the accommodations and the views.

I usually avoid entertainments trumped up for the tourist trade and particularly those held in old castles, but I did get to the medieval dinner at Bunratty Castle and must recommend it. The castle itself is delightful, and it is now acquiring a small medieval village, in the process of being constructed around it.

Dinner is served nightly at the castle till June and then twice nightly during the summer. The management has engaged a group of singers and actors as part of the basic personnel, and they present a first-rate show. The food is prepared by caterers at Shannon Airport and is admirably done. Ancient tradition is observed in the table settings. There are wooden plates and mugs, rather pretty ones at that, but no knives or forks. Guests are offered mead to begin with, but a small amount of protest can bring forth more contemporary drinks. We were first served a delicious soup made with a venison base and filled with good vegetables. Then came spareribs cooked with wine and herbs, which, I was told to my amazement, was actually an authentic fifteenth-century Irish dish.

So perhaps the Irish and not the Chinese introduced spareribs to America. This, by the way, was perfect food to be eaten without benefit of utensils. Next on the menu was capon and vegetables, followed by a version of fifteenth-century salad with many carrots in it. A rather creamy dessert rounded out the meal. Songs, stunts, and general gaiety made this a truly diverting experience.

Just outside Dublin is one of the most unusual restaurants with entertainment I have encountered—the Abbey Tavern Howth. It is well worth the trek, but go when you have all the time in the world and are relaxed enough to forget about the ordinary rules of service. The place is run with a casualness that is difficult to explain. Experienced friends had warned that the waits were long, but one had no idea how long. A reservation is obligatory, but when you arrive you are likely to be sent to hear the folksingers while your table is being readied. The entertainment takes place in a strange barnlike structure at the back of the restaurant, where there are tables, chairs, and benches. You find a place among the crowd and listen, servicing your own table with drinks from the bar. The music is quaint and genuinely old.

On the occasion of our visit, two hours elapsed before our party was finally seated at dinner, but the food warranted the lengthy wait. The Abbey Tavern does exceptional dishes with prawns—the curried version was particularly good—and I can vouch for the excellence of the broiled lobster and the *coquille* of scallops. In fact, this restaurant does greater justice to the native seafood than any other place I visited in Dublin or the surrounding countryside. However, if you eat cold fish at the Tavern, you would be well advised to carry along your own little pot of mayonnaise. Otherwise, you will find yourself eating a salad cream so sweet that it will ruin the flavor of the fish.

I had heard much about a small restaurant in Dublin called the Soup Bowl, near the Shelbourne and Royal Hibernian Hotels, and although I could not believe that a restaurant of that name would be anything but a beanery, I proved to be wrong. Reservations are necessary, and that is not the end of it, for you must also ring the front doorbell to gain admittance to this rather pleasant house—something of a throwback to speakeasy days. There are about ten tables on the first floor and a small lounge on the parlor floor. The décor is that of a comfortable home, the table appointments are exceptionally nice, and the service is efficient and friendly. The warmth of hospitality hovers over all.

The menu is not expensive, and there is variety. Our party had good smoked Irish salmon, smoked eel, potted shrimp, and a *coquille* as appetizers. The *coquille* showed care in preparation and arrived piping hot, a thing never to be taken for granted. We then had, among us, superb kidneys in Madeira sauce, a fillet with marrow, a version of *marchands de vins*, and a beautiful sirloin steak served with a first-rate béarnaise sauce. New potatoes accompanied these dishes, and we also had a salad, for which cruets of good olive oil and wine vinegar were supplied—a scoring point with me, for I find that the usual captain or waiter has far too heavy a hand with the vinegar. All things considered, the Soup Bowl is high on the list of Dublin restaurants, operating in simple, honest fashion with a rare degree of personal attention. After dinner, you can relax over coffee and cognac as you would at your private club.

The hotels of Dublin specialize in French food with strong Irish overtones. Their menus resemble each other, and the service is generally adequate. One finds delicious specialties from time to time, such as the chicken pie offered for luncheon at the Russell. Evidently the chef prepares a plat du jour and puts his best effort into that one dish. If this is true of all Irish hotel dining rooms, it is something to remember. We also had a cold supper in our rooms at the Russell one night, and seldom have we eaten such wonderful cold chicken and ham or such good bread and butter. Hotel dining rooms are considered smart in Ireland. By and large, though, the Irish-French spots are undistinguished, and while the food is not bad, it is likely to be overseasoned and overelaborate, which is bad enough.

The most famous of Dublin restaurants is Jammet. The nineteenth-century décor here is superb, the ambience is one rarely experienced, and if you enjoy people-watching, the clientele is worth the visit. The food is good and well presented, but as you eat your way through a palatable meal you wonder the while what greater glories must have emanated from the kitchen in the past. If Jammet is something of a museum piece, it is still the finest restaurant in Ireland. It prepares local fish and shellfish extremely well, and the old-time captains do certain dishes at table-side with great aplomb. The wine list is excellent. This is a must on your trip to Ireland.[1]

---

[1]Both Jammet and the Soup Bowl have disappeared from Dublin's restaurant scene.

I was greatly disappointed in the Dublin pubs, for I had been led to believe that any one of them you might stumble onto would be teeming with atmosphere and interesting people. Those I explored had little to offer. I shall be promptly disputed, but I believe we have recreated a more attractive and more stimulating collection of pubs in New York and other American cities than now exists in Ireland and England. In the days of Yeats, Joyce, and, more recently, Behan, there may have been an exciting pub life, but today it is no more intriguing than life in our local bars. Some of the brighter ones for décor and character might include Davy Byrne's, Bartley Dunne's, the Bailey, the Brazen Head, and Neary's. Many of the better-known pubs serve food at lunchtime, but a sampling of these turned up only mediocre fare. Of course, if you are a devotee of Irish whiskey, Guinness, and Irish coffee, you'll love drinking in Ireland. The famous coffee varies in quality from pub to pub, but at its best it can be ambrosial.

[1966]

Falling and Rising Stars of Gastronomy

The *Guide Michelin,* despite its occasional lapses, has always been as reliable a guide to eating in France as one could possibly find. However, after a recent gastronomic tour of starred restaurants with two knowledgeable companions, I came away more or less disillusioned with the Michelin firmament. Once a restaurant moves from one star to two, it becomes apprehensive and, for the most part, rests on its specialties, and once a restaurant achieves three stars, it need never change its menu as long as the quality is maintained for the Michelin scout. Thus, year in and year out, the majority of starred restaurants produce the same dishes. Their specialties are listed in the guides, and travelers expect to find them, unless they happen to be seasonal items. Hanging on to one's stars appears to take precedence over the creative impulse and high standards that originally inspired the award. Alas, we encountered two three-star restaurants that proved inferior to many of the one-star places, and several two-star restaurants turned out to be temples of gluttony rather than of gastronomy.

Our tour covered Normandy, a bit of Brittany, the Sarthe, Cognac, Bordeaux, Les Landes, the Basque country, Gascony, and Provence, ending on the Riviera. We consulted three different guides, two of the standard ones—*Michelin* and *Kleber-Colombes*—and Henri Gault's, whenever we were in a district he had covered. We are certain that changes in France since the war have affected its food traditions, but we were not prepared for such differences of expert opinion as those displayed in the three guides, sometimes as totally contradictory as the music or drama critics of the leading New York papers. And so we add our own voice of dissension. We already had notes from previous trips, and among us we were able to sample a large number of dishes. I shall recount some of the high and some of the low spots.

You would probably never have cause to go to the Beauséjour at Lery unless you were driving back and forth to Normandy or perhaps Le Havre. It is off the main road, with nothing unusual about its situation, and carries only two stars. The restaurant is attractive, but the patron is very shy, and therefore the welcome is likely to seem cold. We sampled the two-star specialties. As first courses, *tarte aux moules* was far from good, and the Alsatian onion tart was merely interesting, but the fresh asparagus was superb, as well as the accompanying mayonnaise. The two choices of entrées removed any doubts we may have had about the quality of the restaurant. A *civet* of langouste *à la crème* was the finest lobster dish of the entire trip, and the andouillette (the regional sausage made from tripe and other entrails) was as good a one as I have tasted. Salad proved to be the usual French *salade*, with a little too much vinegar for most American palates. If you are interested in eating what is likely the best langouste dish in the provinces, visit Beauséjour. It earns its two stars solely on this, but it should bring more of its dishes up to the same standard.

Henri Gault, whose books are fast becoming authoritative in France, has a most amusing one describing gastronomic and scenic journeys through various sections of France. It is called *A Voir et à Manger.* In it, Gault recommended a small brasserie in Trouville that is not mentioned in other guidebooks and was not particularly recommended by the concierge of our hotel in Deauville. But if you trek to the Quai de la Souque in Trouville, you will find the Brasserie des Vapeurs and a second unheralded place, both sans stars and both happy experiences. The Brasserie is friendly, rather haphazard, and, in Deauville's *haute saison*, a popular spot at night. Order the *moules à la marinière*, which are the best in the region. (The secret is in the amount of chopped onion and butter that goes into them.) The copious order for one seemed almost more than enough for the three of us, but we finished every mussel and returned for more. The shrimp, served hot with white wine and butter, were also delicious, and so was the grilled sole. The seafood, generally, is excellent, the *choucroute* passable, and the tripe very good indeed, but if they offer you the cassoulet, don't buy— it's canned. Other attractions are the Muscadet, the beer, and the bread.

Still farther down the quai, almost directly across from the fish market, is La Régence, where seafood is wonderfully prepared. The *moules* are good, but not to be compared with those at the Vapeurs, and there is an excellent *friture* of all the tiny fish of the sea, including baby skate and sole. Lobster *à la nage* is also good here, and especially good is the sole *à l'estragon,* an unusually pleasant combination of flavors. The ambience of La Régence is enchanting, and the waiters are more than attentive and knowledgeable. This is an entertaining place to escape to if you are in Deauville and want a breather from all the elegance, although you'll see a few ropes of pearls and evening clothes—no doubt escaping, too.

Although Alençon is noted for a two-star restaurant, it is still, as far as I'm concerned, notable only for lace-making. Petit Vatel, which must have caught the Michelin man on an off day, does little to honor the name of the great chef. The menus are prix fixe, and the more expensive the menu, the richer the fare. The large array of courses would be of interest only to the goutiest individuals. We chose three different menus, and each was equally poor in balance. I began with what promised to be a simple dish—poached eggs with spinach and cheese—which came prepared with both a rich Mornay sauce and a topping of cheese. The spinach was just there for color, I suspect. For the fish course we chose langouste, trout, and *St.-Pierre meunière.* The langouste had been grilled with enough butter to keep a Normandy farmer in money for six months; the trout, which had been stuffed, was buried beneath the same sauce that covered my eggs; and the "sautéed" St.-Pierre was crumbed, fried, and offered with a *sauce rémoulade.* Again, searching for simplicity, two of us ordered the *carré d'agneau,* a house specialty, but the lamb came thickly blanketed with a purée of fresh tomatoes cooked with butter, which overwhelmed the delicacy of the meat and did not particularly blend with the brown sauce served in addition. The other choice of entrée was chicken roulade, which was served with a red wine and herb sauce thickened with blood. So rich was it, after the preceding courses, that it could barely be tasted. There was more to come—a cheese course and then a wagon of eight different flavors of ices and ice creams, all of which you were supposed to take with a sauce. The ices happened to be excellent, but what did it matter at that point? With dessert, we were served dinner-plate-sized *tuiles*, which were worth the price of admission. Otherwise, we had spent thirty-five or thirty-eight francs for thousands of calories we didn't need. *Vulgar* is the only word for such menus nowadays, and surely there should be à la carte service in these havens of Edwardian gustation. Le Petit Vatel, by the way, has an excellent wine list and particularly good Bordeaux. If you go for a long, leisurely dinner and then take a good walk afterward, it might seem more attractive than it did on the occasion of our luncheon. By no means, though, does it deserve two Michelin stars.

If you pass through Nantes, you will find two extremely good one-star restaurants, both of them in leading hotels. The Central Hôtel et Rôtisserie Crémaillière serves as magnificent an array of *fruits de mer* as you'll come across in many a mile. This dish seems to be standard from Nantes to Bordeaux and includes langoustines, *palourdes* (the small French clams), periwinkles, crab, shrimp (both the tiny rose and the gray), and sometimes oysters. It is usually presented with great style. In Nantes, you are in the beurre blanc region, home of that devastating sauce made with butter, shallots, and a touch of white wine or vinegar. When salmon, *brochet* (pike), turbot, and other fish come to you with beurre blanc, your resistance collapses. Here you rather leave off drinking Muscadet and begin with Gros Plant, which is a glorified Muscadet and very palatable when young, as is Muscadet. The Central Hôtel et Rôtisserie Crémaillière deserves more than its single star.

Across the river and down the Loire about eight kilometers from Nantes is a charming small restaurant, Mon Rêve, another candidate for a push from one star to two. We ate rillettes, those delicious bits made by cooking down pork and fat and then potting them, especially satisfying with a bottle of Muscadet. We followed this with frog's legs, tiny ones, cooked beautifully with garlic, butter, and a touch of oil, and a delicate *brochet* with beurre blanc. The strawberries for dessert were picked from the garden ten minutes before.

The next good food we encountered was at Darroze in Villeneuve-de-Marsan. The menu is prix fixe, and the fine wine list is prepared by Raymonde Bazin-Soulé, who is associated with the wine expert Frank Schoonmaker. The meal we had at Darroze included a perfect salmon trout braised in champagne; a salmi of woodcock, rich and delicious, though it could easily have been omitted; *foie d'oie aux raisins*, done with great care and presented beautifully; braised baby lamb with mushrooms and tiny browned new potatoes, *petit pois*, and *haricots verts*; and a salad, followed by cheese and again the king-sized *tuiles*, which I found this year in a number of restaurants. In addition to a blanc de blancs before lunch, we drank a bottle of Meursault Matrot 1962 and a Cos d'Estournel 1947, which gave the meal an air of grandeur. Darroze deserves every encomium.

Between Avignon and Marseilles, there are two three-star restaurants, a couple of two-stars, and several one-stars. One of the two-star restaurants far surpasses both of the three-star restaurants. I consider Lucullus in Avignon, or what is now called Hiély-Lucullus, one of the great restaurants in France. The food has a rare quality of freshness, and the sauces, though there are not many, are perfection. M. Hiély combines classic and regional dishes on his menu, and among them I can especially recommend his gratin of spinach and mussels or clams.

Lamb and beef are done superbly, too, and I recently enjoyed a souris of lamb *à la gardien,* prepared in the style of Provence with herbs, tomatoes, olives, and peppers. The desserts at Lucullus are limited but excellent.

When I first visited Auberge de Noves, just across the river from Hiély-Lucullus, I couldn't believe that Michelin had bestowed three stars on it. Each year I expect to see at least one of them taken away, but somehow Auberge de Noves remains in favor. Close by, in Les Baux, is another three-star restaurant, L'Oustau de la Baumanière. The proprietor, M. Thuilier, has served great food on occasion and good food nearly always, and some of his dishes are justly famous. The service is pleasant and thoughtful. This year, however, at a Sunday lunch, we asked for the sommelier five times in order to take advantage of the superb wine list but were graced by his visit only in time for dessert.

One of my favorite restaurants anywhere is L'Escale, in Carry-le-Rouet, on the coast beyond Marseilles or Martigues, or an easy drive for lunch from Avignon, Arles, Nîmes, or Les Baux. L'Escale is perched above the sea and provides a view that is a joy as far as eye can reach. It is run by M. Bérot, who was the chef on the *Normandie* and is one of the few greats of gastronomy remaining. His bourride, bouillabaisse, and turbot *au champagne* are all worth a visit. Now here is truly great food, along with a view, yet for as long as I can remember, L'Escale has gone along with one star. Who knows but that the lack of stars keeps it great.[1]

[1966]

---

[1]Beauséjour and Central Hôtel et Rôtisserie Crémaillière are no longer listed in the Michelin guide. Petit Vatel and Mon Rêve (now Villa Mon Rêve) have lost their stars. Darroze (now Hélène Darroze), Hiély-Lucullus, and Auberge de Noves currently each have one star; Baumanière and L'Escale have two.

*E*ating My Way Across the Atlantic

A couple of months ago I crossed the Atlantic on the *France*, which Craig Claiborne once called "the greatest restaurant in the world." Well, while it is not really the greatest, it is definitely a miracle of food service when you consider they serve almost two thousand people a day. In first class, where there are about four or five hundred passengers, there is not only a huge daily menu, but by ordering a day or half a day ahead, you can have specialties of your own choosing.

Of course, many passengers never have anything special. There were two people sitting near me who ate practically nothing but smoked salmon, caviar, and steak. They would have smoked salmon and sirloin steak for lunch and smoked salmon, caviar, and a chateaubriand or double filet steak for dinner. And very often, they drank cola with it. They were rather the exception. Most people who sail on the *France* do so because they like to combine the excitement of an ocean voyage with the enjoyment of good food and wine.

The wine list on the *France* is something very special. Considering what one pays in U.S. restaurants for wines right now, it is gratifying to be able to drink good wines, even great wines, at a reasonable price. I discovered a perfectly delicious still champagne, which we don't get in this country because of certain French laws. It was clear and briskly dry, with a very faint bubble. It cost less than five dollars. I also drank a great Château Pétrus 1962, which was about half the price I'd have paid in New York.

I ate extremely well, too. A wonderful choice of fresh fish had been put aboard at Le Havre—turbot, salmon, and an extraordinarily flavorful and meaty fish from the English Channel called *mouline*, which I had at lunch one day with the captain. He is very fond of this fish and has it taken aboard for his own and his guests' enjoyment. But of all the fish I ate, I think the turbot I had one night for dinner was the high point of my shipboard dining, for it was poached to perfection and served with a beurre blanc, one of the great sauces of French cuisine.

While it isn't difficult to make, beurre blanc is a sauce that does demand care and patience. The great secret of preparing it is that the butter is *creamed* in the sauce but not allowed to melt. To start with, you will need a heavy 2-quart saucepan, either enameled iron, heavy-duty stainless steel, or heavy copper with a stainless-steel lining. Take some shallots or, if you don't have shallots, rather mild onions, and chop enough to make 2 tablespoons. Put this in the pan with $1/4$ cup of white wine vinegar, $1/4$ cup of dry vermouth or dry white wine, and about $3/4$ teaspoon of salt. I break with tradition and also give it just a dash of Tabasco. Cook this over brisk heat until it is reduced to a glaze. There shouldn't be more than a generous tablespoon or tablespoon and a half left. Have ready 3 sticks (12 ounces) of unsalted butter cut into $1/4$-inch pieces.

Remove the saucepan from the heat, take 2 pieces of the butter, and beat them in with a whisk or a heavy fork. You want them to cream in the liquid, remember, but not to melt. As soon as they are incorporated, add another bit of butter. Keep whisking in bits of butter, and finally set the pan over warm water or over very low heat with a metal or asbestos pad under it. Keep adding and creaming the butter until the sauce is thick, well blended, and has almost the consistency of a hollandaise. Place the sauce in a small bowl and serve immediately. If you have to hold it for a little while, keep it over barely warm water until ready to serve, but be sure it doesn't harden or melt, or you have a disaster. Beurre blanc is superb with any kind of fish, especially poached fish like turbot or striped bass.

With the excellent food and service you get on the *France*, you can work up a remarkable appetite. One night I had *boeuf à la ficelle*, which is beef (either a piece of sirloin or tenderloin), tied, suspended in a bubbling rich broth until beautifully rare, then served with several different sauces—an unusual and extremely good way to cook tender beef. Another time I had a delicious pot-au-feu, and still another day, a perfectly roasted rack of lamb.

One night for dinner, the chef produced one of the most dramatic and decorative desserts I have ever seen—a ring of cream puff paste, from the center of which rose a shaft of frozen chocolate mousse, surmounted by a crown of spun sugar. It was just as good to the taste as it was to the eye.

If you have never known the leisurely pleasures of a cruise or an ocean crossing on the *France*, I hope that someday you will experience the wonders of their kitchen and wine list. This is to me one of the last great luxuries left in the world.[1]

[1974]

Good Meals on Wheels

When I was young, we used to travel by train from Portland to San Francisco and New York. I always looked forward to those trips, especially the transcontinental ones, because of the interesting things we had to eat—big baked potatoes that the Northern Pacific Railroad advertised, luscious apples, and very often game or trout, picked up en route. Dining on a train was a great adventure and, if you were traveling for several

---

[1]The *France* was bought by the Norwegian Cruise Line and renamed the *Norway*, which is still in service.

days, a pleasant break in the routine. Alas, that is no longer so. Railroad dining has taken a nosedive. On the whole, instead of being a gastronomic treat, it is something to be avoided. Your own packed lunch is better than most of the food you get in dining cars or snack cars nowadays.

That hasn't happened in France, thank heavens. Recently, after a relaxing transatlantic cruise on the SS *France*, always a favorite experience for me, I had a day of traveling by train from one end of France to the other. On disembarking, I took the boat train at Le Havre and breakfasted on good strong coffee, rolls, butter, and preserves, along with a fairly decent croissant, though nothing to equal those on the *France*. Then I changed trains in Paris for the famous Mistral, which tears from Paris down to Dijon, Lyons, and through the Rhône Valley to Marseilles and over to Cannes, a trip that lasts eight and a half hours, with the train traveling for part of the time at eighty miles an hour.

By paying a slight supplement, you can have a seat in a car where your meals are brought to you, so you don't have to fight your way through the train to reach the dining car. The meals on the Mistral are of the quality of an extremely good restaurant, far better than any transportation food I've had in the United States for years; and, mind you, the cooking is done in a cramped train kitchen with every disadvantage. The platters are nicely garnished, the plates are hot, and the service is excellent. I had two meals on the train, lunch and dinner, and although I wasn't actually hungry for the second meal, I wanted to sample the menu.

Lunch began with a wedge of delicious Charentais melon, ripe and sweet, followed by a fish course of *colinotte*, a meaty fish we don't have here, sliced about three-quarters of an inch thick and sautéed in butter with shallots and mushrooms. A touch of white wine was added to the pan to give just a vestige of a sauce, and with some lemon, it made very good eating. As my main course, I chose a brochette of chicken, broiled on a wooden skewer with pieces of bacon and served with a fruity curry sauce. The pieces of chicken were nicely charred on the outside and moist inside. With this came lovely yellow saffron rice, laced with raisins, sautéed onion, and crisply sautéed chicken gizzards, hearts, and liver. There was a choice of wines, and the St.-Emilion I picked was very drinkable. We were then offered salad, a tray of varied and interesting cheeses, and a choice of desserts—puff pastry with a fruit filling or a strawberry sorbet.

For dinner, first came a flavorful fish soup with a crisp crouton floating in it, then, in lieu of the fish course, a little oblong tartlet shell holding an egg *mollet* and tiny tips of canned asparagus (ideal for this kind of dish), topped with hollandaise sauce and garnished with parsley.

It occurred to me that eggs *archiduc*, as this dish was called, would be ideal for luncheon or supper. It is light, unusual, and the components can be prepared ahead of time and assembled at the last minute. You could bake your little pastry shells in the morning and, an hour or so before serving, make the hollandaise and cook the eggs. An egg *mollet* is simmered for five to six minutes, then plunged into cold water and peeled while still hot. The yolk will not be as set as for a hard-boiled egg nor as soft as for a soft-boiled one, but in between, runny in the center and rather firm at the edges. The French often encase the eggs in aspic, but for this dish, you should keep the peeled eggs in warm water until you are ready to use them. The hollandaise can also be held over warm water.

After this course on the Mistral, there was a choice of roast lamb, pinky rare, with tiny potatoes and onions, and watercress; or a veal chop with sautéed potatoes and baby zucchini. Then, once more, salad, cheese, and dessert.

What a contrast this was to the miserable overdone hamburger or tired sandwich that is thrust at one on American trains. I was grateful to have my remembrance of past glories in railroad dining revived.

[1974]

$\mathcal{S}$end It Back

As a nation, we are notably more timid than our European cousins in demanding our money's worth, and nowhere is this more apparent than in restaurants. We accept without protest sloppy waiters, overcooked food, dirty wineglasses, and inferior wines. In modest eating places, we probably don't complain, because our expectations are minimal, and it doesn't seem worth the bother. But in pricey restaurants, especially French and Italian ones, customers are frequently intimidated by the personnel. We have all been put to pasture in bitter fields by overbearing maîtres d'hôtel, captains, and waiters. It is time to strike back, not with anger, but with authority. We should take a lesson from Theodore Child, who wrote on gastronomy at the turn of the century.

"The maître d'hôtel," he notes in his remarkable little volume *Delicate Feasting,* "important, fat, fussy and often disdainful in his manner—serves mainly to create confusion. . . . For my own part, and in the restaurants where I'm in the habit of dining, I refuse to hold any communication with the maître d'hôtel until after dinner when I graciously allow a favored one to descend into the cellar in person and select for me, with his own podgy fingers, a creamy Camembert. . . . This concession I make not because I admit for a moment that the maître d'hôtel is an infallible judge of Camembert but merely because after dinner I am more charitably disposed than before dinner."

Remember, *restaurant* is the French word for restorative. Whether it's a simple bistro with a lot of personality or a grand establishment flaunting double damask, polished silver, and flowers, a restaurant should restore your spirits as well as your appetite. Obviously, you will not cheer up if your food is badly prepared. But the idea of sending it back sometimes causes people even greater anxiety than eating it. This should not be so if you know your food and can state specifically what is wrong.

Recently, I ordered calf's liver and bacon in a small, reputable French restaurant in New York City. I asked for the liver to be cut thin and done quite pink and the bacon cooked not too crisp. When the dish arrived, the liver was thin but overdone, and so was the bacon. I said to the waiter, "You got the slicing right but you missed on the cooking. Would you mind bringing me another order?" He looked surprised but smiled, took back the dish, and returned with a replacement—this time, perfect. No self-respecting restaurateur should take exception to your complaint if you are honest, and what's more, if you speak with assurance.

I've had bad moments in famous restaurants, too. I remember a luncheon at Maxim's years ago, under the watchful eye of the owner, M. Vaudable, who was seated nearby. My companion and I sent back a sole Albert. It was overcooked, the sauce was curdled, and it looked unappetizing. The captain had served it anyway because he knew it would be a bother to change, and he thought we wouldn't complain. When we did, he was chagrined. Vaudable later agreed that we were right to refuse the dish. We tipped the waiter accordingly. And that goes to the heart of the matter, for often the absence of a tip will make your point when nothing else will. Captains and waiters earn their livelihoods with tips, and therefore a gesture of this kind is serious business.

You are not always in the position to send food back to the kitchen, particularly if you are someone's guest or a close friend of the restaurateur. Is it better to unsettle your host or your stomach? A terrible decision. I once had to eat nearly raw kidneys rather than distress the director of a famous New York chain of restaurants, who was supervising an important luncheon of mine. A man of volatile temperament, he had already had several dishes redone, and had he known, he might have exterminated the entire kitchen. You've got to use common sense about when to swallow a mistake and when to speak up.

If you should know your food before registering a complaint, you should certainly know your wines. You can't fool a good sommelier. But if you find a bottle that is corky, that has gone "over the hill," or that is disagreeable, don't be afraid to say so. It is unlikely that your taste will be questioned, unless you are in a mediocre restaurant staffed by poorly trained personnel. If the lesser in command do not agree with you, then call the owner. And if he won't give you satisfaction, then refuse to pay for the wine, as I did once in a restaurant in Carpentras, in the South of France. Although I was accompanied by a wine expert and a friend with an excellent palate, both the captain and the owner argued that the wine was good. It was one of the bitterest encounters I have ever had in a restaurant, and all the more shocking because the place had one star in the *Guide Michelin.* Not only did I deliver a speech to the captain and the patronne, but I wrote Michelin a lengthy protest. Perhaps there were other complaints, because the following year the restaurant was missing from the starry ranks.

Often, however, wine is sent back out of ignorance. One day I was lunching with an editor in a restaurant where I had been working as a consultant. The managing director came to our table and said, "This is a bottle someone sent back last night for no reason. Will you both taste it?" We did and I said, "Forget the bottle we ordered. We'll keep this." It was one of the best wines I had ever tasted.

With wine it is not always a question of flavor. A bottle can be served too cold. If so, simply say, "I'm sorry, would you mind resting it for a while to warm up?" Or, if it's too warm, "This wine needs a little more chilling. Give us a drop to taste now, and we'll drink the rest later."

Few things cause as much disturbance in restaurants as the mysterious hierarchy of seating. We all know that some tables are less desirable than others and that restaurateurs like to place their more celebrated clients where they can be seen, saving other prime spots for regular customers. If you are truly uncomfortable, it does not hurt to ask for another table. A good captain will be glad to help you, providing the restaurant is not too crowded. Don't ask if it's simply a matter of prestige. Of course, you can always become a regular customer yourself and ask for your favorite table when you call for a reservation. Never rely on the big tip to get you the table you want. A renowned maître d'hôtel at one of the most beautiful and most sought-out restaurants in New York was told he was not to accept tips from table-seekers. He ignored the warning, and when he was found out, he was dismissed. He has not held an outstanding position as maître d'hôtel since.

Whether we are talking about inefficiency in a restaurant's kitchen or its dining rooms, it all comes down to the same thing. We are fools to put up with it, and the sooner we speak up, the faster things will improve. The rules are simple: be sure you are right, and be firm, but don't be abusive. Even then, be prepared for some nasty skirmishes along the way. It would be nice if we could show our displeasure as my Chinese godfather used to do. He was an aristocrat. He was also a tyrant, and he could afford to be. He loved to eat. If his chef served him a dish that he didn't like, he dropped it on the floor and ordered the kitchen to send him something else. I was told by his son that when they lived in China they often dined on a barge, with a kitchen barge in attendance to supply the food. It was much easier then, because his father simply dropped dishes overboard. He never lost his temper, however. His contempt was sufficient.

Perhaps this technique should be practiced in restaurants I know of today where the quality of food is wretched and the prices are sky high. The sound of breaking crockery could well announce that Americans are at last sending it back.

[1975]

6

*B*eard struggled with excess weight all his life and with poor health in his later years. Every so often, he went on a diet that was halfhearted and didn't work. It was not until 1976, after a pulmonary embolism nearly killed him, that he capitulated to his doctor. This time his dieting (salt-free, low-fat) was on a live-or-die basis and made the news. "Culinary King James Beard Trims the Fat," said a headline in *People Weekly,* while the *New York Times* more graciously wrote, "James Beard Discovers Life Without Butter." He began to preach what he practiced. "I Am on a Diet" was one such proclamation and signaled the party was over. For Beard. For the rest of us, he continued his gastronomic cheerleading, although we began to see more diet pieces like the ones here on iceberg lettuce, margarine, and "The Friendly Egg" (published the week before he died).

Beard was putting the best face on things, but of course he longed for his butter and cream, and of course he cheated. Two years after "I Am on a Diet," we find him in Switzerland gorging on *choucroute* and *malakoff*—a deep-fried mixture of cheese, egg yolks, kirsch, milk, and bread (see "Swiss Culinary Contrasts").

This is easy to forgive when you read, in "Hospital Food," that he endured four hospitalizations in a single year, none notable for improving his digestion. He recalls the rare good treatment he had experienced years earlier in Doctor's Hospital in New York. That was after his heart attack in 1971, when his hospital room had some of the best food in town. Rudolph Stanish, the omelet king, prepared his specialty at Beard's bedside. A friend on the staff of *Gourmet*, who lived around the corner, rushed in freshly made hamburgers. I made the trek north during lunch hour, bringing along, on request, a fat sandwich of Swedish meatballs or pâté from Nyborg and Nelson. A portable icebox, within the patient's reach, was filled with containers of lump crabmeat and splits of champagne. No wonder Beard says that a gift of food is just the thing to cheer a patient.

$\mathcal{I}$ Am on a Diet

To someone who has spent more than seventy years eating as he pleased and where he pleased, Prohibition has come as a shock.

No longer, luscious slabs of sweet butter to eat with crusty homemade bread. No longer, a bounty of olive oil in my salads. No longer, deliciously aged beef and its rich, fatty trimmings. No longer, that favorite dish of smoked sausages and ham with heaps of steaming sauerkraut. The party is over—for a time, anyway.

What is one to do? Go around with a long face? Not at all. I prefer to see it as a new adventure in eating, somewhat less sensual and joyous than my former style but with its own unexpected pleasures. I have been exploring even more than usual. Sometimes I have a planned recipe in mind. More often than not, I improvise. By ignoring convention, I have come up with wonderful new combinations of flavors. No food is too simple to benefit from a little experimentation.

For instance, I have found that a baked potato (on the diet from time to time) can achieve greater stature if cooked longer than is normally recommended. Take a russet or Idaho, scrub it well, and toss it into a 400° oven. Let it rest there for two hours. Impossible, you say? Just try it. The potato develops a thicker and crisper outer coat while it preserves the floury quality of its meat. It also develops an exciting flavor—not that I haven't always loved potato skins. With a few generous grinds of black pepper it becomes a delectable dish and a boon to my kind of diet.

It is a sane diet my doctor has put me on. Salt and sugar have been banished. I am allowed a certain amount of fat—notably a little olive oil or corn oil—and unsalted margarine (the type that is sold frozen). I am also permitted lean meat and fish and a variety of vegetables. No beets, unfortunately, or celery and very little asparagus, which are surprisingly high in sodium. Without salt, I am beginning to rediscover the natural flavors of food. A raw, unsalted mushroom has a delicate taste quite unlike that in its cooked state. Fish served raw, Japanese fashion, also becomes a new experience. To make up for the lack of salt, I have intensified the use of herbs and additives. My great friends in seasoning are garlic, onion, and shallot; tarragon, basil, rosemary, chervil, and thyme, fresh if possible; lemon and orange; and discreet amounts of bay leaf, cinnamon, nutmeg, and mace. I use quantities of mushrooms, and my pepper grinder is going constantly.

I needn't even give up bread, because there are many salt-free varieties that can be bought or made, such as the flat breads like matzo and crisp rye breads. When I make my own salt-free loaf, I often add some garlic, spice, or pepper to give the flavor a lift.

Certainly I do not feel deprived, and I go into my kitchen each day with the idea that I am going to create something out of the ordinary. Not only that, but friends, restaurateurs, and chefs have gone out of their way to cook for me, observing the rules of my diet while making dishes that appeal to both the eye and the palate. In a sense, my entire circle of friends is on this diet with me, sharing the challenge of cutting down, cutting away. I have heard people express astonishment at how good life can be without salt.

I never doubt that someday I will be allowed to eat as I please again, but that is of no great concern right now. The important thing is to keep the joy of eating. So if you, too, find yourself on a diet, there is no need to feel punished. Adjust to your regime and find new ways to stimulate your palate. It's amazing what a bit of garlic, a drop of lemon juice, or a few grinds of pepper will do to stave off the feeling of martyrdom.

❧ Marcel Dragon's Salt-Free Chicken Salad ❧

$4^{1}/_{2}$- to 5-pound roasting
  chicken
2 quarts water
$^{3}/_{4}$ cup dry white wine
$1^{1}/_{2}$ medium carrots, peeled
1 large onion, peeled
1 rib celery (optional)
2 slices lemon
1 bay leaf

Freshly ground pepper
$^{1}/_{2}$ cup finely diced water
  chestnuts
Mayonnaise (made without salt)
Boston lettuce leaves
2 tomatoes, peeled and
  cut in wedges
1 avocado, peeled and sliced
Watercress sprigs

Place the chicken in a large kettle, pour in the water, and add the wine, vegetables, lemon, bay leaf, and 1 teaspoon of pepper. Bring to a boil, skim off any solids that rise, then cover and simmer gently until tender, 1 to $1^{1}/_{4}$ hours. Remove the chicken and cool. Reserve the broth for future use.

Remove and discard the skin and bones. Cut the chicken into bite-sized pieces, and combine with the water chestnuts and enough mayonnaise to bind, about $^{1}/_{2}$ cup. Chill. Spoon into a salad bowl lined with lettuce. Garnish with the tomato wedges, sliced avocado, and watercress. If you like, sprinkle with pepper to taste. Makes about 6 cups, or 4 to 6 servings.

❧ Roast Split Herb Chicken ❧

$^{3}/_{4}$ cup minced fresh
  mushrooms, about $^{1}/_{4}$ pound
2 tablespoons unsalted
  margarine, softened
6 shallots or 6 to 8 green
  onions (white part),
  minced, about 3 tablespoons
1 tablespoon minced parsley

1 teaspoon crushed
  dried rosemary or
  1 tablespoon fresh
1 teaspoon dry mustard mixed
  with $^{1}/_{4}$ cup water
Two 2- to $2^{1}/_{2}$-pound
  broiler-fryers, split
  and backbones removed

Mix well all ingredients except the chickens. Loosen the skin of the chickens by running the fingers under it. Using about 1/4 cup for each chicken half, spread the herb mixture under the skin. Place the chicken, skin-side up, on a rack in a shallow foil-lined baking pan. Bake in a 400° oven 50 to 60 minutes or until tender. Serves 4.

⚜ Baked Veal Chops in White Wine ⚜

*4 veal loin chops about
  1 inch thick
2 medium onions, sliced
2 teaspoons dried tarragon or
  2 tablespoons fresh*

*1 teaspoon freshly ground pepper
2/3 cup dry white wine
1 tablespoon unsalted
  margarine
Minced parsley*

Trim excess fat from the chops. Place the onions in a foil-lined broiler pan. Sprinkle half the tarragon and half the pepper on the onions. Place the chops on the onions, and sprinkle with the remaining tarragon and pepper. Pour on the wine, dot with margarine, and cover with foil. Bake in a 375° oven 20 to 25 minutes or until done to your taste. Remove the foil, then broil 3 to 4 inches from the heat until delicately browned on one side, about 5 minutes. Transfer to a warm serving dish, pour on the pan juices, and sprinkle with parsley. Serves 4.

Variation: Substitute 3/4-inch to 1-inch pork chops for the veal chops, and proceed as above, using leaf sage instead of tarragon. Cover with foil and bake 20 to 30 minutes or until the chops are done and no longer pink. Finish under the broiler.

✒ Broiled Stuffed Red Snapper with White Wine ✒

1 whole red snapper, about
   3 pounds
1 medium onion,
   sliced very thin
1 medium green pepper,
   seeded and sliced very thin
1 medium tomato, peeled and
   sliced thin

1 teaspoon dried thyme or
   3 sprigs fresh
$1/2$ teaspoon freshly ground
   pepper
1 tablespoon oil or to taste
$1/3$ cup dry white wine
$1/4$ cup minced parsley
Lemon slices

With a sharp knife or kitchen shears, slit the fish to the tail, and lay open. Reserving a few onion and pepper slices, layer the remainder, along with the tomato slices, in the cavity. Sprinkle with thyme and pepper. Line a jelly roll pan with foil, then place a folded strip of foil, about 14 inches long, across the pan to help in turning the fish. Place the reserved onion and pepper slices on the foil, arrange the stuffed fish on this, and brush with oil. Pour on the wine.

Broil at the hottest setting 6 inches from the heat for about 10 minutes, basting occasionally with the pan drippings. Carefully turn the fish, using the foil strip and a wide spatula. Brush with oil, and continue broiling and basting until the fish flakes easily with a fork in the thickest part, about 10 minutes. Remove to a hot platter, and pour the pan juices over the fish. Garnish with parsley and lemon. Serves 4.

Variation: Prepare as above, but omit the foil strip. Bake in a 425° oven, without turning the fish, for 30 to 35 minutes or until the fish flakes easily with a fork at the thickest part.

❧ Baked Shrimp ❧

2 pounds medium shrimp
1¹/₂ teaspoons dried tarragon,
    soaked in 1 tablespoon
    dry white wine; or
    1¹/₂ tablespoons fresh

Freshly ground pepper
    to taste
3 tablespoons olive oil
    or unsalted margarine,
    melted

With a sharp knife or kitchen shears, split the shrimp down the back, almost but not quite through. Peel off the body shells, leaving on the tails, and devein. Spread the shrimp open to "butterfly" them. Arrange in a single layer in a lightly greased 10- to 12-inch round baking dish or pan with a 1-inch rim; a fluted quiche dish is perfect. Sprinkle with the tarragon and pepper. Drizzle with oil. Bake in a 350° oven 10 minutes or until just tender. Serves 6 to 8.

❧ Crab Salad ❧

1 pound fresh or frozen
    (thawed and drained)
    crabmeat, cartilage removed
4 small carrots, shredded,
    about 1 cup
¹/₄ cup minced parsley
2 tablespoons white
    wine vinegar

1 teaspoon freshly
    ground pepper
Grated peel of 1 lemon, about
    1 teaspoon
3 large cloves garlic, crushed
¹/₃ cup plain yogurt or
    to taste
Salad greens

Combine all ingredients, except the greens, in a bowl, and toss. Cover and chill at least 2 hours. Arrange on greens of your choice, and serve. Serves 4.

[1977]

Dieters' Secret

For years, it was not considered the in thing to eat or admit to eating margarine. Yet, traveling around and snooping in my hosts' refrigerators and freezers, I discovered that despite what my friends professed, many of them did use margarine a great deal, either on doctor's orders or because they really liked it.

Well, with millions of us on special diets, margarine, especially the unsalted or "sweet" margarine, is no longer something to hide or apologize for. It's a way of life. Those of us who have to live without salt and without butter find it a great boon, and I think it's true that even those who don't have to cope with restrictions use margarine for many different reasons and purposes.

I grant you, nothing takes the place of the glorious bouquet that issues from freshly churned sweet butter, or the taste of fresh butter on a hunk of homemade bread, or the smell of hot butter in the sauté pan—the aroma given off a by an onion slowly sautéed in butter should be bottled and sold.

Still, it is a question of what comes first, your health or your taste buds and olfactory nerves. There's no sense in being ashamed and feeling you have to hide the margarine. Just tell your guests you are on a diet and are preparing dinner with margarine—or don't tell them at all, and I bet they'll never guess. The other night, I blanched some thinly sliced carrots for about three minutes, then tossed them in rosemary-flavored margarine, added parsley, and let them sauté very gently in the mixture. Several of my dinner guests remarked on the wonderful flavor of the carrots and tried to figure out the combination I had used. Well, it was nothing more than 4 ounces of unsalted margarine, beaten well with $1/2$ teaspoon of finely chopped fresh rosemary, plus a little chopped parsley, added while the carrots were sautéing. Of course, I didn't use the whole quarter pound of margarine for the carrots. I saved some to use another night on a piece of broiled steak, and it is also a wonderful way to dress up a plain hamburger. If you are limited in your sodium intake, herbed margarine can take the place of many forbidden condiments. You have to make your own flavors and stop depending on things like soy sauce, chili sauce, ketchup, and Worcestershire sauce.

It's the simplest thing in the world to combine margarine and chopped fresh herbs such as rosemary, parsley, dill, or tarragon. Beat the mixture with a fork or, to make a large quantity, use a food processor. Refrigerate or freeze the margarine, and put a little dab on your broiled fish or chicken or meat, just for flavoring, and you'll find you never miss salt.

The other night I decided to make a roast chicken for dinner, so I put $1/2$ pound of unsalted margarine in the food processor with 1 cup of chopped shallots (I processed the shallots first, then added the margarine), whirled it until smooth, and added 1 tablespoon of lemon juice, $3/4$ teaspoon of freshly ground black pepper, and $1/2$ teaspoon of dry mustard. (Dry mustard has no salt, unlike prepared mustards, unless you can find one that is labeled salt-free.) I rubbed two $31/2$-pound chickens with the flavored margarine rather sparingly; although margarine has fewer calories than butter, it is still a fat. I put the chickens on their sides in a rack in a roasting pan and roasted them for 20 minutes in a 425° oven, turned them on the other side for the next 20 minutes, and then on their backs for 20 to 25 minutes longer, which to my taste is quite enough (meaning, still a little pink at the joints). I basted the birds with the pan juices as they roasted. They came out deliciously imbued with the flavor of shallots, lemon, and mustard, and beautifully browned.

In summer, I find it is a good idea to roast several chickens this way for a picnic or for a diet luncheon or dinner in the garden. Let the chickens cool at room temperature until just tepid, and they'll be much juicier than if they were refrigerated. Chilled, they lose that just-cooked freshness of flavor. Serve them with sliced ripe tomatoes and a dribbling of oil and vinegar, or with chilled cooked broccoli or cauliflower dressed with oil and vinegar. A big bowl of raw green peas is also nice, along with the tomatoes.

Unsalted margarine, which you can find in your market freezer and should be stored in your own freezer, has innumerable uses in our dietary lives. To be sure, I find I use much less margarine than I did butter. I scrape a little on my breakfast toast or put a bit on a baked potato. I also find it is perfectly adequate for sautéing, and it makes very good pastry and cakes. For one who was a confirmed advocate of the joys of butter over many, many years, this is indeed a testament.

[1977]

*H*old the Vinaigrette

As we are heading into the salad season, I would like to say a few words in defense of iceberg lettuce, a green that has been utterly damned by the food snobs in this country.[1] I like iceberg, and know other lovers of good food—Julia Child for one—who are not above using it. Crisp, crunchy iceberg, a reliable standby that is available at all times in all markets (very often in much better condition than other greens), has a palate-satisfying flavor and texture you find in few other types of lettuce. Everyone fancies

---

[1]Beard was never afraid to change his mind. Eighteen years earlier, he found iceberg lettuce "watery and tasteless" (in *The James Beard Cookbook*).

romaine, one of the greatest of our crisp salad greens, but if you think about it, romaine and iceberg are quite similar in taste and texture. One of my pleasures, while on a calorie-restricted diet, is to break iceberg lettuce into big chunks and have nothing but a little lemon juice on it as a dressing.

The fault I find with most tossed salads is that remarkably few people seem to know how to make a good vinaigrette dressing. This is not only a matter of using the right proportions of three or four parts oil to one part vinegar, but also of gauging the strength and flavor of the ingredients. One should taste vinegar before making a dressing. The superb sherry wine vinegar I use is so strong and overpowering that I have to use less or else dilute it with a little dry sherry if I'm making a big salad.

Because of my diet, I have cut the amount of vinaigrette dressing I use by half, and I add 2 or 3 tablespoons of unflavored yogurt instead. This gives the dressing a marvelous acidity, texture, and zest. More and more these days, instead of tossing the greens with dressing, I serve leaves of romaine or endive au naturel in a bowl or on a plate and either give them a sprinkling of salt and pepper and a few drops of oil or serve a bowl of yogurt vinaigrette as a dip. You really taste the flavor of romaine or endive that way, when it hasn't been dressed to death. Almost any salad green, such as chicory, watercress, and the Italian arugula, can be served like this. If you like, put a few slices of raw mushroom on each salad plate, sprinkled with lemon juice, salt, and pepper.

Cooked beets and raw onions, sliced and put in jars with vinegar and spices and marinated for several days, are good with a great many summer foods. Another favorite of mine, which I like to serve with hamburgers and steaks, is a dish of onions, sliced paper-thin, soaked in ice water in the refrigerator for several hours until crisp, then served with just a sprinkling of coarse salt or a touch of vinegar. It is both a relish and a low-calorie substitute for salad.

Try eating your greens as plain as possible and you'll find that in addition to eliminating the calories of the oil, you'll have a more delicious and palatable salad. Varying your salad routine is also important. The eternal tossed salad can become a bore, and you owe it to yourself and your family to give your meals a change of pace. There are so many things in the spectrum of seasonal vegetables that can be eaten raw and crisp. Snow peas are delicious; so are uncooked asparagus tips. A bowl of freshly shelled green peas, provided they are young and sweet, is great for munching. So save your vinaigrette dressing for where it is really needed—with certain vegetables or with a white bean, rice, or French potato salad.

Should you insist on having your salad dressed, here is a combination I think you will like extremely well—marinated mushrooms and beets with greens.

Slice 1/2 pound of firm white mushrooms into a bowl. Add 3 tablespoons of olive oil, 1/2 teaspoon of salt, 1/2 teaspoon of dried tarragon (or 1 teaspoon of chopped fresh tarragon), and 2 teaspoons of wine vinegar. Toss well, cover, and marinate for 1 hour. Put 3/4 cup of sliced cooked or canned beets in another bowl with 2 tablespoons of finely chopped onion and the juice of 1/2 orange (about 1/4 cup), and let stand 1 hour. When you are ready to serve, break up some greens—romaine, and maybe iceberg lettuce and chicory—into a salad bowl, allowing 5 to 6 cups for 4 servings. Add the mushrooms and beets with their marinades and toss thoroughly. If you feel you need more dressing, you can add 1 or 2 tablespoons of oil and a few drops of vinegar or lemon juice. At the last minute, sprinkle with 2 tablespoons of chopped parsley and serve. This unusually good mixed salad goes well with meats such as lamb, pork, and veal, either hot or cold.

[1977]

The Friendly Egg

The egg has had rather a poor press lately. Dire warnings about its cholesterol content have obscured the fact that it is the cook's best friend. It would be a sad world indeed without soufflés, omelets, custards, quiches, cakes, mayonnaise, meringues, and a hundred and one other dishes that depend on the egg. Our culinary heritage certainly includes eggs in good measure, and all the great nineteenth-century American cookery authors used lots of eggs as a matter of course. They rightly considered them to be suitable food for the ailing as well as the healthy. Mind you, some of the "sick bed cookery" can make alarming reading. The admirable Mrs. Rorer is a case in point.

I've always adored Sarah Tyson Rorer, who was a rival of Fannie Farmer in popularity. A principal of the famous Philadelphia Cooking School and culinary editor of the *Ladies' Home Journal*, she was an author of some repute. In her *Good Cooking*, first published in 1896 as part of the *Ladies' Home Journal Household Library*, there is a grim little chapter entitled "Cooking for the Sick." Mrs. Rorer writes:

"Eggs are not acceptable in all forms of disease. The convalescent typhoid patient is frequently 'set back' by an illy cooked soft-boiled or poached egg, where the albumen is too much coagulated. The stomach digestion being weak and impaired, is insufficient to thoroughly attack and break down the hardened portion of the white. It passes into the duodenum, the seat of the disease, and frequently becomes fastened in an ulcer, causing severe trouble, perhaps death."

This disturbing bit of information (I suspect that Mrs. Rorer's medical information was also ill digested) is followed by a perfectly charming recipe for frothed eggs, which goes as follows:

"Separate one egg, keeping the yolk whole in one-half of the shell while you beat the white to a stiff froth. Heap the white in a dainty bowl or eggcup, make a little well in the center, drop in the yolk, stand the whole in a saucepan containing a little boiling water; cover the saucepan and cook one minute. Serve in the bowl with a tiny bit of butter and a grain of salt."

Naturally, I tried it. You need a "dainty dish" that holds eight ounces. A custard cup or a four-inch-diameter individual soufflé dish is fine. Butter it, or the egg white will stick. Use room-temperature eggs and, unless you like *very* undercooked egg yolk, it's a good idea to cook the dish, covered, for three minutes. Finally, serve with buttered toast fingers to dip in the yolk. Delicious.

Of course, there are people who simply can't stand the idea of eating a soft egg yolk. If you're one of them, or cook for one of them, you might like to try this exquisitely simple French dish, which I have served for breakfast, a light lunch, or a late supper. It's called *les oeufs à la tripe*, though heaven alone knows why. For 2 or 3 servings, hard-boil 4 or 5 eggs. Cut into 1/2-inch slices and set aside. Sauté 1 medium-sized onion, finely chopped, in 4 tablespoons of butter until soft and golden. Stir in 3 tablespoons of flour, and cook, continuing to stir, for 3 minutes. Add 1 teaspoon of salt, about 1/2 teaspoon of freshly ground black pepper, and a few gratings of nutmeg, then gradually stir in 1 1/4 cups of light cream. Stir until the sauce thickens, then simmer gently for 3 or 4 minutes. Taste for seasoning, and fold in the sliced eggs. Heat through quickly and serve on toast.

[1985]

Hospital Food

I speak from experience when I say that hospitals have the worst food in the world, because I have been in four within the last year. The choice of food is unbelievably dreary and absolutely without appeal to the eye or palate, and it is usually cold by the time the tray arrives. I suppose the main reason is that this is mass feeding, but I don't know why in even the smallest hospitals it has to be such bad mass feeding.

This hasn't always been so. The first time I was in Doctor's Hospital in New York, the trays looked inviting, the food was good, and if you were not satisfied, you could order from the menu of the restaurant downstairs. Even when I was on a special diet, the dietician managed to devise attractive menus. You'd think any hospital would realize that serving patients food they really want to eat is of some importance. Last year, when I was hospitalized, I ordered a chicken sandwich for lunch and was brought flabby slices of white bread with about one and a half inches of pastelike, unrecognizable filling. The chicken must have been ground to a pulp and mixed with some gooey dressing. I showed this little horror to a friend who happened to be a trustee of the hospital. He called the head dietician and said such ghastly food should never be served to any human being.

I know it is difficult for a hospital kitchen to prepare three meals a day for patients on all kinds of diets, as well as for the staff (many of whom, I found, prefer to bring their own meals or go out and buy fresh fruit and vegetables). Still, I think most patients would be happy with less food, as long as it was well cooked, hot, and palatable. This isn't impossible. In one hospital, my breakfast was excellent because the eggs were poached and the toast made on the serving floor instead of being brought up from the main kitchen. In another, the soup was outstanding, tasty, flavorful, and not like the library paste one usually gets, so there must have been a cook who loved soup. If it can happen now and then, why not all the time?

Any break from the monotony of the hospital tray is a blessing to someone who has to spend days or weeks in the hospital and can't face another dish of canned pears and cottage cheese, chicken that tastes as if it had cooked around the clock, and fish broiled until it is dry as dust. If you have a friend or relative in the hospital, I suggest that you take a little edible gift—after finding out what they are allowed to eat—instead of flowers or books.

During one of my hospital sojourns, a friend who lived a block away would bring me, every day, a luncheon snack that was delicious, ample, and a great morale booster. Recently, I was sent a jar of salt-free jellied chicken consommé that soothed my parched throat and tasted like nectar.

Another thing that is easy to eat and soft on the tongue is a good custard. You might take a friend three little cups of custard, each with a different flavor—add a touch of vanilla to one, mace or nutmeg to the second, and a small bay leaf to the third (this may sound strange, but a bay leaf in custard is an old English trick that gives a brisk and pleasant flavor). Wrap the cups in plastic or foil so they can be refrigerated and served for three meals. If sweets are permissible, apart from things like custard, make a small sponge cake or homemade cookies. Or just provide good fresh fruit—grapes, a peach, or any seasonal exotic fruits, like mango or papaya. Nurses, too, enjoy a little treat, so if you are making cookies, set aside a few for the staff.

Another good gift for the patient is cold soup. It could be taken along at lunchtime in a plastic container or left in the hospital floor refrigerator for a later meal—but be sure to put the patient's name on the container. With this, you might have a small loaf of homemade bread, sliced so it won't be any trouble to serve, or pack thin sandwiches of good bread and butter. I'm going to give you a couple of ideas for soups with a yogurt base that practically any patient would be allowed to have.

For avocado-yogurt soup, put the pulp of 1 ripe avocado in the blender or processor with 1½ cups of hot chicken broth and 1 tablespoon of chopped fresh tarragon or 1 teaspoon of dried tarragon. Blend until smooth. Taste for seasoning. Combine with 1 cup of yogurt, and chill well. Add a few chopped chives or tarragon leaves for a garnish. Makes 3½ to 4 cups.

For cucumber-yogurt soup, peel, seed, and cut in strips 2 medium cucumbers. Cook in 2 cups of chicken broth with 1 tablespoon of chopped onion until just tender. Blend or process until smooth, taste for seasoning, and add 2 teaspoons of chopped fresh dill or 1 tablespoon of chopped fresh mint. Cool, then beat in 2 cups of yogurt. Makes 4 cups.

[1977]

7

$\mathcal{T}$he food community remembers James Beard as a prophet of American cooking, but his culinary interests had no borders. He was almost equally at home in French cooking, and he had a respectable knowledge of cuisines around the world. In 1979, he did a series of articles for *American Way* in which he discussed a variety of cuisines with their leading practitioners—represented here by Indian cooking, with Madhur Jaffrey, and Chinese cooking, with Cecilia Chiang—the latter especially interesting because it was a cuisine Beard scarcely mentioned, although it was close to his heart and part of his early history. In other articles, he presents highlights of Swiss cooking and finds a good deal to admire in the much-maligned English kitchen.

"The Food of Provence" was the outcome of Beard's long stay in St.-Rémy-de-Provence in 1963 while finishing up his memoir, *Delights and Prejudices.* I spent two weeks with him during this period, on a working holiday that was also a gastronomic education. Beard managed to fit himself in the front passenger seat of a two-horsepower Citroën, and we would set off to explore the food of Aix, Arles, Gordes, Les Baux, and other Provençal towns, on one occasion doing two three-star restaurants in a single day.

Beard returns to native ground in the final piece, in which he takes stock of current (1982) trends in so-called American cooking.

A Salute to Women

People always ask me who make the best cooks, men or women. It's an impossible question. If I said men, I would be accused of a sexist bias. Yet if I said women, I would be faced with the argument that none of the great chefs in history have been female. Well, there's a reason for that, but it's not a matter of gastronomic skill.

In the days when there were legendary chefs like Carême, apprentices were sent into their kitchens to learn the profession from the very bottom. These were boys of eight or nine. They started by scrubbing vegetables, carrying garbage, cleaning pots and pans. They also had to lift heavy utensils and heavy boxes of food. As they learned to become deft with their hands, they developed muscle. This was not a job for a girl. It was beyond her physically, and it was hardly the proper moral environment for a young lady in the last century. Therefore, the tradition of the hero chefs grew up in the male image.

If women have failed to make their mark on gastronomy as chefs, they have unquestionably done so as food authorities. In this country, in the early part of the nineteenth century, we had Miss Leslie, who wrote a number of popular cookbooks and was a tremendous force in American food. Mrs. Hale flourished mid-century, wrote *Receipts for the Millions* and other books, and was equally influential. Later came Mrs. Rorer, who had a cooking school in Philadelphia, lent her name to various products (including gas ranges), and really dictated the eating habits for her generation, as did two competitors in Boston, Mrs. Lincoln and Miss Fannie Farmer. As a matter of fact, the followers of Mrs. Rorer and Miss Farmer became so intensely partisan they would have nothing to do with one another.

Then we had Irma Rombauer of *The Joy of Cooking*. And in these last thirty years, there has been another wave of talented, dedicated women teaching cookery, writing about it, and even doing excellent work in the field. Though they never seem to reach the stature of a Pierre Franey or other contemporary chefs, they are a vital, positive force in American food and deserve more recognition.

No one in recent times has swayed the eating habits of this country more than Julia Child. She teaches effectively and entertainingly on television, she writes, she cooks, and she creates. Along with Miss Farmer and Mrs. Rorer, she is certainly entitled to the high bonnet of a chef.

I can think of only one woman in our day who has actually achieved that bonnet and challenged male supremacy—Mère [Eugénie] Brazier, who has reigned in France for many years. She first became famous for her *volaille demi-deuil*, or chicken in half-mourning, a simple, flavorful dish made with a good fat chicken or capon with thin slices of black truffles inserted under its skin, which is poached in a rich broth and served with a *sauce suprême*. That dish, coupled with another, much richer creation—an artichoke bottom filled with foie gras—established a firm reputation for Mère Brazier, and she soon found herself with two restaurants, one in Lyons and another about fourteen miles outside the city [in Col de la Luère], both bearing her name.

Since it is a rather interesting recipe, I'm going to tell you how to do Mère Brazier's *volaille demi-deuil* for yourself. Although the success of the dish depends on the quality of the bird and the availability of truffles, it can be approximated in anyone's kitchen with a reasonable amount of care. If you don't want to spend the money on truffles, it will still be worth your time to try poaching a chicken in this fashion. It makes a delectable main course and is a pleasant change from other routine ways of preparing chicken.

⌇ Volaille Demi-Deuil ⌇

First make the poaching broth. Put 2 or 3 pounds of chicken necks, backs, and gizzards in 2 quarts of water, add an onion stuck with 2 cloves, a sprig of parsley, and a teaspoon of thyme. Bring to a boil, skim off any scum that rises, then reduce the heat and simmer for 2 to 2½ hours. Strain it, discard the chicken pieces, and let the broth cool. Chill overnight if possible to allow the fat to congeal at the top. Then remove the fat before using the broth.

The chicken for this dish should be a fresh roaster of 4 or 5 pounds. If you can afford a truffle or two, slice it very thin, loosen the skin on the breast of the chicken with your fingers, and slide the slices underneath. Otherwise, just salt and pepper the cavity of the chicken, and throw in a sprig of fresh rosemary or about ½ teaspoon of dried. Truss the chicken so it will hold its shape and look attractive after cooking.

Heat the broth in a deep kettle, add about a tablespoon of salt, and bring to the boiling point. Add the chicken, bring back to a boil, then cover and reduce the heat to produce a bare simmer. Simmer for 45 minutes to an hour or until the chicken is just tender. If overcooked, it will fall apart. Transfer carefully to a warm dish, remove the trussing strings, and keep the chicken warm while you prepare the sauce.

Spoon off any excess fat from the top of the broth. Melt 4 tablespoons of butter in a saucepan, add 4 tablespoons of flour, and cook over medium heat for about a minute. Add 1½ to 2 cups of hot broth, and stir over medium heat until the mixture thickens. Taste for salt and pepper. Let simmer over very, very low heat for 5 or 6 minutes, and then add about ⅔ cup of heavy cream. Bring gently to the boiling point, and cook for another 2 or 3 minutes. Add a dusting of nutmeg or mace, and stir in 1 or 2 teaspoonfuls of lemon juice, being very careful not to break down the sauce.

Serve the poached chicken on a hot platter surrounded with mounds of freshly cooked rice and garnished with a bit of chopped parsley. Pass the sauce separately. For a vegetable accompaniment, serve a purée of spinach or a purée of carrots. Drink a beautiful chilled white burgundy, and raise your glass to toast a great woman chef.

[1974]

Chinese Cuisine

Chinese cuisine is different from any other in that it is based on flavor and texture, which the cooking techniques are designed to accentuate and enhance. To the Chinese, one eats in order to pursue the characteristic flavor of things. Therefore, the blending of flavors in a dish must be so subtle and skillful that the original taste is never lost, even though it may have been improved upon by the artifice of the cook. In this, it is totally unlike classic French cuisine, with sauces designed to give food a different dimension of taste and provide infinite ways of merging the flavors of ingredients in a dish.

To explore and understand the mysteries and intricacies of the Chinese cuisine, one must know the underlying philosophy and principles. I am much indebted to a fascinating book called *Chinese Gastronomy* by Hsiang Ju Lin and Tsuifeng Lin, the wife and daughter of author and artist Lin Yutang, which explains these principles in a scholarly but very clear way. In Chinese cooking, there are certain words of great importance, each expressive of a certain nuance of the cuisine. First come the words that express flavor and aroma: *hsien, hsiang, nung,* and *yu-er-pu-ni. Hsien* means the true, natural flavor of a food, be it a piece of fresh bamboo shoot, fat pork, fresh fish, or sweet butter. *Hsiang* is the word for aroma, foods that give pleasure by their fragrance as well as their taste—meat roasting on a spit or onions sautéing in butter, for instance. *Nung,* in contrast to *hsien,* is used for dishes that are strongly spiced or flavored with meat stocks, an embellishment of the natural flavor. *Yu-er-pu-ni* is a word that means something that has the luscious taste of natural fat or oil without being greasy and unpleasant, the wonderful unctuous quality you get, for example, in an avocado, sweet butter, rich fish roe, or perfectly cooked pork.

The words for texture, *tsuei* and *nun,* are direct opposites. *Tsuei* means crisp and crunchy, a texture mostly achieved or brought about by cooking—crisply roasted duck skin, sautéed shrimp, blanched asparagus. *Nun* is applied to things that are soft and tender without being mushy. An egg *mollet* in jelly or a smooth mousseline of salmon would be considered *nun.*

These subtle yet profound nuances are an essential part of Chinese cuisine, which you will be able to notice when you eat perfectly cooked Chinese food. There is an art to bringing out natural flavors through seasonings that blend in so well they are never noticeable. A tiny drop of wine or vinegar, a touch of light soy sauce, a pinch of sugar, the flavors of ginger and garlic extracted by hot oil; all are used to enhance a dish, but you should never be conscious of them.

Then there are the procedures intended to control flavor, such as blanching, steaming, boiling, stir-frying; and the ingredients that modify flavor, such as soy, sesame oil, vinegar, ginger, oyster sauce, each of which has a very specific purpose. Finally, there are the ingredients that control texture. For instance, cornstarch is used to bind the juices of meat with seasonings. Brine, as in salt-cured duck, extracts water and makes meat and fat firm.

All of these things are part of the complex structure and philosophy of Chinese cuisine, a cuisine that can only be experienced and appreciated at its greatest when practiced by a fine Chinese cook who knows how to bring flavor and texture into balance. The endless variation on a theme within a very defined structure is what makes Chinese cooking unique. It has had no written history, as French and English cooking have had since the seventeenth century. The cooking tradition is imparted by one generation to the next. A trained Chinese chef has no need to rely on a recipe.

In my lifetime, I have been lucky enough to know some great Chinese cooks, starting with Let, the chef in my mother's kitchen. Many years after, in San Francisco, the late John Kan, his wife, Helen, and their restaurant chef, Puy, blessed me with beautiful dishes. Today I have as my friend and mentor Cecilia Chiang, owner of the Mandarin restaurants in San Francisco and Beverly Hills and a woman with a great knowledge of fine Chinese cuisine. She is also an accomplished and creative cook with impeccable taste. I will never forget the first time I dined in the Mandarin at Ghirardelli Square and watched her prepare a barbecued lamb with incredible grace and ease and a superb sense of timing. That lamb was one of the choicest morsels I have ever eaten in a Chinese restaurant.

Madame Chiang's chef in San Francisco is exemplary in his ideas and presentation, and many people have learned the basics and finer points of Chinese cooking by attending the lessons he gives in the kitchen. I have been to one or two of these classes, in which Danny Kaye participated. Kaye is one of the greatest exponents of Chinese cooking in this country, a fast hand with a cleaver and a master of the arts of stir-frying, poaching, steaming, roasting, and smoking. He has worked with both Kan's and Cecilia Chiang's chefs and produces magnificent Chinese feasts at his home in Beverly Hills.

When I was in San Francisco recently, Cecilia Chiang and I had a long discussion about the uses of wheat flour in Chinese pastas, which have been a part of Chinese cooking for many centuries. At a dinner she organized, we had pasta in four ways, each quite different to the bite and the palate. As an opener, there were thin, cold noodles in a spiced meat dish. Crispy yet tender, with a texture beyond what the Italians call al dente, the noodles absorbed flavors from the other ingredients in a wonderful way. Then came noodles in a simple chicken broth with an overtone of chicken fat, which had permeated the noodles so that they were unctuously soft. For the next dish, heavier noodles had been stir-fried with vegetables. Lastly, we had various little dumplings, their delicate dough encasing fillings of crabmeat and chicken with vegetables.

After the pastas came a tantalizing dish of stir-fried tripe and chicken gizzards called "black and white," typically Chinese in the simplicity of preparation and use of textures. Another intriguing dish consisted of clams steamed with ginger and pepper. A further study in textures was provided by abalone, done very simply with bamboo shoots, and by an entirely different texture, shark fins, tasteless in themselves but with a sauce that glamorized them without robbing them of their very distinctive quality. The dinner ended with a sweet rice dish "of the eight precious perfumes," a dish I don't care for because it has too much sweetness and certainly its own texture—the softness and gluey quality that rice gets when cooked in a special way. Exquisite to gaze upon, this dish is considered one of the great sweet delicacies of Chinese cuisine, which is not noted for desserts. They are all, to me, far too cloying.

I am going to give you some of Cecilia Chiang's recipes, including one for a red-cooked pork shoulder, a simple but classic dish she prepared for me at her home. It is nothing more than pork poached in water, soy, and sherry with ginger and sugar, but unbelievably delicious.

As a contrast to the classic Chinese dishes served at the Mandarin, I love to go to the enormous Hong Kong Teahouse when I am in San Francisco, where they serve a variety of teas and a parade of small delicacies called *dem sem* or *dim sum*, some steamed, some deep fried, some sautéed. Scores of dishes that are suited to this type of service are brought around in a seemingly endless array on trays or big carts laden with small plates, and this continues from eight o'clock in the morning to three o'clock in the afternoon, the longest lunch hour on record. You can find similar teahouses in New York, San Francisco, Honolulu, and various other cities, and it is well worth your while to visit one.

At the Hong Kong Teahouse, I sampled at least five different types of dumplings, formed in various shapes, some with a crescent form, some like little bags, and others made with a yeast dough that looked like small mountains. We took a peek into the kitchen, and it was rather awe inspiring to see everyone working fast and furiously, shaping the dumplings beautifully and popping them on huge bamboo racks to steam. This is yet another aspect of Chinese cooking, and while great restaurants like the Mandarin or David K's (in New York City) may occasionally give you a few little *dem sem* as a first course of a large meal, they do not serve a tea lunch, which is reserved for the teahouses.

Obviously, it is not possible to cover the entire scope of Chinese cooking in one article, but if you want to conduct your own tasting of superb Chinese food along the lines I have indicated, by all means make a reservation at one of Cecilia Chiang's Mandarin restaurants. When ordering your meal, the ratio is usually four main dishes for four people, plus one for the table, as it were. But if you are smart, you will gather together twelve or more people so you can order twelve to sixteen courses and have a fascinating panorama of the various flavors, textures, and techniques of Chinese cuisine. You are in for some lovely surprises. I have long loved Chinese food, I have eaten a great deal of it, and I am still being surprised.

ॐ Red-Cooked Pork Shoulder ॐ

For red-cooked pork shoulder, you will need a whole pork shoulder of 5 to 6 pounds, with the bone in and skin left on. Wash the pork, and make a few slashes with a knife on the skinless side of the meat to allow the sauce to penetrate more easily during cooking. Place the pork in a heavy, medium-sized pot, and add enough water to cover. Cover the pot and bring the water to a boil over high heat. Skim off any scum that forms, then add $1/4$ cup of dry sherry and 5 or 6 slices of fresh ginger. Cover again, turn the heat to low, and simmer 1 hour. Drain off a third of the liquid, and add $1^1/4$ cups of soy sauce to the pot. Simmer on low heat for another $1^1/2$ hours, then add $1/3$ cup of sugar (preferably rock sugar, which will give the skin a more glazed appearance), and cook for a further 30 minutes, basting the skin continuously with the hot sauce. To test for tenderness, pierce the meat with a fork or chopstick. If it penetrates easily, the meat is done. If not, cook a little longer. Place the whole shoulder and sauce in a deep dish. Slice the meat thinly, and serve with the sauce.

ॐ Black and White ॐ

Cut $1/2$ pound of honeycomb tripe in $1^1/2$-inch by 2-inch pieces, and score in a crisscross pattern with a knife. Put the tripe in a bowl with cold water to cover and 1 teaspoon of baking soda. Let soak overnight, then drain.

Combine in a bowl the white part only of 3 scallions, shredded; 1 tablespoon of dry sherry; $3/4$ teaspoon of Oriental sesame seed oil; 1 teaspoon of vinegar; 1 teaspoon of salt; 2 tablespoons of chopped fresh coriander; and 1 teaspoon of cornstarch mixed with 1 tablespoon of cold water. Mix well and set aside.

Trim and rinse $1/2$ pound of chicken gizzards, and score them in a crisscross pattern also. Bring 1 quart of chicken broth to a simmer in a pan, add the tripe and gizzards, and poach gently for 5 to 6 minutes. Remove from the stock. Heat 2 tablespoons of vegetable oil in a wok that has been heated over a high flame, add 1 large sliced garlic clove, and stir-fry for 1 minute. Then add the mixture from the bowl, the tripe, and the gizzards, and stir-fry briskly over high heat for 2 minutes. Serve at once.

❧ Sauté of Bean Sprouts ❧

Heat 2 tablespoons of vegetable oil in a wok over very high heat until it starts to smoke. Add 1 tablespoon of soy sauce, 2 tablespoons of dry sherry, $1/2$ teaspoon of salt, and a pinch of sugar. Then toss in $1/2$ pound of bean sprouts. Stir-fry only 1 minute so the sprouts retain their crispness. Add a few drops of Oriental sesame oil and serve immediately.

[1979]

Indian Cooking

To most people in the Western world, Indian food is what they call a curry—of meat, fowl, or seafood in a thick sauce spiced with commercial curry powder. The French flavor their classic béchamel with curry powder, combine it with chicken or veal, and also dub it curry. The British and Americans will make a yellowish brown sauce with sautéed vegetables, curry powder, and other spices, and mix in some pieces of cooked lamb, chicken, or shellfish. They serve it forth with boiled rice and an array of condiments in little dishes: chopped peanuts, chopped hard-boiled eggs, chopped parsley, grated coconut, Major Grey's chutney, and—if they are really being fancy—the odoriferous dried fish known as Bombay duck, and *pappadums,* fried in hot oil, to be sprinkled on top of the dish. Even the Chinese and Japanese, who as Asians might be expected to know better, are apt to use stale, packaged curry powder for curried dumplings or rice. All of these dishes that are lumped under the heading "curry" or "curried" are supposed to be representative of Indian cuisine. Then there are those who think they are adding an exotic Indian touch by mixing raw curry powder into a mayonnaise, vinaigrette, or cream sauce, when all they are doing is ruining a perfectly good thing with the uncooked flavor of a blend of ground spices, which usually includes a lot of harsh-tasting turmeric, the spice that gives curry powder its bright yellow hue.

Who knows how curry powder came into being? It doesn't exist in India. The general belief is that the word is an anglicization of the Tamil word *kari,* meaning "sauce," or the spice known as kari leaf. But in India and other Asian countries, where the subtly spiced, stewlike dishes known in English as curries are eaten, no one spice blend is used. Instead, each dish is flavored with a combination of spices that are ground fresh daily and varied according to the food they are to flavor and enhance. It is this use of spices that characterizes Indian cuisine and brings such enormous variety to the standard range of foods available in each region of the country.

I never really comprehended the underlying principles of Indian cooking until the past few years, when I was fortunate enough to work with Madhur Jaffrey, a beautiful and multifaceted woman, who is the author of *An Invitation to Indian Cooking*. She is a fine cook and food researcher, as well as a skilled actress who has appeared in a number of Indian and Anglo-Indian movies and television plays. Madhur's theatrical training has given her a platform presence and ease with the public, which is evident in the trips she makes around the country lecturing and demonstrating Indian cooking. She gives cooking lessons in her New York City apartment, and she has, on occasion, also taught classes at my house. I vividly remember one evening when she was downstairs teaching in my kitchen and I was upstairs in bed, recovering from a stint in the hospital. The fragrance of the spices she was frying wafted up the stairs, driving me quite mad with the thought of those lovely spicy dishes that I could smell but not eat. I finally fell asleep, my nostrils still tingling with tantalizing aromas.

Madhur grew up in Delhi in the northern part of India, a member of a well-to-do family that had become partially westernized. They ate Indian meals but observed the British custom of breakfast, high tea, and a large lunch and dinner. Although her father felt a meal was not a meal without meat, Madhur and her mother delighted in the simpler dishes the servants prepared for themselves, the food of the people, and often asked them to make a little more so they could share it.

Like most well-brought-up Indian girls, Madhur did no cooking. In her student days in London, she became terribly homesick for the food of her own country. So with help from her mother, who would send her recipes and advice, Madhur ventured into the kitchen, and she has been cooking ever since.

As Madhur says, it is hard to generalize about Indian food because there is not one style of cooking but several. Eating habits vary from state to state in this vast country, depending on geographical conditions, local produce, and religious beliefs. If you think in terms of Europe, it would be like trying to characterize collectively the food of countries from Italy to Sweden. There is little shipment of food from one area of India to another, and people tend to eat what they grow. The northern part of the country is cold, the southern, tropically hot, so the main rice-eating areas are in the south. In the northern grain-growing areas, wheat breads are the staple, although many Indians do eat both rice and bread. Saffron is native to Kashmir, so you find saffron-flavored and -colored dishes in Kashmiri cooking. Black pepper and ginger are indigenous to the tropical southwest coast and have been major exports for many centuries—ginger, since the time of the Venetian traders.

In India, spices have been regarded for thousands of years as medicinal and are therefore used not only for their flavoring power but also for their beneficial qualities. Cumin, for instance, is thought to be cooling to the body. A mixture of ground cardamom, peppercorns, cumin seeds, coriander seeds, cloves, and cinnamon, used to flavor vegetable and meat dishes, is known as *garam masala,* or "hot spices," not because of its fiery taste but because it is supposed to provide heat for the body. According to Madhur, all foods are characterized by their physical effects, for in Hinduism there has always been great emphasis on the functions and biochemical balance of the body through the use of spices and certain healthy, cooling, and digestion-aiding foods such as yogurt. Yogurt is a very ancient product and is used widely in India in marinades, in cooking, diluted as a drink, and in the refreshing *raitas*—mixed with cooked or raw vegetables and seasonings.

Among the many, many spices and herbs of the Indian kitchen, most are familiar to us—cinnamon, cumin, coriander seeds, cloves, fennel seeds, nutmeg, poppy seeds, saffron, garlic, fresh gingerroot, and fresh green coriander (also known as Chinese parsley or cilantro). Then there are fried red and fresh green chili peppers in their various degrees of strength and hotness; turmeric, with its great coloring qualities, a spice you find in some Middle Eastern dishes and in our mustard pickles; the flattish yellow fenugreek seeds, with their distinctive bitter taste and interesting perfume; and mustard seeds—the black are preferred, but yellow may be substituted. And there are such lesser-known exotica as *kalonji*, or black onion seeds; *anchoor*, a raw mango, dried and ground, that has a sour, brisk acidity; tamarind paste; and asafetida, a resin with a rather unattractive odor that is used in small quantities in some vegetarian dishes. (I can remember when in winter American children were made to wear lumps of asafetida, sewn into little bags, around their necks, to protect them from germs and infection. I can't say what effect the smell had on germs, but it certainly did nothing for the popularity of the unfortunate children.)

Spices for Indian cooking should be bought whole and fresh in small quantities, then ground as needed, either in an electric blender or, preferably, in a small electric coffee mill, used for that purpose alone. Freshly ground spices release much more flavor and aroma.

To me, the fascinating thing about Indian spicing is the enormous change in taste that can be produced by different combinations. Sometimes the spices are roasted until they turn color and then are crushed, and at other times they will be gently "popped" in hot oil in order to modify or change their flavor. The order in which spices are added to a dish or the manner in which they are used is equally important. For instance, turmeric, which burns quickly and turns bitter, usually is added when there is liquid in the dish, as you'll notice in Madhur's recipe for shrimp with cauliflower cooked in the Bengali style, where a wide range of spices comes into play, adding subtlety and excitement to what is basically a simple preparation.

Spicing also plays an extremely important role in Indian vegetarian dishes. Almost 80 percent of the Indian people are vegetarians. Some of them will not even eat eggs, although nonvegetarian Indians eat seafood, poultry, and certain meats that are permitted by their religion, as well as eggs and dairy products. You'll find the richest cooking and the most lavish meat dishes in the northern regions, such as Delhi and the Punjab, where the Mogul emperors brought their own Persian-inspired tastes to the local cuisine. Some of these dishes can now be found in the better Indian restaurants in the United States, dishes like the elaborate *biryani,* or marinated meat or poultry and spiced rice, garnished with almonds and raisins, intriguing kebabs of ground spiced meat, or dishes colored and flavored with saffron.

One of the great strengths of the Indian cuisine is the enormous number of vegetable dishes that have originated in this most vegetarian of countries. The daily meal of many Indians consists of either rice or a wheat bread with vegetable and lentil dishes, plus buttermilk or yogurt, a seemingly frugal but actually perfectly balanced diet, for the dairy products provide any proteins not supplied by pulses and rice. Again, most of the vegetables are those we know—onions, tomatoes, potatoes, carrots, eggplant, spinach, okra, cauliflower, peas, beans, mustard greens—with a wide range of dried pulses, such as chickpeas, black-eyed peas, and many types of lentil.

At a typical Indian table, you'll find a variety of dishes. These are eaten in small quantities with rice, a dal or lentil dish, and perhaps one of the unleavened breads—*chapatis, pooris, or parathas*—or, in the north, the delicious leavened *naan*, baked in the clay tandoor oven, where meats and chicken are roasted over an open fire, tandoori style. There will be one or more meat, poultry, or fish dishes, some moist and stewlike, others fairly dry in consistency; one or more vegetable dishes; and an assortment of cooked and raw relishes that could be likened to our salads and condiments. These might include a cooked chutney, a fresh uncooked chutney, pickled vegetables (onion, turnip, carrot), chopped raw tomato, onion and cucumber, and a yogurt *raita*. Dessert is most often fresh fruit.

The chutneys go far beyond the familiar mango or tomato chutneys we know. They may be sweet, sour, sweet and sour, salty, hot, or cold, and they are intended to add an exciting fillip of flavor that will stimulate the appetite—very necessary in a predominantly hot climate. Madhur told me that fresh chutneys, the kind made with mint, coriander, and fresh coconut, subtly spiced and mixed, perhaps, with fruit or yogurt, were served every day in her home. The favorite was a combination of mint, fresh coriander, fresh green chilies, salt, and sometimes a little garlic or onion, all ground together. It both refreshed the mouth and was a source of vitamins. She also remembers the pickles her grandmother used to make and cure in the sun from different seasonal fruits and vegetables.

I have included some of Madhur Jaffrey's recipes for you to try. Together they make a complete light meal and serve as an introduction to the world of Indian cooking.

❧ Shrimp with Cauliflower, Bengali Style ❧

1 pound medium-sized shrimp,
    peeled and deveined
$1/8$ teaspoon ground turmeric
1 small head cauliflower, or
    about $1^{1}/_{2}$ pounds
9 tablespoons mustard oil
$1/2$ teaspoon whole black
    mustard seeds
$1/8$ teaspoon whole black onion
    seeds (kalonji)
$1/8$ teaspoon whole
    fenugreek seeds
$1/4$ teaspoon whole
    fennel seeds
$1/4$ teaspoon whole
    cumin seeds

A piece of fresh ginger,
    2 x 1 x 1 inches, peeled and
    finely grated
1 teaspoon ground
    coriander
1 tablespoon ground cumin
$1/8$ teaspoon cayenne (or to taste)
3 whole fresh hot green chilies
    (optional)
1 teaspoon salt
$1/8$ teaspoon ground
    cardamom seeds (may
    be crushed in a mortar)
$1/8$ teaspoon ground cinnamon
$1/8$ teaspoon freshly ground
    black pepper

Rub the shrimp with the turmeric, and set aside. Break up the cauliflower into delicate flowerets, no wider at the end than $3/4$ inch and no longer than 2 inches.

Heat 6 tablespoons of the oil in a deep 10-inch skillet or sauté pan over medium heat. When hot, put in the cauliflower. Stir and fry for about 2 to 3 minutes. The cauliflower should be half cooked and still crunchy. Remove with a slotted spoon and set aside.

Add the remaining 3 tablespoons of oil to the skillet. When the oil is hot, put in the mustard seeds, onion seeds, fenugreek seeds, fennel seeds, and cumin seeds. (This particular five-spice combination is known as *panchphoran* and may be purchased already mixed from Indian grocery stores. If bought in this form, use $1^{1}/_{4}$ teaspoons of the mixture for this recipe.) Ten seconds later, put in the ginger, ground coriander, ground cumin, and cayenne. Stir for half a minute and then add a cup of water. Keep cooking on medium heat for half a minute. The sauce should turn a bit thick. Now put in the shrimp, cauliflower, green chilies, and salt. Cover, lower the heat, and simmer 3 to 4 minutes or until the shrimp are opaque and the cauliflower is cooked. Stir gently a few times during this cooking period. Remove the cover, sprinkle with ground cardamom, cinnamon, and black pepper. Serve immediately. Serves 4.

⟡ Aromatic Rice with Peas ⟡

3 tablespoons vegetable oil
1 stick of cinnamon, about
    1¹/₂ inches long
3 bay leaves
4 whole cardamom pods
5 whole cloves
1 cup peas, either freshly shelled
    or frozen peas thawed in very
    hot water and drained

1¹/₂ cups long-grain rice
    (not parboiled)
2³/₄ cups chicken broth
³/₄ teaspoon salt (1¹/₄ if the
    broth is unsalted)

Heat the oil in a heavy 2- to 2¹/₂-quart pot over medium heat. When hot, put in the cinnamon, bay leaves, cardamom pods, and cloves. Stir the spices for 5 seconds. Now add the peas. Stir and fry for a minute. Add the rice, and turn the heat to low. Stir and fry the rice for about 3 minutes. Now add the chicken broth and salt. Bring to a boil. Cover with a tight-fitting lid, turn the heat to very, very low, and cook, undisturbed, for 25 minutes. Turn off the heat. Let the rice rest, covered and in a warm spot, for 10 minutes. Mix the rice and peas gently with a fork, and serve. Serves 4 to 6.

Note: The whole spices in this dish are for flavoring only and are not to be eaten.

❧ Yogurt with Cucumber and Mint ☙

1 cup plain yogurt
1 cucumber, peeled, seeded,
   and coarsely grated
1 tablespoon minced fresh
   mint leaves

$1/_2$ teaspoon salt
$1/_8$ teaspoon freshly ground
   black pepper
$1/_{16}$ teaspoon cayenne

Mix all ingredients together, and serve cold. Serves 4.

[1979]

Swiss Culinary Contrasts

While I was in Switzerland last fall, I stopped on the way from Lausanne to Gstaad for a cup of coffee in Gruyère, an incredibly picturesque village that is the home of Switzerland's greatest cheese. With the coffee came a platter of tiny molded chocolate cups, filled with the richest, most delicious cream. I thought how absolutely indicative this was of Swiss cuisine. The combination of chocolate and cream, two of the outstanding products of that part of Switzerland, expressed much about the eating habits and the gastronomic treasures of this small country, which is only about twice the size of New Jersey.

Many people think of Switzerland in terms of the Alps and yodeling, but there's a lot more to it than that. It is a country of fascinating contrasts and of mixed culinary influences, drawing on the finest of raw ingredients. Over the years, I have lived for varying periods of time in French-speaking Switzerland and German-speaking Switzerland, but never in Italian-speaking Switzerland, although I have visited there, and I have been amazed at the way these three very different cultures blend so smoothly throughout the country.

Switzerland is a land of good food rather than show-off food. I am always struck by the fact that you can go to almost any small town or village and find something attractive to eat, most likely a local specialty drawn from the products of the surrounding countryside. I can remember unpretentious restaurants on the shores of Lake Geneva, where one could sit at an outdoor table and be served huge platters of delicate, fresh lake perch, filleted and sautéed, which you ate with thin, crisp, homemade french fries, a green salad, and local white wine until you couldn't eat any more.

Last fall, four of us dined in a small restaurant in a village between Lausanne and Geneva, where the simple menu, served every day, started with a big platter of charcuterie—smoked and raw cured hams, thinly sliced sausage, and that exquisite air-dried beef that is unique to Switzerland, *viande de Grisons.* The beef—defatted, spiced, and brined before being dried—is served sliced in paper-thin curls and is indeed a delicious morsel. Its almost spicy quality enhances many dishes. Combined with fresh asparagus, it is divine. This came with wonderful home-made *cornichons,* pickled onions, and good bread. Switzerland has a great variety of excellent breads. After having been in the South of France, where the breads have deteriorated dreadfully, I was pleasantly surprised to find good, firm, honest bread everywhere I went.

After the charcuterie came the local delicacy, *malakoff,* a mixture of shredded cheese combined with eggs and a touch of kirsch, mounded on small rounds of bread and then deep fried until it puffed and browned and came out looking like a baby soufflé. The bread was crisp, the cheese firm on the outside and meltingly soft and runny inside, and the whole thing was so addictive that we kept on ordering more. We all managed three apiece, and I imagine heartier eaters have been known to down four, five, even six.

This is so typical of the way the Swiss use their cheeses: Gruyère, probably the finest firm cheese in the world; Emmenthaler (which we refer to as "Swiss cheese," as if there were no others), with its big holes; Appenzeller, exciting to nose and palate; Vacherin, which is to my taste one of the very great soft-ripening cheeses, brilliantly flavored when aged, but seldom found outside of Switzerland; and other lesser-known cheeses that form the basis of Swiss cooking. Who but the Swiss have come up with anything to equal fondue, made with Gruyère, sometimes with an addition of Emmenthaler, white wine, and a fillip of kirsch? On a winter's day or evening, to dip chunks of bread into this lovely seething mass of melted cheese until one's hunger is satisfied, washing it down with drafts of beer or Swiss white wine, is an experience to satisfy soul and body.

Then there is raclette, a country dish beloved of skiers, for which half a wheel of raclette—a cheese from the canton of Valais—is put in front of an open fire or a special electric grill to melt. The melted part is scraped off onto a hot plate and served with tiny boiled potatoes, sour pickles, and beer or wine. It's a marvelous snack, and I was pleased to discover that Swissair recently introduced it on its flights between Zurich and New York.

If you would like to make raclette but don't have a fireplace or grill, just put two or three paper-thin slices of the cheese (sold as raclette or sometimes as Bagnes) on a metal or other heatproof plate, and melt them in a preheated 450° to 500° oven. Serve with boiled potatoes and pickles on the side.

Each part of Switzerland has its distinctive foods and dishes. The German-speaking section has the greatest variety of sausages and all kinds of pastries. The traditional dish of Berne, Berner Platte—a collection of sausages and pork with sauerkraut and boiled potatoes, very similar to *choucroute garnie*—

combines French and German influences in a typically Swiss way, while in the Italian-speaking region, you spot a definite Latin influence on the rather "Zurichoise" cooking.

When you think of the great chefs of the world, the Swiss do not immediately spring to mind. Hoteliers and restaurateurs, definitely, but not chefs. Yet it has been my privilege in the past twenty-five years to know three really great chefs who were Swiss—German-Swiss, Italian-Swiss, and French-Swiss.

The first was the late Albert Stockli, with whom I worked off and on for about fifteen years during the time when that incredible collection of great restaurants known as Restaurant Associates was forming. Albert was more or less the inspiration behind the food—the guiding hand. Like all great chefs, he was temperamental, but he was a remarkable man and one whom I greatly respected. He had a deep love for the mountain country near his home city of Zurich, and he would bring forth dishes of his homeland that would delight and startle you. Albert made better *rösti* than anyone I ever knew.

As you probably know, this national potato dish of German-speaking Switzerland consists of partially boiled, shredded potatoes cooked as a flat cake in butter in a skillet until crisp and brown on each side. The dish is a triumph of potato art—the center mealy, with shreds of potato held together by their natural starch. One finds *rösti* everywhere in Switzerland, served with everything.

I can remember, too, the superb veal dishes Albert made at the Newarker restaurant at Newark Airport. One was the Zurich specialty of veal cut in julienne strips, sautéed with shallots, and served with a white wine and cream sauce, and of course with *rösti*. There was a similar dish made with strips of calf's liver, a tiny bit of vinegar, and cream, which charmed even those who normally shunned liver.

My second Swiss chef is Seppie Renggli, the incredibly creative executive chef of the Four Seasons in New York City. Just visiting this man in his kitchen before lunch, where he takes over the grill section, is an extraordinary experience. His worktable is piled with julienne vegetables; shredded vegetables; tiny mushrooms of all varieties, both cultivated and wild; and a glorious display of seafood—scallops, bay shrimp, large shrimp, crab, and bits and pieces he feels might blend well with other ingredients. These he puts together in salads and vegetable combinations, which are served along with the grilled meats and fish in eye-pleasing arrangements that are beautiful but never chichi; the blended flavors are of first importance. Seppie is a chef who has never disappointed me and who has at times really reached the heights.

Now I want to tell you about the young Swiss chef who is currently the talk of the food world and possibly the most creative and remarkable of all the great European chefs—Frédy Girardet. Girardet's simple, comfortable restaurant is on the first floor of the town hall of Crissier, an unassuming suburb of Lausanne, where he grew up. To eat here is to have a unique experience, for it is not like visiting a famous three-star restaurant where the chef is known for certain specialties that people write ahead to order for their dinner. You have the feeling that instead of being in a restaurant, you are in the workroom of a man who is devoted to his métier, constantly experimenting and originating.

We were there twice within three days, first for dinner on a Saturday evening. Monsieur Girardet came out of the kitchen and asked if we would accept the dishes he had chosen for us, which we did with alacrity. He had also chosen the wines— from his private cellar—all of which were Swiss, for he is staunchly devoted to the excellent products of his country, particularly the wines and cheeses. I couldn't have been happier with his selection, for it gave us a sense of his creativity, an inspired working out of flavors, textures, and contrasts. One course led harmoniously into the next, like a perfectly orchestrated piece of music. Girardet's food is not complicated or contrived but the essence of simplicity and purity.

The opening course of our dinner was fresh duck foie gras, sliced thickly, seared on each side in butter until it was crisp outside but pink within, then given a little dash of vinegar and additional butter, which blended with the unctuous texture of the liver to make this a dish to remember.

Then came a subtle progression of seafood courses, starting with the small delicately flavored Belon oysters, briefly heated through in a light, creamy sauce; followed by crayfish and minute squid; scallops poached in fish stock and dressed with a drift of fresh dill; and pieces of poached lobster topped with shreds of black truffle and surrounded by ovals of finely puréed broccoli. With these courses, we had a young and an older Traminer d'Yvorne, a Swiss white wine in short supply.

As this was the season for game, the main course was little medallions of young venison in a light *sauce poivrade*, circled by a froth of red cabbage, along with chestnuts and sautéed apple slices, with which we drank a pinot noir. Then came a platter of Swiss cheeses: a young, fresh and an older, riper chèvre; a perfect ripe and runny Vacherin; and an excellent Appenzeller. For dessert came the most ethereal of soufflés with a passion fruit sauce. The dinner was possibly one of the three or four greatest gastronomic experiences of my life. Girardet is without doubt a supreme master of his art.

On our second visit, for lunch on a Tuesday, we had the privilege of doing some photography in the kitchen and watching

Girardet's brigade at work. They are all young—mostly students from the Lausanne Hotel school—and they work with an enthusiasm and devotion that is heartwarming. Girardet was not there that day, but again he had chosen the dishes he wanted us to eat. We knew he had so instilled these young men with his spirit that they were trying with all the skills they could command to emulate his great cooking hands and to perfectly produce his inspirations. This, too, was an exciting meal, but even more exciting was to watch the dishes being cooked, assembled, and arranged.

We watched cabbage leaves being blanched and trimmed, then rolled around langouste tails, forming little packages. These were poached briefly and topped with a comma of fresh beluga caviar and a smidgen of finely chopped sweet red pepper. Other dishes were a terrine *de légumes,* a jewel-like mosaic of tiny colorful vegetables with pink duck liver nested in the center, garnished with herbs and a reduction of tomato; tiny kidneys and livers of rabbit with crayfish and wild mushrooms; and pigeon with truffles and a purée of watercress. Again, it was the kind of eating experience to which you abandon yourself completely.

I shall never forget these two meals at Girardet's and the excitement I felt at meeting this man and discovering his highly individual attitude toward cooking. I hope he will choose to remain in Crissier and let the world come to him instead of being seduced, as others have been, by the plaudits of the gastronomic press into taking his talent beyond his own little corner of Switzerland.

[1979]

The Food of Provence

No matter what spot I aim for in Europe, I am bound to end up in Provence for a day, a week, or a long stay, drawn by those magnificent chalky hills, the Alpilles, the colors of the tiled roofs, the Mediterranean light and sea, the Roman antiquities. I love the sight of the long rows of tall, pointed cypresses protecting fields and farmhouses against the mistral, the arbors of sycamores shielding streets from the hot sun—and most of all, I love the taste of Provençal food.

Last year, I settled down for several weeks on a farm named Lou Barcarès on the outskirts of St.-Rémy-de-Provence. From the terrace of the long tiled farmhouse, I looked out over fields of cultivated herbs—marjoram, tarragon, and chervil—and brilliant flowers. Beyond were the Alpilles, which looked deceptively like great distant mountains in the pure atmosphere but were, in fact, only hills and within walking distance, changing color through the day. At the foot of these hills I often gathered bay, rosemary, and thyme, growing wild.

The Provençal countryside is blessed by the sun and rich in the bounty of the earth. The early young vegetables are so good they are frequently eaten raw as crudités, bathed in spicy marinades and sauces. Melons perfume the air around Cavaillon. Luscious figs, apricots, and richly flavored raspberries abound. And everywhere you encounter the ripe rosy tomatoes, purple aubergines and green courgettes, garlic and onions, and superb olive oil, which laves the inimitable dishes for which Provence is so rightly famed.

To welcome me to Lou Barcarès, the owner, Mme. Yvonne Baudin, invited several guests and prepared an aïoli. This classic sauce, of which the essential ingredient is garlic, is the very breath of Provence. It was once said that if you wish to appear in public in Marseilles on a Friday afternoon, you should eat aïoli out of self-defense, if for no other reason. Aïoli always accompanies other foods—especially the fish dish known as bourride, a specialty of Marseilles—and it is the traditional Christmas Eve saucing for snails. Mme. Baudin's aïoli was served at table in the huge marble mortar in which it was made, ringed with a wonderful and colorful assortment of fish, vegetables, and other accompanying foods.

The traditional way to make an aïoli is to pound the garlic in a mortar in a steady, revolving motion. For 8 persons, pound about 12 garlic cloves or more if you like, then add 3 egg yolks. Continue the grinding motion. Finally, pound in olive oil, drop by drop, until the mixture has the texture of a thick mayonnaise. Add salt and lemon juice to taste. Should the emulsion break down, remove it, clean the mortar, and start again, using 1 garlic clove, 1 egg yolk, and a little oil. Then spoon in the first mixture, and continue stirring until the emulsion thickens.

Modern cooks say you can make aïoli by whirling the garlic cloves in a blender with an egg yolk and a little oil, after which the paste is combined with a heavy homemade mayonnaise. Thus, you would blend 12 garlic cloves with 1 egg yolk and 3 tablespoons of olive oil, and when this is thoroughly blended, beat it into a mayonnaise made with 3 egg yolks and 3 to $3^1/2$ cups of olive oil, or more, depending on the size of the yolks. The mayonnaise can be made in a blender, in an electric mixer, or by hand.

For the accompanying foods for 8 people:

Buy 2 pounds of filleted salt cod in one piece. Soak it in water to cover overnight or for 8 to 10 hours. Change the water once during the soaking. Drain and cover with cold water. Bring to a boil, and simmer for 10 minutes or until tender. Serve hot.

Peel and boil 10 to 12 medium-sized potatoes in salted water until just pierceable. Drain and dry over low heat. Serve hot.

Scrape 10 carrots and cook in boiling salted water until just done. Lightly peel 12 small zucchini and cook them in salted water until just pierceable. Poach 12 medium white onions until just tender. Cook 1 artichoke for each person. If asparagus is in season, cook 2 pounds until tender but still firm.

Serve 2 or 3 snails in their shells to each person.

Poach striped bass, red snapper, or halibut in a court bouillon. Serve hot or cold with a garnish of sliced cucumbers.

Allow at least 1 peeled hard-cooked egg per person.

Arrange the assortment of foods on platters, place around the aïoli, and let each person help himself to the sauce and accompanying foods. French bread and a good white wine or rosé of Provence are perfect with this dish.

Aïoli also makes a delicious sauce for hot or cold fish, cold vegetables, cold fowl, or hot or cold meats. It is often served with boiled lamb or boiled beef, together with capers and the ever-present black olives.

Avignon is the closest town of any size in the vicinity of St.-Rémy, and thus it was my major shopping center. On the main thoroughfare, there is a great two-star restaurant, Lucullus. M. Hiély, the patron, serves superb food and adheres strongly to the traditions of Provence.

❧ Mussels Lucullus ❧

2 to 3 quarts mussels
1 cup white wine
3 to 4 pounds spinach or
   2 packages frozen spinach
4 tablespoons olive oil
3 tablespoons butter

Salt and pepper to taste
1 cup heavy cream
4 egg yolks, lightly beaten
Pinch of saffron
Fine bread crumbs

Place the mussels in a heavy pan with the white wine, and steam them until they open. Shell and beard the mussels. Strain and reserve the liquid. If fresh spinach is used, blanch for 3 minutes in boiling water. Drain well and chop. If frozen spinach is used, thaw, drain, and chop. Heat the spinach in the olive oil and butter. Season with salt and pepper. Place in a gratin dish and top with the mussels.

Prepare a sauce by combining the heavy cream, $1/2$ cup of mussel liquid, and the beaten egg yolks, and cooking over low heat until thickened. Do not allow to boil. Season to taste with salt and pepper, and add a pinch of saffron. Pour the sauce over the mussels, sprinkle with crumbs, and glaze in a hot oven for 5 to 10 minutes. Serves 6 to 8.

One of the characteristic dishes of Provence is a daube, which usually resembles a stew, but sometimes the meat is cooked in one piece, which makes it nearer a pot roast. There are many varieties of daubes. Here is one that originated in Avignon.

☞ Daube Avignonnaise ☜

1 leg of lamb, boned	1 carrot, sliced
1 onion, stuck with 2 cloves	$1/4$ cup olive oil
2 sprigs parsley	1 teaspoon thyme
8 cloves garlic	1 bay leaf
Salt	Red wine
Strips of larding pork soaked in cognac and rolled in chopped parsley	6 large onions, coarsely chopped
	1 pig's foot, split
	3 or 4 slices salt pork, diced
2 onions, sliced	1 large piece of orange rind

Save the bones from the lamb, and ask the butcher for an extra one or two. Place the bones in a pot with the onion stuck with cloves, 1 sprig of parsley, and 2 cloves of garlic. Add 2 quarts of water, and cook down to a good broth. Season with salt to taste. Strain the broth and chill. Remove the fat from the top.

Cut the lamb in good-sized pieces. Lard each piece with a portion of the larding pork, and place in a large bowl. Combine the sliced onion, sliced carrot, olive oil, thyme, bay leaf, remaining parsley sprig, and 3 cloves of garlic, crushed, and add to the bowl. Pour in enough red wine to almost cover the lamb. Marinate for several hours or overnight. Drain off the liquid but reserve all the seasonings, along with the meat.

Make a bed of some of the chopped onion in a deep casserole. Add half of the pig's foot, then half of the marinated meat, more onion, the salt pork, the remaining meat, and the other half of the pig's foot. Add the orange rind, the reserved marinade seasonings, the remaining 3 cloves of garlic, and enough of the broth to cover the lamb. Put aluminum foil over the casserole and cover tightly. Cook very slowly on top of the stove or in a 275° oven for 3 to 4 hours. Remove the meat, skim off fat from the surface of the sauce, and reduce it over high heat. Cut the meat from the pig's foot, and add it to the sauce. Arrange the lamb on a serving dish, and pour the sauce over it. Serves 6 to 8.

Northwest of St.-Rémy is the town of Maillane, where the poet Frédéric Mistral was born and died. Mistral, who looked rather like our Buffalo Bill, wrote copiously and sentimentally about Provence and did a great deal to record and preserve Provençal customs and folklore. His lovely house has been made into a museum.

Across the street from the museum is the tiny Oustalet Maillanen, one of the typical small restaurants in Provence, where the food is prepared by the owner, in this case Mme. Fraize, a superb cook.

❦ Mme. Fraize's Alouettes sans Têtes ❧

2/3 pound ham, ground
  with 3 garlic cloves
3 tablespoons chopped parsley
1 teaspoon rosemary
Sprinkle of nutmeg
Salt and pepper

18 scallops of veal,
  pounded and trimmed
Olive oil
6 or 7 slices of bacon, cut in
  small pieces
Bay leaf
2/3 cup white wine

Combine the ham, parsley, rosemary, nutmeg, and salt and pepper to taste. Spread the mixture on each of the veal scallops, roll them up, and tie firmly with thread. Brown in olive oil. Add the bacon and let it cook down. Then add the bay leaf and white wine. Cook over low heat until the meat is tender, turning the rolls 2 or 3 times. You may cover the pan for part of the cooking time. The sauce may be thickened, but it is best when served as is over the meat. Rice and a gratin of eggplant are perfect accompaniments. Serves 6.

About a mile from Lou Barcarès, in a farmhouse called Mas Rouge, nestled at the foot of the Alpilles, lives an American friend of mine who has spent many years in Provence. He introduced me to this unusual Provençal treatment of pork. There are many versions of this dish. You find it in Spain and in the north of France as well.

❦ Drunken Pork ❧

1 boned leg of pork, with skin,
  about 8 or 9 pounds
7 cloves garlic
3 small onions
1 teaspoon basil
Red wine

3/4 cup pine nuts
Salt
Brown sauce or beurre manié
1/2 cup raisins, sultanas,
  or currants

Place the pork in a deep bowl with 4 cloves of garlic, the onions and basil, and enough red wine to almost cover the meat. Allow to marinate for 5 to 6 days, turning once or twice a day. Remove the meat and dry thoroughly. Reserve the marinade.

Make several gashes in the pork and force into them $1/4$ cup of the pine nuts and the remaining 3 garlic cloves, sliced. Rub the meat with salt. Roast at 325° on a rack in a roasting pan, allowing 25 to 30 minutes per pound.

While the pork is roasting, reduce the marinade to $1^1/2$ cups. Thicken with brown sauce or a beurre manié, and add the raisins and remaining pine nuts.

Serve this sauce with the roast, along with rice or polenta. Serves 8 to 10.

With St.-Rémy as home base, I often set out for neighboring points of interest on an hour's outing or perhaps a full day's journey. You could radiate in any direction and find antiquities, a fascinating hill town, or a charming stretch of landscape. Travel farther on into the Alpilles, and you encounter an eerie succession of rocky crags, some carved in strange fashion by the force of the mistral over the centuries, some hollowed out by men, for these limestone mountains have been quarried since the time of the Roman Empire.

Atop one isolated hill is perched the old town of Les Baux (named after bauxite, which was discovered in the vicinity). And below the town, tucked into a deep valley between two towering crags, is L'Oustau de la Baumanière, a three-star restaurant and inn, and one of the oldest showplaces of Provence. Since the opening of the restaurant, the owner and chef, M. Raymond Thuilier, has spent most of his time creating new and delicious dishes. His delectable *gigot en croûte* has become world famous.

❧ Gigot en Croûte ❧

2 or 3 lamb kidneys
4 to 5 tablespoons butter
1/3 cup Madeira
3 or 4 mushrooms,
    coarsely chopped
1/8 teaspoon thyme
1/8 teaspoon rosemary
1/4 teaspoon tarragon

Salt
Leg of baby lamb, 2 to 2 1/2
    pounds, with leg bone
    removed and shank bone
    left in
1 pound rough puff paste
1 egg beaten with 2
    tablespoons cream

Cut the kidneys into small pieces and toss them in hot butter until lightly browned. Deglaze the pan with Madeira. Add the mushrooms and herbs, and sprinkle with salt. Stuff the boned part of the leg with this mixture, re-form the leg, and secure it with a skewer.

Rub the leg with butter. Roast on a rack in a 450° oven for 10 minutes, reduce the heat to 375°, and roast for 10 to 12 minutes more. Remove from the oven and cool.

Roll out the rough puff paste about 1/2 inch thick, and wrap it around the leg, leaving the shank bone exposed. Cut out small pastry leaves and decorate the leg. Brush with the beaten egg and cream. Return to a rack, and bake at 375° until the pastry is brown and crisp, about 20 to 25 minutes. Serve with a gratin of potatoes. Serves 2 to 3.

Even if there were nothing but the beautifully arbored Cours Mirabeau, with its fashionable shops and cafés, Aix would be well worth a visit. But there is much more to explore along its handsome streets—fine houses, churches, museums, galleries. And when you tire of wandering, you can feast at the Provençale or the Croix de Malte. The Provençale offers from time to time a delicious entrecôte, which is simple to prepare and could be adapted as a variation on a favorite American outdoor dish.

❧ Entrecôte Provençale ☙

1 minute steak per person,
  about 6 to 7 ounces each
Olive oil
¹/₃ cup white wine

1 cup homemade
  tomato sauce
³/₄ cup green olives

Sauté the steaks quickly in oil and remove to a hot platter. Deglaze the pan with the white wine, and add 2 or 3 more tablespoons of olive oil, the tomato sauce, and the olives. Heat to the boiling point, correct the seasoning, and serve over the steaks.

If you prefer to grill the steaks, prepare the sauce separately. Sauté 1 clove of garlic, finely chopped, in 3 tablespoons of olive oil. Add the tomato sauce, olives, and a dash of sherry or dry vermouth. Heat to the boiling point, and simmer for several minutes. Correct the seasoning.

To the southwest of St.-Rémy lies a beautiful town important in Provençal history and celebrated in poetry and song—Arles. On Arles' principal, handsomely arbored boulevard, you will find the Jules César, a hotel regal in appearance, which serves good, honest Provençal food. A more modest—though entirely satisfactory—eating place, directly across from the ancient Gallo-Roman arena, is called Café des Arènes.

One of the specialties of Arlésienne cooking is this version of sautéed chicken.

❧ Poulet Arlésienne ☙

1 frying chicken, 3 to 4
  pounds, cut up, or legs
  and thighs
4 to 5 tablespoons olive oil
2 cloves garlic, chopped
1 teaspoon salt

1 tablespoon chopped
  fresh basil
¹/₂ teaspoon freshly ground
  black pepper
1 teaspoon dried basil
²/₃ cup white wine

For the sauce:

3 onions, finely chopped
1 clove garlic, chopped
3 tablespoons olive oil

2 cups homemade tomato sauce
1 hot pepper, finely chopped
1/4 teaspoon Tabasco

Sauté the chicken pieces in oil until delicately colored on all sides. Add the seasonings and 1/3 cup of wine, and simmer for about 20 minutes, turning once. Meanwhile, prepare the sauce: sauté the onion and garlic in the oil until just soft, add the tomato sauce, and simmer for 20 to 25 minutes. Add the hot pepper and Tabasco, and correct the seasoning. The sauce should be thick and piquant.

Remove the cooked chicken to a hot platter. Deglaze the pan with the rest of the wine and pour the juices over the chicken. Serve the sauce separately. Serves 4.

To the south of Arles is that strange, isolated region formed of the delta of the Rhône known as the Camargue. Only recently has it become fashionable for tourists. One of the principal industries of the Camargue is cattle raising, and it is here that France has its own version of the cowboy—the *gardien.*

⚞ Beef à la Gardien ⚟

4 or 5 strips bacon, cut
    thick and diced
2 tablespoons olive oil
3 large onions, coarsely
    chopped
3 pounds chuck, cut in cubes
1 onion stuck with cloves
1 teaspoon rosemary
1 leek

1 or 2 cloves of garlic
Strip of orange rind
Salt, cayenne, and pepper
    to taste
2/3 cup small green olives
1 cup black olives, pitted
3 or 4 potatoes, cut in thick
    slices

Render the bacon in a heavy skillet. Add the olive oil and the chopped onion. Cook until golden. Add the meat, and brown on all sides. Add the remaining ingredients and about 1 cup of water. Cover, and cook slowly until the meat is tender. Uncover, and let the sauce reduce. Serve with rice. Serves 6.

I have always loved the tough, raucous port town of Marseilles, with its beautiful harbor and enchanting Old Port. The screaming fish-women, the rough-and-ready sailors, the odd assortment of other characters all go to make up an exciting atmosphere that is both warm and harsh. There is nothing quite like the color, smell, and noise of Marseilles. Where else would you find a garlic market?—which is held here in July.

Marseilles has innumerable small and great restaurants where you can feast on bourride and *soupe de poissons.* Bourride, to my mind, has always been a better dish than the renowned bouillabaisse when it is done with care, as it is at the Brasserie Catalan. [See recipe page 34, "Hearty Luncheon Dishes."]

Drive thirty kilometers west of Marseilles along the water and you are in another world. Here are lovely little villas, beautiful trees, and the bluest of Mediterranean water. This is Carry-le-Rouet. The restaurant on the hill, L'Escale, is run by M. Bérot, once chef for the French Line. One of the great specialties for a first course at this superb restaurant is clams au gratin.

☜ Clams au Gratin ☞

½ cup finely chopped mushrooms
½ cup finely chopped
  shallots or onions
Butter
2 tablespoons finely chopped
  parsley

2 tablespoons finely chopped
  tomato
Salt and pepper
36 small clams on the
  half shell
⅓ to ½ cup bread crumbs

Sauté the mushrooms and shallots or onions in 6 tablespoons of butter for 3 minutes. Add the parsley, tomato, and salt and pepper to taste. Spoon this over the clams. Sprinkle with crumbs, dot with butter, and bake at 400° for 5 to 8 minutes or until the clams are just heated through. Serves 6.

There are wonderful oval gratin dishes in various parts of Provence, known as *tian,* which are used to cook unusual concoctions of vegetables, vegetables and fish, and vegetables and eggs. The secret of most of these dishes is slow cooking in oil—olive oil, of course. There is no end to the variations possible. Here is an example:

⚜ Gratin of Greens ⚜

2 pounds spinach
Olive oil
2 pounds Swiss chard
2 pounds zucchini
Salt to taste

1 cup cooked rice
3 cloves garlic, chopped
6 eggs, well beaten
Fine bread crumbs

Wash and dry the spinach, chop rather fine, and cook in a little olive oil in a heavy skillet over medium heat until just wilted. Drain. Chop the chard and cook in the same manner. Dice the zucchini, and cook in 6 tablespoons oil until just tender. Combine the vegetables with salt to taste, the rice, and the garlic. Transfer to a well-oiled heavy baking dish. Add 3 to 4 tablespoons olive oil, and bake in a 300° oven for 20 minutes. Add the eggs, sprinkle with crumbs, and return to the oven until the eggs are just set. Eat warm or cold. Serves 6 to 8.

Another great dish of Provence is *brandade,* which is basically codfish. It is something you want only once or twice a year, but when you have it, it must be superb. There is a restaurant in Paris that serves delicious *beignets de brandade,* made by dropping the *brandade* mixture by spoonfuls into hot 365° fat to cook until completely browned. The English cookbook author Elizabeth David claims the finest *brandade* she knows comes from a small shop on the rue Avignon in Nîmes. I found that the local charcutier in St.-Rémy made a most acceptable *brandade,* too.

✸ Brandade ✸

Soak 1 pound of filleted salt codfish for several hours or overnight. Change the water once. Cover with fresh water, bring to a boil, and simmer for 5 to 6 minutes. Drain. Flake very finely, discarding any bone. Using a mortar and pestle, a blender, or an electric mixer with a dough hook or paddle attachment, pound the fish to a paste with 2 cloves of garlic while adding $2/3$ cup of warm olive oil, spoonful by spoonful, alternately with $1/3$ cup of warm heavy cream, until the mixture becomes well integrated. It should look rather like wet mashed potatoes. Serve warm with fried toast. Serves 6 as an appetizer or luncheon dish.

[1964]

In Praise of English Food

The English are inclined to be modest about their food, and there are those who assert that there is plenty to be modest about. Yet many a discriminating American traveler in England has learned that there is good food aplenty if you know where to look and what to ask for.

It generally turns out that the most vocal of complainers about English food have eaten at good restaurants and hotels but have ordered the most familiar dishes. Seldom, I find, have they experimented with the more distinctive English foods, although the country abounds with magnificent gastronomic specialties.

First of all, England offers some of the world's greatest fish and seafood. Foremost of the fish is Dover sole, which doesn't have much resemblance to the fillet of sole served in American restaurants. It is the greatest white fish known to the *fine bouche*. It has a firm texture, is heavily meated, and has a rich and subtle flavor that lends itself to variety in preparation. It comes with sauces, elaborately stuffed and rolled, or plain sautéed. The English know and appreciate their Dover sole. They serve it sea fresh, usually grilled or sautéed, and with plenty of butter, a delicate sprinkling of parsley, and a punctuation of lemon.

I also find turbot an exciting fish. A turbot weighs about ten pounds, but they can grow much larger. Thirty-pound turbots swim in cold waters off the coast of Yorkshire and Devonshire. This is a superior fish often served at gatherings of epicures. I like my turbot simple. I've always felt that poached turbot, served hot with lemon butter or cold with mayonnaise, is as satisfying to the palate as any highly sauced dish. Hunt out the small restaurant on the coast or a good grill specializing in fish and try this delicious member of the Rhombus family.

Plaice, a form of flounder, abounds in English waters. It is not to be confused with the plaice caught around the island of Nantucket. The latter is actually summer flounder, a smaller fish, lighter in texture. English plaice may weigh ten pounds. It has firm white flesh, and when broiled or sautéed, with the addition of a few slivered almonds, it is delicious.

If you visit England during the "R" months, start your fishfest with a first course of oysters. The chilly seas that surround Great Britain may be responsible for the superiority of the English oyster. They are firm, with just the right amount of fat and a delicate taste of the salt sea. Try Whitstables or Colchesters, both beloved by oyster fanciers the world over. Other English oysters I find delectable are Rochesters, Miltons, and Burnhams. In London, go to Bentley's on Swallow Street or to Wheeler's or any of the oyster specialty houses and feast on this delicacy, along with English ale or sturdy stout; or, if you prefer, a bottle of Chablis. With oysters, the English serve thinly sliced, well-buttered brown bread.

Shrimp and prawns are also exceptionally good in England. Do not miss Dublin Bay prawns, subtly flavored and toothsome. They remind me of France's langoustine. Cold Dublin Bay prawns with a touch of lemon juice and a bit of mayonnaise make the perfect first course or snack, and they go well with a bottle of good ale or a brisk white wine.

No discussion of superior English foods can go on for long without coming to cheese. Someday I'm going to treat myself to a special cheese tour of England. In few places is cheese so perfectly aged. Besides the many local cheeses worth hunting down, there are, of course, those of international fame. I suppose the three greatest are cheddar, Cheshire, and Stilton. English cheddar is usually well aged and has just enough bite to make it stimulating to the tongue and palate. Cheshire is similar to cheddar but softer, more crumbly, and has a more delicate quality. Less well known is an amazing cheese called Wensleydale—white, sharp, and very rich. Then there is Stilton, a blue-vein cheese that ages and cures into a ripe, creamy, highly flavored product. Good Stilton is never cut with a knife, but with a fork or wire to prevent it from crumbling. Some people cure Stilton with port, and good it is, but I prefer the ripe cheese by itself.

Speaking of port, the English are the world's biggest consumers of it. (They have a true appreciation of all fine wines.) In England, you can taste the greatest ports available anywhere.

As you travel through the countryside, you will be served a good deal of chicken. It has a natural, good country flavor. English chickens benefit by growing up in a rather unsophisticated, quiet atmosphere. They are not hormonized or vitaminized or reared under glass.

Duck is usually simply cooked—nicely roasted (the English are roasters and meat-cookers par excellence) and seldom embellished with more than a savory stuffing. Sometimes it is served with tart applesauce. Like the chickens, the ducks have an honest country flavor. They have neither been fattened for market by a special process nor so larded that they cook away to a pan of grease. They are well breasted, firm textured, and delicately flavored.

I am weary of the talk that cabbage and Brussels sprouts, poorly cooked, are the staple vegetables of the English menu. I well remember eating the first new potatoes, the first tender young peas, and the first scarlet runner beans from my aunt's garden in Wiltshire. And I have bought fine fresh vegetables from greengrocers in London and found they always had a good, earthy flavor. The English are born with green thumbs. They love gardening and are blessed with a climate that encourages a slow maturing for vegetables and fruits. Their garden produce is grown by local farmers and brought immediately to market, ripe and luscious. And what this means to the flavor of a strawberry! English strawberries are astonishingly red, juicy, and sweet.

Raspberries, rhubarb, red and black currants, greengage plums and damson plums (which make a fabulous preserve), and gooseberries are other English fruits that are exceptional. English gooseberries often grow as big as plums. They are memorable when poached in sugar syrup until just tender but still firm and served up with thick cream.

Most people seem to believe that roast-beef-and-Yorkshire-pudding is the basic English meat dish. Although roast beef is prevalent and delicious, there are many meats that are just as typically English. Mutton, for example. A perfectly grilled mutton chop or a well-roasted joint of Southdown mutton is an eating joy. Southdown is a particular breed of sheep that produces fine wool and distinctively flavored meat. And I don't ever spurn really good boiled mutton with caper sauce. Spring lamb from the same breed is also delicious, especially when served up with tiny new potatoes and the first tender green peas of the season. And I can recommend the hams and bacon from the Wiltshire countryside, which are cured and smoked in the old-fashioned manner. Their texture is firm and their flavor rich.

These are a few of the foods I have found outstanding in many trips to England over the past thirty-five years. If you order wisely, you can find much of the best in leading London restaurants, but let me urge you to enjoy country produce close to the source.

If English food is sometimes abused by bad treatment, one must remember that the English have no monopoly on bad cooks. Yet there is a distinct difference between the average British inn or restaurant and its counterpart across the Channel. In France, the boss is likely to be the chef; in Britain, he is frequently an absentee who owns the establishment as an investment. So it will pay you to search out one of the fine old inns, such as the Fellbridge Hotel near East Grinstead in Kent, where the owner takes justifiable pride in her food.[1] The inn is small enough to have a friendly, intimate quality. It is the center of countryside activities, and the local people gather at the small snack bar. On Saturday evenings, they all come to dance.

---

[1] The Fellbridge Hotel is not listed in current guidebooks.

What a joy it was to relax here—to awaken after a comfortable sleep in linen sheets to a cup of freshly made tea and the crackle of a newly lit fire, and to gather your wits before dressing for breakfast. And what a breakfast! The English breakfast is unequaled. First of all, there is porridge. This is not something dumped from a box and served five minutes later. This is porridge that has bubbled, sputtered, and simmered for hours over hot water. It has the real flavor of meal. You anoint it with sugar, plenty of rich country cream, and perhaps a dab of butter.

To follow, there is bacon from the best Wiltshire hogs, served in gargantuan rashers. With it come small tomatoes that are found only on English breakfast plates, each one completely, deliciously ripe. Or there are sausages, plump and pungent. Sometimes your breakfast plate also includes a grilled mushroom cap. And eggs? Of course, and the eggs you find in inns and private homes must come from very happy hens. They have gleaming whites, brilliant yolks, and that subtle flavor of freshness.

One of my greatest pleasures in an English breakfast is the toast rack. I like crisp, fresh toast of homemade bread, and I do not want it smothered in a napkin. This I enjoy with plenty of butter and marmalade, when I am through with the main dish, punctuating each bite with a swallow of steaming hot tea.

Other English breakfast treats are grilled kidneys, finnan haddie, and that traditional pair, kippers and bloaters. Somehow the smell of a really good kipper or bloater (not one inoculated with artificial smoke) heating on the hearth or stove is most tantalizing early in the morning.

Sunday lunch at the Fellbridge Hotel is another occasion. Then the owner serves beefsteak and kidney pudding, and many neighboring families come in to feast. This dish, which can be unbelievably bad if not properly made, at the Fellbridge is fantastically good. The meat is tender and flavorful, the suet crust thin and light. I could have eaten a second helping if I had not known that fresh strawberries from the Kentish fields were to follow. A big plate of these, with the stems left on and a neat pile of powdered sugar for dipping, served with a slice of light sponge cake, is worth remembering.

Another choice country spot is the elegant and very Georgian Ivy House Hotel at Marlborough in Wiltshire. If you are interested in a jaunt to Cornwall, the beautiful rugged land of Arthurian legend, go to the Punch Bowl Inn in Lanreath. Here, too, are fine foods and wines, and don't pass up the cider. This is apple country, and true old-fashioned hard cider is a local specialty.

If you inquire locally or consult a British travel service, you will find such inns in almost any area you care to visit. You might pick, for example, the famous dairy country, Devonshire, home of one of the world's gastronomic delights, Devonshire cream. This is the heaviest of heavy creams, warmed very, very slowly over low heat for hours until it forms thick clots. This clotted cream is wonderful eaten with fresh fruits, such as strawberries, raspberries, or peaches.

The making and serving of tea is a well-known English specialty. One of my earliest memories of London is tea at the Ritz. I keep going back, and the proceedings are still as impressive as they were years ago. Perfectly trained waiters prepare your tea as you order it. The water is brought to a thundering, rolling boil before it is poured over your favorite leaves—Assam, pekoe, Darjeeling, or oolong. The tea steeps in a hot pot for four or five minutes and is brought to you with milk (not cream), a bowl of sugar, and fragile cups. With this comes a choice of foods. The English have always excelled in making sandwiches that are well filled but thinner than paper. At the Ritz, they bring platters of finger-sized sandwiches bursting with mustard cheese, shrimp paste, thinly sliced chicken, or delicious ham. Or you might decide to have a piece of crisp, hot buttered toast or a scone. After this come slices of cakes: Genoa cake, Madeira cake, Dundee cake—rib-sticking, rich, buttery, and often fruited cakes. There are also trays of small, delicate pastries, and as if this weren't enough, you may be offered slices of heavier, creamy pastries, made to tempt the eye and enlarge the waistline.

Tea at my aunt's country home in Wiltshire, with a view across Salisbury Plain, is another sort of experience. (If you ever receive an invitation to an English country home for tea, by all means accept. It will undoubtedly be a memorable treat.) The teapot still brews the same wonderful blend that I knew as a youth. The table groans with my aunt's own variety of currant-studded buns. There are thin slices of homemade white and brown bread, buttered and waiting to be heaped with raspberry or wild bramble jam. Sometimes there are crumpets, their spongelike texture oozing with melted butter. In addition, my aunt serves feathery home-made sponge cake; little jumbles that she calls "rocks," heavily meated with walnuts and raisins; tiny, flaky Eccles cakes; and an old favorite of mine, Banbury cakes. Sometimes, too, there are lemon cheese tarts or jam tarts, tender and delicious.

One experience no food lover should miss when in England is a visit to Fortnum and Mason's in London. This magnificent shop is a monument to the finest English taste in food. For over two centuries, Fortnum and Mason's has been supplying an amazing array of delicacies. During the latter part of the nine-teenth century and the Edwardian period, they became famed for their magnificent hampers of elegant picnic food and for the great crates of fine food they shipped around the world, wherever Englishmen were stationed away from home. Last year I visited this shop on its two hundred fiftieth anniversary and found it as fabulous as ever. I trudged around the ice counters admiring game pies, cooked game, poultry, meats, the incomparable Scotch salmon, and the "made" dishes for which Fortnum and Mason's is so famous.

If you lunch at Fortnum and Mason's, you will eat remarkably well from a list of good staple foods of the British Isles: Scotch beef, fine fresh fish, crabs, lobsters, traditional meat and game pies, and potted shrimp, one of the most inviting appetizers I know. The tiny shrimp are mixed with softened butter, with a touch of mace added, and then stored in little pots and chilled. They are served unmolded on greens and make a much tastier dish than any shrimp cocktail.

Here are a few other places in London for English food I find especially satisfying:

Scotts in Piccadilly serves excellent fish and game, especially good sole, dressed crab and lobster, fine English cheese, traditional English desserts, and good wines, beers, and ales. The Café Royal on Regent Street has a somewhat Edwardian atmosphere and specializes in grills, meats, and seafood, with an excellent wine list. The Savoy Grill has a menu with an international flavor, but it includes traditional English specialties. It is elegant and expensive. The Ivy, 1 Wert Street, features such delicacies as plovers' eggs and Scotch salmon. Bentley's on Swallow Street is notable for its seafood and wines. The Antelope in Eaton Terrace, S.W. 1, is a good, simple pub, serving hearty food. So is Fleet Street's famous Cheshire Cheese. Brown's Hotel on Dover Street is a fine hotel in the old English tradition. Its restaurant menu includes Continental items, but look for the English specialties. Rules on Maiden Lane serves typical English dishes in a setting of faded Edwardian elegance.

[1958]

"American" Cooking

People are trying very hard to make American cooking as phony as nouvelle cuisine sometimes has been. They are dreaming up food that is about as American as Peking duck, though without its crispy succulence, and everybody seems to have a different theory as to what our cookery is all about. Sometimes I get the feeling that if the ingredients are not still twitching or just off the branch, one-quarter the normal size, and produced by a farmer in the outer reaches of New Hampshire or Oregon, your dish can't be labeled true-blue American.

Well, the truth of the matter is that the way people eat is an unconscious reflection of the way people live. We have a great tradition of home cooking and restaurant cooking that spans three centuries. We are now, I hope, in a new epoch of gastronomic excellence that, with a liberal seasoning of common sense, will draw on the best of old American cookery as well as on the technological advances of the new.

Great excitement has been engendered over the fact that Belon oysters can now be raised from French seed on the Maine coast, and I am quite sure there will be a tremendous hullabaloo if a company named Agri-Truffle is successful in its attempts to grow French truffles under California oak trees. These efforts are made in the name of the new American cuisine, though I'm not quite sure why.

American food, as defined in an earlier age, was, of course, regional. Planes and refrigerated trucks didn't rush lettuce and seafood and strawberries from one side of the country to the other. Recipes were perfected by women who came from practically every country on earth and used traditional family methods and locally available ingredients. Many of these recipes found their way into little fund-raiser cookery books put out by ladies aid societies, missionary societies, hospital volunteer groups, and women's exchanges. Thus we developed a tradition of such things as New England clam chowder, Manhattan clam chowder, New Orleans court bouillon, San Francisco cioppino, Oregon crab soup, and, in the Midwest, catfish-head soup. All different, all delicious.

As the nation became more industrialized and kitchen help vanished and more women took up careers, shortcuts in the kitchen were the order of the day. Now, in the age of the cooking school, it appears that the average cook—man or woman—is expected to turn out slices of lobster pâté adrift in a sea of asparagus sauce (complete with a tomato "rose"), pheasant pot-pie with a dome of puff pastry six inches high, and a mousse of watercress. All this in an hour or less after getting home from work. There is a difference between good American home cooking and good American restaurant cooking, but the distinction is becoming blurred.

American home cooking, generally prepared without help but with superb mechanical aids, such as the food processor, uses ingredients that are as fresh and natural as possible. It is done in a relatively short time. Company cooking, on the other hand, is usually a weekend effort.

My advice is to avoid treating the much-touted "new American cuisine" as if it were some kind of patriotic endeavor one simply must pursue. It's mostly journalistic hype, and it's pointless to try and name a "Vestal Virgin of American Cuisine," a "King of the New American Restaurants," or a "Queen of the New American Cafés." I have yet to meet any culinary vestal virgins, kings, or queens in the food world—just ordinary folk, who are all contributing to the development and betterment of our eating habits.

To my great amusement, masses of garlic are now considered very new and chic in a number of the more avant-garde restaurants. Well, garlic is nothing new. In former centuries, garlic was treated as the vegetable it is. When cooked slowly, unpeeled, for a long time, it becomes mild and mellow to the point where you can pop the creamy pulp from the husks and eat the purée on crusty bread or add it to a sauce or a cheese soufflé mixture.

I am giving you a recipe that is originally Hungarian and was found in a manuscript cookbook of a midwestern housewife. This dish serves eight to ten persons. It's old, it's new, it's red, white, and blue. What more could you ask?

❧ Garlicked Goose ❧

Rub a 12- to 14-pound goose well with salt and pepper. (If frozen, it should be thoroughly defrosted.) Stuff the cavity with 2 pounds of garlic, broken up into cloves but not peeled. Sew up the goose, place it on a rack in a roasting pan, and cover it with foil. Roast in a 375° oven about 2 hours. Remove the foil, and prick the skin of the goose very well. Pour off the fat from the pan and reserve it. Continue roasting the bird $1/2$ to $3/4$ hour longer until the skin is brown and crisp and a meat thermometer registers 175°.

Serve the roast goose with braised red cabbage and mashed potatoes, to which a little of the goose fat and garlic purée have been added. To make the purée, simply squeeze the creamy pulp from the unpeeled garlic cloves roasted inside the goose.

[1982]

8

*T*his trio of pieces is largely autobiographical. "An American Attitude Toward Food" is as much about Beard as about food, taking the reader on a quick whirl through his life, from his beginnings in the Pacific Northwest to his professional coming of age in New York. It could serve as his résumé.

"Berrying" is an affectionate reminiscence of boyhood days. It is one of a number of fragments that Beard taped for a final book and has never been published. It complements the piece that follows, "Life at Its Best," which is an excerpt from Beard's earlier memoir, *Delights and Prejudices,* and appeared in *Harper's Magazine* two years before publication of the book. This charming segment recalls the joys of family summers at the beach in Gearhart, Oregon, where his mother's sure hand in the kitchen and cookouts by the sea gave Beard the underpinnings for a life in food. Time and again in his writings he returns to his Pacific Northwest heritage, and many a piece begins, "When I was growing up in Oregon . . ." For Beard, food was autobiography.

$\mathcal{A}$n American Attitude Toward Food

I grew up in a kitchen, and I guess the scent of food is like a perfume. It has stayed with me all my life. My mother ran a small residential hotel in Portland, Oregon, and eating was an experience in our family. We were three distinct personalities, my mother, my father, and I, and we all liked food cooked in a different way. Let, our Chinese cook, spoiled us, really, because he'd take a dish and do it separately for each of us.

Let was originally my mother's chef when she ran the Gladstone Hotel. At the turn of the century, she had an international approach to food that would be revolutionary even by the standards of the last ten years. She was of English and Welsh background, and the majority of her kitchen staff was Chinese, with intermittent French head chefs. Portland was clearly too small to contain the Gallic temperaments of the latter, so after a few months they'd leave, but their technique and style would have been perfectly mastered by the Chinese. The food was sort of the precursor of our "new cuisine," a combination of quick sautés, French sauces, and American ingredients.

My father loved food, too. His family, over a period of sixty years, had trekked from the Carolinas to Oregon, and he had what I think of as old southern—closely related to Scottish—ideas about food. He felt that spinach should cook for about four hours with a piece of hog jowl and that string beans needed about three hours of the same treatment.

But he also loved game, and among my earliest memories is the row of brilliantly colored ducks and pheasants that would hang in the larder. There were always teal, too, and I developed a great love for them because they are delicate and small enough to eat whole at one sitting.

When we had teal, it was always reserved for the household, never served to guests. These tiny members of the duck family are devastatingly good when roasted simply and quickly—basted with butter and seasoned with only salt and pepper—and, like squab, eaten with the fingers. As an accompaniment, we often ate braised celery or tender raw celery, and potatoes cooked in the oven with broth. Several years ago, when I was staying in Yucatán, I had teal served to me—it migrates there from the Northwest—and it was the most sentimental meal I ever had eaten. I relished each bite. In France, too, one occasionally finds teal. It is called *sarcelle* and is as good there as it was in Oregon in my youth.

Little did I think, back in those days before the First World War, that food would become the foundation of my career. I started out wanting to be a singer and an actor—I'm not quite sure what kind of actor—and my family encouraged me to pursue these interests. For the most part, I'd have to say I succeeded. I got in at the beginning of radio, and I did a stint on the New York stage in the late thirties. To make ends meet, I taught at a country day school in New Jersey, where I got the first grade going on bread making.

It was around this time that I had a real identity crisis. I decided I was never going to earn enough money working in the theater and radio to keep my life going in the manner in which I would have it. Noel Coward did not seem to be rushing to write plays for me, after all, and the only thing that matched my love of theater was my love of food. I'd always been exposed to good food. My mother had had several friends in the restaurant business who ran really excellent establishments, and I learned early in life to appreciate them.

And then there was New York. New York in the late twenties and the thirties teemed with wonderful restaurants and restaurant chains—Schrafft's, Longchamps, and Child's—where a little bit of money bought a lot. At six foot four, I always had an appetite, and it usually took more than three "squares" to make a whole.

As luck would have it, around this time I met a man named Bill Rhode and his sister, Irma. As we were all in search of a career, we hit on the idea of capitalizing on America's mania for cocktails. The repeal of Prohibition had set the cocktail party into full swing, and in America the *cinq-à-sept* was reserved for drinks and finger food. Something, we agreed, should be done about the food. We had eaten too many pieces of cottony bread soggy with processed cheese, anchovy fillets by the yard, and dried-up bits of ham and smoked salmon. The ghastly potato-chip dip invention had only begun to spread across the country. So we opened a small, exclusive catering shop called Hors d'Oeuvre Inc.

There were, we gauged, at least 250 cocktail parties every afternoon on the Upper East Side of Manhattan, and we felt certain that all we needed was the better mousetrap. I remember Mother's saying that a good sandwich at teatime was hardly to be found anywhere. It would be a fine idea, I thought, to offer New York perfect tea sandwiches, also larger ones for evening entertaining—"reception sandwiches," I believe they are called officially. We called them "highball sandwiches."

Next we had to decide on our bill of fare. We discovered the trick of using various smoked sausages and meats as cornucopias and developed a dozen stunning ways to offer stuffed eggs. For the cornucopias, we used salami, bolognas, hams, smoked salmon, and the specially cured pork loin called *lachsschinken*. We also made rolls of salmon, tongue, and the rarest roast beef, and there were sandwiches of veal.

The fillings we created were appetizing and varied. For the most part, the base was a mixture of cream cheese and sour cream. This, with various additions, could be forced through a pastry bag, which speeded the work considerably. I became the squeeze-bag artist. The salami filling contained *fines herbes,* with the addition of dill and sometimes a bit of garlic; the *lachsschinken* filling included horseradish and perhaps a little mustard, if customers liked their food piquant; the salmon filling was flavored with a combination of onion, capers, freshly ground black pepper, and a touch of lemon juice. As for the rolls, the beef was spread with a very hot kumquat mustard and the ends dipped in chopped parsley, while the tongue was spread with a Roquefort or mushroom butter and sometimes garnished at either end with a sprig of watercress. Our veal sandwiches—two thin slices of veal cut in rounds—were filled with an anchovy butter or a herring butter, both of which were tremendously popular.

Incidentally, I wrote my first cookbook, *Hors d'Oeuvre and Canapés,* during this time, and thirty years later, when I went back to revise it, I was surprised by how little needed to be updated and by how many of our selections had become caterers' standbys. Not infrequently, when I'm at a cocktail party, a tray of canapés is passed before me, and among them I see old friends.

At this time, too, Americans were becoming more exposed to foreign foods, through luxurious ocean liners and the grand hotels that dotted the country. It was with the dawning of the New York World's Fair in 1939 that food in all its extraordinary variety was set before the American public in ways they had never seen before. A window was opened on the food world that even the dreadful war could not close. The scents from those multinational kitchens—the Swiss Pavilion, the Belgian, the Italian, the Russian (where caviar cost practically nothing), the Swedish, and, of course, Henri Soulé's French Pavillon— would eventually lead us to what we've come to know as the American attitude toward food. Even now it's not fully realized.

Well, when the war came I had to give up the catering business because rationing made it impossible. We couldn't buy enough butter or enough meat, but the incredible exposure to all those cuisines I'd sampled at the Fair sustained me through the bleak years until peace returned.

I have to say I was lucky, though, because I spent the war years working for the United Seamen's Services. Basically, we performed the same duties as the USO and the Red Cross, but entirely for the Merchant Marines. We had clubs all over the world, and given the circumstances, we served really top-notch food. I traveled a great deal for the USS, starting in Puerto Rico and going to Brazil, Peru, and the Canal Zone, then on to Morocco, Italy, and France. I never ceased to marvel at how people could make do. They learned to conserve and substitute—for example, making eggless, milkless, butterless cakes. Those were the years, too, when frozen foods began to take hold. They seemed like a miracle. (Mr. Birdseye, who had very particular ideas about food, would set his freezing equipment right out in the middle of acres of strawberries and freeze them on the spot.) And of course, all the meat and poultry that was served in Europe was shipped in refrigerated containers.

By the late forties, in a sprint to recoup those lost years, people seemed to rush into the future, trying to rebuild their lives, their careers, their families. Food reflected this sense of urgency. Along with frozen foods, there were fast foods in nascent form. Pizza was beginning—there were about three pizza places in New York that were very good. Soda fountains everywhere produced milk shakes and malteds. Another staple of this time, still popular today, was the clubhouse sandwich, a meal in one course. I have particular ideas myself about this dish. To me, it's two slices of toast, not three; lettuce (if you like lettuce); sliced breast of chicken, not turkey; bacon; sliced ripe tomato; and mayonnaise.

When you look back, you see periods of time inextricably linked with some person, some place, some thing. For me it was often food. The twenties, for instance, were the era of hot dogs and speakeasy food, some of it very good indeed. Hamburgers didn't really become popular until the forties and fifties, although I can remember being in Los Angeles around, oh, 1930, when there was a string of absolutely sensational hamburger stands. They would put everything on the burger, wrap it in a diaper of paper, and put it in a little bag. This magnificent construction cost fifteen cents. It was a full meal, because you had, in addition to the hamburger, lettuce, tomato, onion, pickle, mustard, and relish. This would be followed by a serving of hot apple pie with melted cheese. Deadly, when I think about it now, but good it seemed to me then.

By the fifties, there I was right in the midst of this burgeoning interest in food. People were taking the time to cook complex dishes, international dishes. Don't get me wrong—people had always taken the time to cook good food, but it was only now that the general public began to realize the varieties and possibilities of food. With this sophistication came a quest for diversity. No longer was eating simply a necessity; it became a pleasure. It seems at this time I found material for cookbook after cookbook, and—wonder of wonders—people were buying them. Suddenly I was in demand to teach cooking classes (I was one of the first to do it—for NBC—on the infant medium television), and corporations sought me out as a consultant to elevate the quality of their goods for consumers who were more demanding than ever before. All this, combined with the boom in technology, helped to channel as well as to unleash my own attitudes toward food in America.

In a way, though, it wasn't until the sixties that some of the jigsaw puzzle of my life came together. That was when I met

Joe Baum, president of Restaurant Associates. I worked with him and the association on a number of restaurant projects, but most of all on New York's the Four Seasons. It proved an ideal collaboration: my sixty years of experience, Joe's enthusiasm, and the excitement of using all-American seasonal products. Our ideas and approach seemed as fresh as the ingredients we sought out. For example, baskets of freshly picked vegetables would be brought to your table so you could choose the ones you wanted. In asparagus season, there were perhaps twenty different ways you could have asparagus prepared. We had fiddleheads and wild mushrooms and many other things both weird and wonderful.

It was Joe Baum's premise that this was a restaurant for New Yorkers. Certainly it proved to be a complete change from everything we'd seen before. If for no other reason, the fact that our menus and format were copied so much convinced us we were right. We had an inimitable group, with Joe Baum, of course, Albert Stockli as executive chef, and Albert Kumin as first pastry chef. I worked a great deal at the Four Seasons. Apart from being consultant on the food, I did the wine list and held wine classes for all the captains every week for two or three years. I've gone through several beginnings in my life, and this is the one I'm most proud of.

I sometimes wonder if my being just one generation from the covered wagon makes me feel so allied to this country's gastronomic treasures. The pioneers lived off the land they traveled, and necessity sired invention. I'm always asked what the dominating factor in American cuisine is, and my reply is that it's the many ethnic groups, each of which brought its own ideas of food to this country. When they first settled here, they often could not find the ingredients they were used to, so they adapted their dishes and invented new ones, using whatever was available.

As people became neighborly and exchanged ideas about all sorts of things, they exchanged ideas about food, too. If you go back into the cookbooks written by the Ladies Aid Society of the Methodist Episcopal Church, or by the Hadassah, or by any such organization, you can almost trace the history of American food. In some books, you find a recipe done three different ways, and you can pretty well choose who had the original.

There are many dishes that could be considered completely American. Indian pudding is one, and it's coming into vogue again. Then we often forget that layer cakes—particularly baking powder layer cakes—are our invention. And while the Europeans have always had tarts, and the English originated apple pie and many deep-dish pies, the cream pies and what I think of as "gooey" pies, along with a lot of fruit pies, were certainly developed in this country. And we have many hot breads, like muffins, biscuits, popovers, and baking powder coffee cakes.

Every country near an ocean developed a fish stew, and ours are New England clam chowder and California's cioppino. And what could be more American than a clambake? I remember splendid ones from my childhood, and you never see them in Europe.

Chili has become virtually an American creation. I don't think I could possibly choose just one kind, because part of the charm of this dish for me is that I can always make it differently, and it never disappoints. I must not forget to add barbecues either—the real southern kind that are smoke cooked—for although they were first introduced by the French settlers in Louisiana, they are surely an American classic. The original idea was to feed a large outdoor gathering by roasting an animal, perhaps a whole sheep, goat, or pig, in front of or over a fire on a homemade spit that pierced the animal from *barbe à la queue*— literally, from whiskers to tail. Thus the word *barbecue* came into our language and spread all over the world.

My father was able to tell me something of the pioneer culinary tradition, which he remembered from his trip by covered wagon from Iowa to Oregon. As a child of five or six, together with his brothers and other boys of the same age, he would shoot birds while his elders hunted small animals. These were usually cooked on wooden spits over a wood fire. According to my father, there was invariably a dispute among the members of the wagon train as to how the cooking should be done. I can only imagine that the dispute was settled by dividing the food so each group could cook in its own fashion—in other words, this was regional cookery standing up for its rights.

As outdoor cooking developed throughout the country, there were great chicken fries for church benefits, and in the South, there were the famous fish fries, where the meals were prepared by servants or slaves after a hunting or fishing party returned to the plantation. These fries were supplemented by enormous hampers of food from the main kitchen. Although lavish barbecues still flourish, outdoor cooking is generally done on a small scale these days. The custom has grown to the point where anyone driving through the suburbs on a summer weekend can smell more beef and chicken being charred, scorched, and burned than in all previous history.

[1983]

$\mathcal{B}$errying

My father had very definite likes and dislikes. One of his likes was green currant pie. Tiny currants turned a brilliant green before ripening, and my father's idea of spring delight was to have them picked—and they were difficult to pick—and made into a pie with sugar in a double crust. This he ate with really heavy cream—and with great relish. The currants were tart, certainly, and resembled the gooseberry in some ways.

Of course, the reddened currants were something entirely different when they came along, and we had plenty of them in our garden. They made the ubiquitous currant jelly, which I never liked and still don't, but which people felt had to be served with game, especially venison, and it had a place in a number of desserts. Fortunately, they're harder to get nowadays and are seen less and less on the market.

The only forgivable instance where currants were used a great deal was in a summer pudding, where they were combined with raspberries. Now that people can't get enough of them for this dish, other berries are substituted—blackberries, loganberries— and I think summer pudding is better without them.

An interesting bit about summer pudding, which to me is one of the three or four best desserts in the world, I learned a number of years ago when I was in England. I was visiting with Lee Miller, the famous photographer, who became Lady Penrose. Lee was a great cook, and she adored summer pudding. She dreamed up the idea—and I have since found it's most practical—of freezing it. She would surprise people at Christmas by toting out a thawed pudding or two that had been made at the height of the berry season.

I now sometimes think summer pudding tastes better after freezing than when freshly made. Quite a few years ago, a class of mine at Seaside, Oregon, did a big benefit for the local school to buy equipment for the home economics kitchen, where we were working, and for that party we made eighteen summer puddings. Some we froze, some we didn't, but they were paraded forth in great style and were one of the successes of the evening.

I have an earlier memory of that part of the world, before the nearby forests were logged out and there were still plenty of wild huckleberries. Now, wild huckleberries are related to the blueberry, but they're not blueberries. They have a taste and bouquet like that of no other berry I have known. They're absolutely ravishing. Only last year, someone came from the West Coast carrying with great care two quarts of wild huckleberries, which we used judiciously, I can assure you. It was nostalgic as hell to once again taste that magnificent wild mountain flavor.

We used to have them in many ways. One was with dumplings, slightly heavy and yet delicious. The huckleberries were cooked and then little dumplings were dropped into the boiling fruit, which we had with extra fruit and cream.

To do our berrying, we ventured into the hills on the other side of the railroad tracks at the beach. One day I was out with our neighbors, Mary Hamblet and her father, a man who was soft spoken and temperate in all things, a true New England Brahman, I would say. Anyway, we had climbed up into the woods and found wonderful patches of our blue huckleberries. We were picking away when Mr. Hamblet suddenly turned, dropped his bucket, and said, "For Christsake, run for your lives. Drop the berries!" Well, he had good reason to warn us. Down the path, not too far away from us, came an enormous bear, and bears love huckleberries. So our labors for the day were wasted, but we saved ourselves. I never again heard an expletive out of Harry Hamblet.

Another treat, found all along the coast, were wild blackberries. Not the ordinary big, fat, very seedy wild blackberries, but what in England would be called wild brambles. The vines trailed over logged-off land and brought forth these luscious little berries that had somewhat the taste of the wild huckleberry.

We used them for a heavenly jam and for delicious pies. In the days when people would motor from Portland to Seattle with great ease, they would plan a stop in a little town in Washington called Chehalis. A small hotel there served wild blackberry pie, for months on end, that was absolutely glorious. They must have had all the schoolchildren in town out berrying, because the quantity they used through the year was startling. Those purplish reddish berries baked in a crust, oozing rich sauce onto the plate, were worth mouthwatering for a hundred miles. One producer of commercial jams finally made a wild blackberry syrup for use with pancakes, waffles, ice cream, puddings, and such. It captured that wild and rich blackberry flavor.

Apart from our jaunts into the wilds for huckleberries and blackberries, we also gathered wild strawberries and occasionally raspberries. Then there were wild black currants, which were something else again. But the bushes were carriers of a plant rust, and when I was about ten or twelve, black currant bushes were pulled up by the government and destroyed, and there was a ban on growing them. However, three years ago when I was on the West Coast, I had a fairly good harvest of black currants brought to me. I don't know if someone was breaking the law or if the danger has receded, but there they were in their glory.

Black currants aren't too enticing raw with sugar and cream, but the English adore them in jam, and the French use them in a heavy syrup called *crème de cassis.* There is both an alcoholic and a nonalcoholic version, and their rich, indefinable flavor makes them a great additive to sauces, puddings, sorbets, ice creams, and drinks. And the color! If you've never drunk a Kir, which is a nice cool white wine with a few drops of *crème de cassis* in it, or a champagne *cassis,* where you have a brisk, dry champagne with a few drops in it, you have missed a good deal. A *cassis* sorbet is one of the classics of sorbetology, and if it isn't smothered by too much sweetness or added flavors, it can be pretty blissful to eat slowly after a big meal, especially if you add a few drops of *crème de cassis.*

In one little field at the beach in Gearhart, and in that one field only, there were a great plenty of what might be called bush blueberries, which I always felt some New Englander brought and planted in that spot. They never spread outside of it. Few people knew about them, but my father discovered them. He had a passion for the berries, which he called not blueberries but "swale huckleberries." I don't know where he got the name or what "swale" has to do with it, except that he said they were low growing. He would spend hours gathering those berries when he visited the beach and would tote them back for my mother to prepare for him, perhaps in a pie or in a sauce. She also often used them in small tarts, with the addition of just sugar and perhaps a drop of lemon juice or vanilla. It's surprising what a drop of vanilla will do to certain fruits when they're being cooked, and certainly vanilla seemed to make these little blueberries something they weren't before. While they did have distinction and goodness, they couldn't be compared with our wild blue huckleberries. As a result, my father seemed to be the sole celebrator of the swale huckleberry season.

[1984?]

Life at Its Best

When I was a boy in Oregon, life was organized around the seasons. Next to the mammoth winter preparations, I suppose our greatest activity was organizing for summer at the beach.

Since we spent three to four months there each year, including visits in spring and winter, Mother had to be certain that things were in order for every possible emergency. My father, who didn't enjoy life at the beach, could be expected to join us only for an occasional weekend.

A huge trunk journeyed back and forth from Portland to the beach, along with an enormous packing case of general supplies, for Mother felt there was nothing in the stores near our destination but inferior merchandise. Thus, she would make a special visit to the paper company for the sole purpose of buying a summer's supply of wax paper, wrapping paper, and toilet tissue. Then she would commence to select food to be packed and shipped—such staples as dried beans and rice, spices and seasonings, and a few jars of vegetables and jams. She hated the musty smell that linens took on when stored at the beach, so there were fresh linens to be sent, too, and new dishes.

Two or three days before we left, the household was in a tumult. A ham was being cooked, a batch of bread was baking, and miscellaneous tidbits were being prepared to see us through the first two or three meals. All of this was stored in a large willow picnic hamper. Then our clothes were packed, the bags were closed, and the express man came to collect everything and check it through to Gearhart. I have gone to Europe for a year's stay with less packing and far less strain.

Finally, the day arrived. In the early morning, Mother fixed a luncheon to take along, although the train left at eight-thirty and we arrived at the beach shortly after noon. You never knew who might be on the train, and a few sandwiches and cookies would be just the thing. Usually this meant thin slices of bread with marmalade, sliced egg and cold chicken sandwiches, and perhaps a tidy pound cake. Mr. McKiernan arrived to drive us to the old Spokane, Portland, and Seattle station.

This railroad had a branch line on which the train tore down along the bank of the Columbia River to Astoria at the astonishing rate of twenty miles an hour or better. We rode in the same venerable parlor cars year after year, and the porters were like members of the family. We had to arrive at the station early or I made a frightful scene, for it was absolutely vital that I have a certain chair on the observation platform. Oh, what train travel lost when the observation platform went out! I have never enjoyed trains as much as I did then, sitting in the open air getting covered with coal dust and clinkers. I had a feeling of personal contact with the world passing by—as if I were touring the countryside on my back porch.

The first stop of any importance was Rainier on the river. Mother had friends in Rainier, who were advised as to the exact time of our arrival, and they always came down to the station to pass a few minutes of pleasantry. Then we set off again, and before long we were unpacking the sandwiches, especially if friends of mine were aboard. Children and mothers alike shared our picnic, the porters brought us ginger ale, and there was a festive air about the entire trip.

Beyond Astoria at the mouth of the Columbia River, where sometimes more friends were on hand to greet us, we went over an endless trestle spanning Young's Bay. This thrilled me beyond words, for it was just like going to sea.

Gearhart was on the coast about eighteen miles below the mouth of the Columbia River. It was a heavenly spot, with lush timber; beautiful meadows; a wide white beach, delightful for walking, driving, or riding; and a tossing, roaring surf, perfect for bathing. It was, and still is, a unique little community, for its commercial life has been kept at a minimum, and there are no amusements other than a golf course. Today it continues to have a sort of isolated charm that attracts the same type of people who lived there when I was a child, and many of the houses are occupied by the families who built them, soon after the turn of the century. Our first year there was 1908, and in 1910 we built a small house in what was then considered a rather remote part of the meadow. It is still not too built up. No place I have ever been gives me quite as much pleasure. I adore the ocean, the sand, the solitude.

Mother would have written asking the Tybergs or William Badger to have the house opened and to meet us and pick up the trunks and assorted packages. It was like the arrival of a celebrated prima donna. As soon as we reached the house there was the fuss of getting unpacked, getting a fire going, getting a bit of lunch ready—invariably, it seems to me, cold ham and pickles, bread and butter, and cheese and tea. Then we set to work on the house, and by evening it was so well organized we might never have been away at all. We would have a long walk on the beach to see if its familiar contours had been altered. Most likely there would be a dinner invitation for us, and people we knew began to drop by. Among them were sure to be the Hamblet family.

The Hamblets were close friends of my mother's and so interlaced with our gastronomic life that I must pause to introduce them here. Harry Hamblet was a New Englander, a man of medium height and comfortable proportions and the most thoroughly generous and outgoing man I think I ever knew. His wife, who became known to my generation of Portlanders as "Grammie," was one of my mother's intimate friends over a period of more than fifty years. And the last Hamblet—Mary—is still one of my best friends, another friendship of over fifty years.

To say that the Beards and Hamblets ate hundreds of meals together is an understatement. And what a treasure-house of good food this part of the world was for us! The sandy soil was perfection for vegetables and small fruits, the evening dew and temperate climate were good for growing and ripening, and the nearby waters provided an inexhaustible supply of fish.

The Columbia River abounded with salmon, sturgeon, and halibut; and the ocean, with the small turbot, grunion, and a tremendous variety of small fish. The Pacific's greatest blessing, though, was the Dungeness crab, to my mind unequaled by anything in the shellfish world. In addition, there were the superb razor clams, which flourished in the days of our beaching and continue in small supply nowadays—definitely a sportsman's catch. They have a rich flavor, akin to that of scallops, and a delicacy of texture different from any other clam I know. And they are larger than most clams, with a tender digger and a somewhat less tender body. So distinctive are they that one should have them cooked as simply as possible in order to savor their natural goodness.

We also had mussels by the ton, but there is something in the water or the life cycle of this mollusk that makes them inedible in the West for a long period of the year. This greatly upset Mother, who had a passion for mussels and looked longingly whenever we saw them clinging to the rocks. In the rivers and streams around us, there were also thousands of small crawfish, trout, pogies (not to be confused with the eastern porgies), tomcod, catfish of a type, and other delights.

Harry Hamblet was interested in the first oyster beds to transplant eastern oysters to the Pacific coast. As a result, bags of oysters arrived each week from not-too-distant Shoalwater Bay, and these added to our bounty. It's no wonder we existed almost entirely on the riches of the rivers and the sea.

One of my memories is of my mother and Harry Hamblet, in early morning, cooking dozens of freshly opened oysters in butter by the pound. There were two big iron skillets going. The oysters were floured, dipped in egg and cracker crumbs, and cooked quickly in deep butter till golden on both sides. The butter was not hot enough to blacken them, and the oysters were not deep fried but merely sautéed just fast enough to heat them through. A squeeze of lemon and some freshly ground pepper was all they needed, together with a garnish of bacon and crisp buttered toast. On such occasions, I'm certain that more than a dozen oysters were consumed by each person. Anyone who says you should never cook an oyster has never tasted these after a long walk along the beach in the sea air. They were ambrosial, and this isn't just nostalgia, for I tried them again lately just to see.

Sometimes after an early morning session of clamming we had a breakfast of fried clams, fresh from the sands. The razor clam spits through the sand and leaves an indentation known as a clam hole. As soon as one of us spotted this marker, he dug a shovelful of sand, then fell to his knees and searched until he struck the clamshell. Sometimes it was a struggle to bring a clam to the surface, so strong was its digging power. A take of five to six dozen in a morning was not unusual.

Mother thought clamming a great sport and would arise at five in the morning when there was a good low tide, don her best alpaca bathing suit, and be off to the beach, equipped with shovel and basket. She would meet a number of friends there, mostly men, for few women would bother to go clamming. I often went with her in later years, but my special joy at first was crabbing. The Dungeness used to hide in deep pools accessible at low tide, and if you wandered through with a rake you could trap a fair quantity. You had to be alert, though, and early, for everyone else wanted them, too.

Thus, we often went home with five dozen clams and six or eight crabs. If she was in the mood, Mother would clean a dozen or so clams and remove the diggers, which she brushed with flour and sautéed quickly in butter. Most people cooked the whole clam. Mother was independent enough to think that only the diggers were fit to eat in this manner. The rest of the clam could be used for other dishes. Nowadays, alas, you are lucky if you can get the clams to sauté in their entirety. I am certain that if the razor clam existed in France, the recipes for them would be classic. As it is, Helen Evans Brown and I go on singing their praises.

Mother took a dim view of the average clam chowder, as did the Hamblets. The one we loved was magnificently creamy and filled with the smokiness of bacon and piquancy of thyme. The clams and their juice were added at the moment of serving, and this timing, together with the seasoning, made it, we thought, better than any other chowder on the beach.

Clam broth we had by the quart. The portion of the clams Mother didn't use for sautéing were tossed into a large pot, together with their shells, onions, celery, carrots, parsley, and water to cover. This was allowed to steep for an hour or so till the concentrated flavor of the clams had permeated the broth. This was strained and served hot in small cups, or chilled, with a tiny bit of salted whipped cream on it. And it was also used as a base for soups and sauces, bestowing a flavor that was wonderfully delicate. The same, less choice portions of the clam were sometimes minced and made into the lightest of fritters, served with a genuine tartar sauce—not a concoction with dill pickle and garlic added.

Our scalloped clams, another delight, were made with cracker crumbs (not cracker meal, but rather coarse crumbs of good unsalted soda crackers), clams, butter, milk, cream, egg, chopped parsley, and that was all. Sometimes Mother would use much the same base and add beaten egg white to make a form of soufflé I have never had anywhere else. It was puffy, subtly flavored with clam, and as airy a dish as ever existed. And this was baked in the oven of a woodstove, which was like a pet to my mother; she could almost tell it what to do.

Dungeness crab is now sent across the country, but to eat it freshly cooked and to eat it after refrigeration are two different experiences. And to have Grammie Hamblet's deviled crab! I have maintained all my life that this was the best cooked crab I have ever known. It was made with finely chopped, crisp vegetables, cracker crumbs, and butter, seasoned well and cooked just long enough to heat the crabmeat without turning it mushy. Served with a very brisk wine—a Muscadet or a Chablis—it was indescribably delicious. Grammie Hamblet deserved a seat in gastronomic heaven for having thought that one up.

❧ Grammie Hamblet's Deviled Crab ❧

Chop enough celery to make 1 cup. It must be cut finer than fine. Add 1 good-sized green pepper also cut exceedingly fine, 1 cup of finely sliced green onions, $1/2$ cup of chopped parsley, 2 pounds of crabmeat, $2^1/2$ cups of coarsely crushed cracker crumbs, 1 teaspoon of salt, $1^1/2$ teaspoons of dry mustard, a healthy dash of Tabasco, $1/2$ cup of heavy cream, and 1 cup of melted butter. Toss lightly and spoon into a buttered baking dish. Top with additional crushed cracker crumbs, and brush with melted butter. Bake at 350° for 25 to 30 minutes or until delicately browned. Serves 4 to 6.

We had salmon during the entire season. Harry Hamblet and the Peter Grants saw to that. The Grants were in the cannery business and commuted all summer between the plant in Astoria and Gearhart. About once a week, they would ask if we wanted a fish, and that night a salmon would arrive, caught the same morning, sometimes sent along with a package of salmon cheeks, which the Hamblets and Beards preferred to almost anything else in the fish world. The cheeks were easy to get in those days, for no one thought of cutting them out when the heads were removed. Nowadays they are as scarce as white caviar and nearly as expensive, if you can get them. We feasted on them sautéed in butter or occasionally grilled over the fire.

The rest of the salmon we poached, baked, or cut into steaks to grill. The poached was usually accompanied by an egg sauce or a parsley sauce, and the baked was done with onions, tomatoes in season, peppers, and a few rashers of bacon, all of which were served up with the fish.

Almost any way you treat a fresh Columbia salmon, it is good, but it must not be overcooked. It should be moist, tender, and just cooked through. Since my Gearhart days, I have eaten a variety of salmon and learned a number of ways to prepare it. It is a fish with great distinction, and I feel it has never had the acclaim in this country it deserves. Too many people think of it as something that comes from a can or is sold smoked. How delicious it was when I had it as the Indians used to do it, barbecued or smoked over an open fire, attached to a forked spirea branch (which won't burn) or spitted and roasted over charcoal or wood coals. How good, too, prepared with a soufflé mixture and served with a mousseline sauce; or poached and served cold with a *sauce verte* or simple tarragon mayonnaise.

Then there was trout. In Switzerland and the Alpine section of France, live trout are tossed into an acidulous court bouillon to make a dish as delicate and as great as any piscatorial delight—*truite au bleu*. This is usually offered with melted butter or a hollandaise. We seldom had trout this classic way in Gearhart, because they were generally brought to us by fish friends who came down late in the morning from their jaunts. Thus, we would have a simple, impromptu lunch, the trout being served meunière or cooked in a coating of cornmeal with bacon. I have been severely chastised by a gourmet-according-to-the-books for even mentioning the idea of bacon and trout together. But is it any more improbable to add the flavor of bacon than to add lemon or vinegar, as in *truite au bleu*? I hope someday to have the chance to offer this critic a perfectly sautéed mountain trout with bacon. I'm certain he will eat it with gusto, protesting the while that it should not be.

Mother and I usually had breakfast together. We were both early risers. If we had already been clamming, crabbing, or swimming, by seven o'clock or seven-thirty we were ravenous. We might have sautéed clams for ourselves or clam fritters, sour milk griddle cakes with bacon, or scrambled eggs with bacon. If Mother were in the mood, she might make popovers, which she did with a flair, and these would be eaten with fresh jam and probably a boiled egg. I could easily manage three of the light puffs and was then quite happy to set out for an adventure at the beach or in the woods.

If we were home and not picnicking, luncheon might be just cracked crab with Mother's fine mayonnaise or a crab salad with finely shredded young cabbage, a tiny bit of celery, a touch of onion, and plenty of good crabmeat—two parts crab to one of vegetables—tossed with a judicious amount of mayonnaise. This was fantastically good eating and was often served as a company lunch, along with legs of crab as a garnish and thinly sliced hard-boiled eggs. We had big peach-blossom Chinese bowls for salads, and the dish looked extremely handsome as it was brought to table. With this lunch went thin homemade bread and butter, hot rolls or muffins, and fresh fruit, a tart, or one of Mother's quick coffee cakes.

Another favorite lunch for guests was a huge piece of cold salmon that had been pickled with vinegar, oil, bay leaves, peppercorns, lots of sliced onion, and a little garlic, as well as some of the broth in which the fish was cooked. This was drained and arranged on a platter with chopped parsley and chives, thinly sliced cucumber, and tomato. A mayonnaise was served with this, along with homemade bread and sometimes a vegetable salad. If good fruit was available, there would be a fruit tart for dessert or a soufflé.

If we had a meat dish, which was not too often, it might be a meat pie with kidney and vegetables or a really good pot-au-feu, with all the seasonal vegetables in the broth and plenty of marrow bones. The extra beef was pressed and used cold in a salad. Occasionally a piece of corned beef from Portland provided a pleasant change of fare. It was ideal for picnic sandwiches or as a snack for supper.

And from time to time we would come by a fine fowl, procured from the people who sold eggs, and this would make a rich fricassee, or it was used for Mother's special smothered chicken—a type of daube—in which the chicken was browned and put to simmer with vegetables, seasonings, and liquid, to which cream and thickening were added. The vegetables were removed and served separately, together with boiled potatoes in jackets or rice. This dish could last for a couple of days if the weather was right, for refrigeration at the beach was somewhat primitive.

Mother was critical of the way most people lived at the beach, looked down her nose at the food served in other houses, and, except for meals with the Hamblet family, she usually refused invitations to eat out. "No use giving up the pleasures of eating just because you're on vacation," she would say. "Who wants to eat a lot of horrible stuff out of jars and cans and that ghastly baker's bread that tastes like cotton batting? To hell with it. I'd rather have a cup of tea, some of my own bread, and cracked crab than eat all that stuff that's bound to give me indigestion."

The Hamblets, the Beards, and two or three good friends who would share our house for a fortnight or so seemed to have noses for wild berries. Mother and Grammie Hamblet, especially. They could almost scent it in the air when the wild strawberries were just right, and off they'd go with the rest of us in tow, all laden with buckets. Five- and three-pound lard pails made good berry containers in those days.

The wild strawberries at Gearhart and up the beach took hours to gather, but they were so good that no one seemed to mind. They grew on long stems, like the European *fraises des bois*, and had a sugary, wild flavor that has lingered on my palate all these years. Occasionally in Spain or in the remote parts of France, where the *fraises des bois* are not cultivated to tasteless pulp, one finds the same flavor; and in the countryside and mountains of the Northwest and sometimes in New England one discovers them in small quantities. No one has experienced the real flavor of strawberries until he has had a plate of these or tasted a good preserve made with them.

Fortnum and Mason's have done a superb job of bottling little scarlet berries in preserve, and I urge you to send for some or buy some the next time you are in London. Incidentally, only strawberries of the wild variety grew in England until the sixteenth century, and it was an Englishman, Cardinal Wolsey, who started the fad of eating strawberries with cream. Mother was deeply indebted to him. She loved to skim heavy cream from a pan of milk onto a plate of berries.

During our berry jaunts, we would also find yellowish pink salmonberries. These were good enough to eat from the vine, my mother pronounced, but not good enough to carry home—too gross in flavor. The same thing went for the thimbleberry, a variety of wild raspberry.

Mary Hamblet practically lived on her horse—her sister and brother spent as much time on theirs—and the trio would come prancing down to our house to announce the discovery of a new patch of berries or the fact that there had been a good catch of crab, and how many could we use, or how many oysters? Such a gastronomic courier system is rare these days.

Three miles from Gearhart was a bustling resort, Seaside, quite the opposite of our reserved community. There were shops, amusements, dance halls, restaurants, and hundreds of tourists. People there lived in cottages built close to one another and without the splendid isolation that Gearhart provided. At any rate, we had many friends there and often spent the day, visiting, seeing a movie, then taking the late train back, or walking the three miles at night in a spirit of adventure.

One place in Seaside fascinated all of us children and drew us back each time we were in town. This was West's Dairy, where they made a five-cent milk shake that resembled the *granitas* of Italy and offered twenty-eight different flavors. We always resolved to sample each of the flavors before the season was over. I doubt that we ever made it, although we'd invade West's five at a time, order five flavors, and try each other's flavor. And what flavors!—claret, wild blackberry, tutti-frutti, grenadine, blue huckleberry, cherry, pistachio. I can see the soda jerks now, scraping ice from a tremendous block, putting it in a mixing glass, and adding the flavor and then whole milk. It was probably the biggest five cents worth of anything I ever had, and it was the only time I consented to drink milk.

Those days on the Oregon shore were among the most memorable in my life. I can remember several occasions when an equinoctial storm came up suddenly, catching us still on the beach. I reveled in being out in the driving rain and high winds and in watching the surf go wild. It was equally exciting to scurry home, draw the shutters, and sup on good food while listening to the wind and beating rain. When the storm had passed, it left a calm of indescribable beauty. I would rush out to the beach to see if any damage had been done to the other houses or to the bulkheads and to see what new treasures had been washed ashore.

Then, for complete peace, there was nothing like the week between Christmas and New Year's when we stayed at the beach. Few houses would be open, and the sense of removal from the rest of the world was even stronger. Mother kept certain items stored in the house for this off-season visit, but as always, we went to the sea for our food, and it sustained us perfectly.

[1962]

❧ Recipe Index ❧

343